D1493875

ECONOMICS AND SOCIETY No. 10

British Industrial Relations

ECONOMICS AND SOCIETY SERIES

General Editor: Professor Colin Harbury

ECONOMICS AND SOCIETY SERIES

BRITISH INDUSTRIAL RELATIONS

GILL PALMER
The City University

London
GEORGE ALLEN & UNWIN
Boston   Sydney

George Allen & Unwin (Publishers) Ltd,
40 Museum Street, London WC1A 1LU, UK

George Allen & Unwin (Publishers) Ltd,
Park Lane, Hemel Hempstead, Herts HP2 4TE, UK

Allen & Unwin Inc.,
9 Winchester Terrace, Winchester, Mass 01890, USA

George Allen & Unwin Australia Pty Ltd,
8 Napier Street, North Sydney, NSW 2060, Australia

First published in 1983

British Library Cataloguing in Publication Data

Palmer, Gill
 British industrial relations.
1. Industrial relations—Great Britain
I. Title
331'.0941   HD8391
ISBN 0–04–331091–5
ISBN 0–04–331092–3 Pbk

Library of Congress Cataloging in Publication Data

Palmer, Gill
 British industrial relations.
(Economics and society series; no. 10)
Bibliography: p.
Includes index.
1. Industrial relations—Great Britain. I. Title. II. Series.
HD8391.P26 1983   331'.0941   83–3811
ISBN 0–04–331091–5
ISBN 0–04–331092–3 (pbk.)

Set in 10 on 11 point Times by Preface Ltd, Salisbury, Wilts.
and printed in Great Britain
by Biddles Ltd, Guildford, Surrey

For Dene

Contents

the history of industrial action in the UK; the challenge of domestic bargaining; growing legislation on individual rights and tripartite administration; alternatives to the free collective bargaining tradition in the UK; conclusion

Acknowledgements

I should like to acknowledge my debt to the editor of this series, Colin Harbury, whose prompt, perceptive comments and unfailing encouragement brought this book to completion. I am also indebted to the following for their invaluable help with various drafts of the manuscript: H. A. Clegg, A. Fox, H. Gospel, S. Kessler, R. Lewis, C. R. Littler, R. Loveridge, A. Marsh, J. E. Mortimer, D. Sapsford, S. Wood.

I gratefully acknowledge permission to reproduce the following: Figure 3.1 from *The Development of the Labour Process in Capitalist Societies* by C. R. Littler, published by Heinemann, (1982); Table 6.2 and 6.3 from R. Price and G. Bain 'Union Growth Revisited', *British Journal of Industrial Relations*, Vol. XIV, No. 3 (1976); Table 8.1 from *Are National Agreements Dead?* by R. Elliott, Occasional Paper, Aberdeen University Department of Political Economy, 80:13; Figure 8.2 from *The System of Industrial Relations in Great Britain* by H. A. Clegg, published by Blackwell (1972).

This book adopts the conventions of referring to 'industrial relations' as a singular noun and 'he' as meaning 'she and he'.

Chapter 1

Introduction

Industrial relations is one of the most discussed, least understood subjects in the United Kingdom. Stories of strikes, wage demands and industrial disruption are constantly in the news. The subject looms large in political debate, dominating recent elections and throwing up major policy differences between the political parties. In the last twenty years industrial relations has developed into an issue of widespread public interest and concern, but this growth in attention has not been matched by growing understanding. Instead of analysis there is often confusion and anxiety. Industrial relations becomes like mugging, the subject of 'moral panic'. Feelings of frustration and fear are whipped up by stories in the media and, in the absence of any systematic analysis, crude assumptions are made: that there is a terrible problem caused by 'too much union power' or by 'modern technology'.

Industrial relations suffers the fate of any subject that becomes a political issue in the absence of analytical debate. Simplistic assumptions lead to drastic and ill-conceived policies. The problem with such policies is that they tend not to have the expected results, and failed policies generate yet more confusion. This book concentrates on the need to understand and analyse the subject that now generates such concern.

WHAT IS THE SUBJECT ABOUT?

Studies of industrial relations coverage by the press and by television show that, as far as the media are concerned, the subject is about trade unions, and in particular, about strikes. Surveys for the 1977 Royal Commission on the Press, and by the Glasgow University Media Research Group show that 'industrial action' accounts for 40 per cent of all television news time and 36 per cent of national press stories on the subject. The media treat the subject as 'trade union activities' and this definition is followed by most politicians and, presumably, the public at large.

However, we need a wider definition of the subject matter if we are to analyse and understand trade unions, and the conflicts that dominate the news. No subject can be understood if it is too narrowly conceived. Just as the complexities of family relationships could not be grasped by looking at divorce, at the activities of Women's Institutes, or at the legal terms of marriage contracts, so no analysis of industrial relations will get far if it looks only at strikes, trade unions or collective bargaining agreements. We need to go behind the dramatic events that hit the media and look at the more basic social processes that underlie them.

For many years academics in the UK followed – or led – the media in seeing the subject as the study of trade unions. As a result, much work took the form of detailed descriptions of unions, or union–management arrangements, numbing the student with facts but giving little insight into what was going on. British studies started the move to overcome this tradition in 1965 when Allan Flanders argued that industrial relations should be seen as the study of the 'institutions of job regulation'. This raises the focus from trade unions, to include employers' associations, the government and any other institution concerned with terms and conditions of employment. Flanders also tried to define more precisely what these institutions are concerned to do. He picked up ideas published in the USA (Dunlop, 1958) and argued that work is governed by a mass of rules and regulations covering criteria for recruitment, effort, performance, hours, pay, holidays and a myriad of other details. Flanders argued that these rules and regulations are what industrial relations institutions try to determine.

Flanders' approach opened the way for a more conscious attempt to understand what trade unions are about, but it has itself been criticised for defining the subject too narrowly, for taking for granted the particular institutions we have at the moment, and for focusing on rules and regulations at the expense of less visible controls. If the subject is only about trade unions, employers' associations and the government, it will miss the importance of informal groupings – like regular meetings of personnel officers in an industry, or the temporary importance of institutions like the National Association for Freedom, the Workers Revolutionary Party, the Police or the Army in a major dispute. If the subject is only about rules and regulations it will ignore the importance of personal attitudes and beliefs – for example, the antagonism between a managing director and union official that can sour relations for a decade. Finally, a focus on rules and regulations may lead us to expect order, where order may not exist.

The more people have tried to analyse what is happening in industrial relations, the wider they have had to cast their net to catch significant institutions, interactions and events. For this reason this book will define the subject as *the processes of control over the employment relationship*. This definition should help us move beyond the simple description of institutions and events, to the more important and more urgent job of analysis.

The employment relationship is an economic, social and political relationship in which employees provide manual and mental labour in exchange for rewards allotted by employers. The details of this exchange take many forms. On the 'rewards' side, rewards can be economic, social and psychological. Rewards from employment may give the employee wealth, power and social prestige, or a despised, dead-end job below the poverty line. On the side of the provision of labour, employee contributions range from scarce, highly marketable skills to semi-skilled or unskilled labour. Employees may find the effort they are expected to provide is rigidly specified and controlled, or left free to individual interpretation. We can contrast journalists with factory assembly-line workers, and university lecturers with airline pilots, to find surprising variations in the type and autonomy of labour exchanged for rewards.

The employment relationship can envelop much of an employee's life – like the Japanese large-firm employee whose house, leisure and future work career will all be on company premises – or the relationship with any particular employer may be as fleeting as for the casual labourer on a British building site. The relationship may be set in a capitalist firm or in a workers' co-operative; in the culture and legal system of the UK, or the Ukraine or Ulan Bator. Potential variations are enormous, but of one thing we can be sure: the relationship is important. It is important for employees in determining their life-style and future prospects; for the employer concerned to control an organisation; and for society at large. The forms of employment relationship that develop, the criteria for recruitment to the most desired jobs and the mobility between types of job will all have an impact on the society's political and social culture and on the antagonism between different social classes that emerges. Given this importance, it is hardly surprising that there will be many people and groups interested in influencing the employment relationship, or that the processes that shape the relationship should form a complex area for study.

ISSUES IN THE EMPLOYMENT RELATIONSHIP

In any society there are a number of economic, social and political issues to be resolved in structuring employment relationships. It has become conventional to distinguish between substantive and procedural issues. Substantive issues cover the details of the reward–effort exchange. Procedural issues surround the question of how the substantive issues are decided, for example, who has the power to set substantive terms, and through what administrative or bargaining arrangements.

Substantive issues include pay, holidays and any less direct 'fringe benefits' like pensions, private health company subscriptions, company cars, training and the prospect of promotion to better paid jobs. There may be many questions surrounding pay determination, not only on how basic levels of pay are set, but also on whether there is a regular fixed rate of pay or whether earnings vary according to effort or performance. Most industrial disputes appear to arise from issues concerned with pay but the 'effort' as opposed to the 'reward' issues in employment relationships can be equally difficult to resolve. In any society decisions are needed on what work is done, and on the way the labour process, required to complete this work, is divided up between jobs. This division of labour affects the type of skill, the skill level, specialisation and monotony of the effort required of employees. The level and intensity of effort also need to be determined. Surrounding these details of the reward–effort exchange will be personnel issues, for example the criteria of recruitment to jobs, whether recruits are trained and offered careers or given only short-term contracts, the criteria for dismissal and any compensation for dismissal or redundancy.

If the substantive issues that can surround the employment relationship look complex, the procedural issues are often more so. What people or groups control the substantive decisions? Are decisions taken by the employers of private enterprise businesses? Are rules laid down in legislation by the state? What influence do employees have? If more than one party has some influence on these issues, what mechanisms are or should be used to reach jointly agreed decisions? What is the balance of power between the parties in joint decision-making bodies? In Chapter 2 we take an initial look at the highly contentious political debate surrounding these procedural questions, a debate to which we will be returning throughout the book.

WHO IS INVOLVED?

There are over twenty million employees in the UK, employed by national or local government, by private companies ranging from foreign-owned giants to small local shops, by nationalised industries, single domestic employers or co-operatives. Millions of people are directly involved in the employment relationship, yet more are concerned to influence the shape it takes. However, in this book we shall be concerned not so much with individuals as with groups. Groups can mobilise more resources than individuals and can exert more pressure to achieve their ends. The way groups form is important, for groups help articulate values and interests, and identify issues which a number of people are prepared to support. Group formation and the relative power of different groups will have a fundamental impact on the way employment relationships develop.

The groups most frequently associated with industrial relations in the UK are the unions, and in Chapters 5 and 6 we look at trade union objectives, structure, government and power. We also look at workplace pressure groups and non-union institutions formed to represent occupational interests.

Employers and managers are too often neglected in discussions of industrial relations. Here too it is groups that exert most influence; the individual employer acting alone, like George Ward in the Grunwick dispute of 1976–7, is now largely a matter for history. In Chapter 3 we discuss the structured groups – the organisations – that employers build to achieve their objectives and we analyse the strategies that have been used on the division of labour and the control of the labour process. Chapter 4 discusses employer groups more directly parallel to trade unions – the employers' associations formed to co-ordinate employers' labour policies.

There are many other groups which may be concerned to influence the employment relationship: religious or political groups; institutions like the press, the BBC or ITV, trying to endorse or encourage what they see as 'reasonable behaviour'; pressure groups like the Campaign for Workers' Control or the National Association for Freedom. However, the most important body apart from the groups formed by employers and employees is the state. The state acts as employer for a substantial proportion of employees, but even when not in this role, government policy, law and the activity of government departments or agencies, fundamentally affect employment issues. Chapters 2, 7, 8, 9, and 10 discuss the state's involvement in industrial relations.

CONFLICT OR CO-OPERATION?

Given the range of issues to be decided, and the people and groups concerned with those decisions, what assumption should be made about the extent to which harmony or conflict is inherent in industrial relations? The basic premises here may seem obvious, but as this is an area that causes much confusion and lies at the heart of much of the political debate, basic premises need to be emphasised. The employment relationship, like any other social relationship, will involve both co-operation and conflict between those involved. Co-operation is needed for *any* social interaction to persist – studies of the relationship between prisoners and their guards show that some form of co-operation invariably develops. The employer and employee can be expected to have a more positive relationship than this. On the other hand, the most voluntary, loving relationships generate conflict over ends, means to ends, values and priorities. Employment relationships obviously provide plenty of scope for conflict on substantive and procedural issues.

Can we be more specific about the degrees of conflict and co-operation to expect? The many assumptions and assertions that exist in this area are introduced in Chapter 2. For the purpose of introducing the subject matter, we need only emphasise that it would be absurd to start with the assumption that employment issues will be non-problematic; easy to resolve to everyone's satisfaction. There is no industrial society in the world that does not have strikes and industrial disputes – even though in some countries they are illegal. There is no organisation, whether it is run on principles of managerial prerogative, co-operation, workers' control or state control, that does not experience conflicts in this area. Even small, self-managing worker co-operatives generate conflicts over the allocation of people to jobs; over supervision; over differences in interests between occupational groups and between individual versus collective goals (Cockroft, 1977). Conflicts like these arise from the basic need to organise people for work, they arise in some form whatever the particular type of organisation used.

Industrial relations is a subject, like politics, where there are likely to be conflicting expectations and demands on limited resources, where there are no perfect answers capable of satisfying everyone involved. Conflict will never be eliminated but the *form* it takes, and its *severity* can vary. Policies adopted by different groups will affect the extent to which conflict is exacerbated or contained. But no policies will achieve the impossible aim of resolving all the issues to the satisfaction of all the goals of all the people involved.

I have emphasised the inevitability of conflict in industrial relations because there is a widespread bias against accepting this idea. This bias contributes to the distortions and confusions to be found in much public discussion of the subject in the press, broadcasting and elsewhere. Anyone who expects relations in employment to be harmonious and problem-free is likely to react with bewilderment and anxiety when difficulties arise. If one feels that everything in a relationship *should* be based entirely on co-operation, then one is likely to believe there has been a serious rending of the social fabric – that society is in danger of disintegration – when major confrontations occur. Alan Fox made this point nearly twenty years ago when he suggested that there are two broad perspectives on industrial relations, a naive 'unitary' and a realistic 'pluralist' perspective (Fox, 1965). People who look at work relations with a *unitary perspective* see conflict as abnormal, only arising when work organisations are not working correctly because of, for example personality disorders, inappropriate recruitment or promotion, the deviance of dissidents or poor communications. In a 'normal' organisation everything will be peacefully ordered. A rational, all-powerful, all-knowing and authoritative management will arrange things in everyone's interest. From this perspective any sign of conflict will be a cause of great concern and it will be assumed that someone is acting irrationally and illegitimately. Conflict will be dealt with by attempts to stamp it out.

Fox suggested that a more realistic perspective on work life accepts the inevitability of conflict at work. This *pluralist perspective* sees organisations as complex social structures formed of a plurality of potentially conflicting interest groups. Conflict is bound to arise as people enter the employment relationship with expectations that cannot be matched with scarce resources and as groups form with conflicting interests and values. From this perspective conflict is not only inevitable but necessary. '. . .Conflict, however distasteful it may be in process, has a consequence that is useful for society, namely to determine the next steps it will take. . .' (Dubin, 1960). The pluralist's response to conflict will not be to try to eliminate it, but to try to find a method of handling conflicts that will produce the most desired results.

In 1965 Fox suggested that many managers in Britain were operating with the unitary perspective. No doubt there are managers who believe that conflict at work is immoral and that all the issues surrounding employment should be resolved in harmonious agreement, but such managers are rare. Most managers are far more aware of the complexities of the social situations they are in. The unitary perspective is probably not, in practice, believed by many people in management, or even in the press or broadcasting. Nevertheless, the perspective still underlies much public debate, and industrial relations is often discussed on the basis of a set of assumptions which, if challenged, would be acknowledged to be absurd.

There are many reasons why widespread and dominant ideas about a subject may fail to reflect the realities of how people actually behave. The idea that conflict is an inevitable part of social life is disquieting; most people find the prospect of continual conflict threatening. Secondly, the idea that particular conflicts are unjustified or immoral is very convenient for anyone trying to maintain a particular authority or cast doubt on the legitimacy of dissenting views. Later in the book we will examine the value of ideological appeals in support of group strategies. Here we need only note that the common bias against the idea that conflict is inevitable in work situations can easily blind the analysis of industrial relations.

In summary, the issues in the employment relationship are

varied and complex. It would be remarkable if everyone acted in agreement and harmony over the organisation of people and resources at work. If an organisation like Cockroft's small print co-operative generates problems, then the employment problems thrown up by British Rail, British Leyland or ICI are likely to test the social skills of managers and workers alike. Conflict must be expected: it is the form that conflict takes and the way it is dealt with that should be the subject of discussion and analysis. The form industrial relations conflict takes will depend on how work is organised, the way group interests form, the strategies and relative power of the various interested groups and the institutional arrangements for handling their conflicts. These areas are the subject of this book.

Chapter 2

Perspectives on the Employment Relationship

How should we approach the analysis of industrial relations; what types of theory should we use? This question is not easily answered, for most writing in the area has been prescriptive or descriptive rather than explicitly concerned with theory. Prescription lies at the centre of public debates on the subject. Over the last few years there has been an unending succession of prescriptions for changes in trade union law, for new attempts at incomes policy, or for the introduction of worker participation schemes. Such proposals are usually highly contentious, the theoretical assumptions on which they are based are rarely spelt out and the debates on public policy are full of theoretical confusions. Academic studies have traditionally emphasised description rather than theoretical analysis. There are generally accepted middle range theories – for example on trade union growth or workers' propensities to strike – but at the level of macro-thoery there is little agreement on how the subject should be interpreted. The development of theory has been backward.

Prescriptions and descriptions often purport to be based on pragmatic, non-theoretical common sense. Of course there is no such thing as non-theoretical common sense, for any discussion of social behaviour requires that some assumptions and generalisations be made. In industrial relations, the existence of contentious and conflicting policy proposals suggests that, whatever the assumptions are, they are certainly not 'common' to all. While some people assume that British trade unions are more powerful than the employers, others assume the reverse. While some assume the government adopts a neutral stance on industrial conflicts, others assume the government is always active, but disagree over whether governments usually act for unions or for employers. If we try to sort out the theoretical generalisations and assumptions behind different public policy proposals, we find ourselves faced with a great range of different approaches. As they are not presented as clearly delineated theories, we can speak of the existence of a number of theoretical perspectives on the nature of employment relations.

This chapter introduces the main theoretical perspectives on employment relationships, through a discussion of different prescriptions. It reviews the different types of prescription currently put forward on British industrial relations. It assesses the theoretical assumptions that lie behind them and it notes the different value judgements often associated with certain perspectives. Readers who find themselves overwhelmed by such an early introduction to theoretical issues can leave this chapter until later. For those who continue, the chapter should show how the subject matter can be analysed and give an initial insight into the controversy and the depth of feeling surrounding industrial relations in the United Kingdom today.

UNITARY PERSPECTIVES AND PRESCRIPTIONS

As was noted in Chapter 1, the unitary perspective assumes that conflict at work is both unnatural and unnecessary. Few people involved in industrial relations actually see their world in these very simple terms, but the perspective has an ideological appeal and two types of prescription are associated with it.

The suppression of dissidents
If one assumes that there are no genuine, significant differences in the interests, objectives or values of people at work, then any sign of conflict between employer and employee must derive from deviance. Individuals concerned to subvert the peace for political or personal reasons must have generated the problems, aided by the sheep-like ability of their co-workers to be led astray. If the militants were removed by dismissal, or if their behaviour was suppressed by the law, all would be well. This agitator theory surfaces at times in media comment, as journalists or broadcasters search for quick, easy explanations for involved and opaque problems. An example occurred in the 1970s when Alcan built an aluminium smelter north of Newcastle. The construction site was plagued by industrial relations problems, culminating in a thirteen-week unofficial strike by the electricians. A government agency was sent to investigate and found the local press and television ready with explanations of what had gone wrong. Their interpretation was that the trouble was caused by agitators. One of the employer's spokesmen pointed out that the eloquent leader of the electricians' unofficial strike was a known communist and a picture built up of troublemakers fomenting strikes for political reasons. Closer investigation of the Alcan site quickly demolished that theory. Indeed, no one on site who had detailed knowledge of the situation presented agitators as the major problem. Instead they pointed to complex and deep-seated factors common at the

time on large sites, exacerbated in this case by fixed cost contracts given to many separate firms. Unco-ordinated policies between different firms had given rise to bizzare pay structures across the site, so that men working next to each other on identical jobs earned radically different pay, and the skilled electricians found themselves earning less per hour than the unskilled men in several other companies (CIR Report 29). Problems associated with co-ordinating personnel policies on large sites were well known within the industry. However, such problems were complex, and took time to understand and to communicate to an uninitiated audience. In contrast, an agitator theory was simple, and neatly fitted popular stereotypes of the industrial relations world.

Individual personalities may, of course, have an impact on the course of events, but individuals operate in social and economic contexts that are ignored by agitator theorists. The removal of leaders may alter the behaviour of the led, but it will not turn complex social situations into a unitary utopia where everyone is of one mind.

The good management of human relations

More sophisticated unitary prescriptions argue the need for the very careful handling of employment relations by managers, to remove the sources of potential conflicts. There are many managerial prescriptions on human relations at work and they are not all premised on unitary perspectives. However, some major managerial theories have apparently been based on unitary assumptions about conflict at work, or at least the theorists have held up the prospect of harmonious, conflict-free employment relations as an incentive for the adoption of the managerial techniques they favour. The Human Relations theories which emerged from the USA in the 1930s emphasised the need for consultation and participative supervision, and later neo-Human-Relations theorists called for job enrichment. These schools of thought did have protagonists who implied that they had identified the source of conflict at work and that their proffered solutions could cure the problems of industrial relations. Today, with the growing economic importance of Japan, the USA has been replaced as the fount of managerial wisdom. A new generation of business consultants prescribes Japanese managerial techniques and makes similar claims that the right technique will eliminate all the problematic conflicts of employment relationships (see, for example, Ouchi, 1981).

Japanese and Western managerial techniques will be contrasted in the next chapter. In this chapter it is sufficient to say that, although management theorists may choose to present their arguments from a unitary perspective, their prescriptions are not necessarily adopted on the basis of naive assumptions. Certainly the impact that such policies have when they are adopted is best viewed from a pluralist perspective. Managerial techniques undoubtedly have an effect on the way interests are perceived and expressed but they do not eliminate the problems of conflict at work.

All the remaining perspectives on employment relations are pluralist, in that they recognise that there are conflicts of interest between people at work and that power will be used in the resolution of those conflicts. As was noted in Chapter 1, most prescriptions and analyses in industrial relations are pluralist in the sense that they recognise a complex plurality of interests in employment. However, that does not imply a simple solution to theoretical problems, for the plurality of interests and the inevitability of conflict can be interpreted in different ways. There are conflicting notions about what are the significant conflicts and which the significant interest groups. There are different views about the balance of power between groups – whether some have a dominant position, exploiting the rest, or whether there can be a balanced, mutual alliance that satisfies everyone. There are disagreements over which group, if any, has wider, more legitimate interests than the others. Underlying all these differences are radically different evaluations of conflict. Even pluralists who see conflict as inevitable are not neutral to its existence. Some only accept conflict if it is expressed in certain ways. Others value it only when it is the result of some group successfully pursuing desired policies, for example policies leading to 'higher productivity', or to 'democracy' or 'equality'. We review these differences in terms of four broad types of pluralist perspective.

LIBERAL COLLECTIVISM AND COLLECTIVE BARGAINING

The dominant school of thought in British industrial relations accepts the inevitability of conflict between employers and employees on economic issues and argues that employees need to act collectively in order to protect their economic interests. It prescribes collective bargaining as the fairest and most efficient method of institutionalising and resolving conflict at work. These ideas are sometimes, rather confusingly labelled 'pluralist' in industrial relations literature, but as there are other analyses that assume a plurality of interests, we shall label this school the 'liberal collectivists'. It is liberal because it advocates a limited, passive role for government and the use of contracts, freely negotiated between conflicting parties, as the best method for resolving disputes. It is collective because, unlike the liberal individualists we mention later, it accepts the legitimate right of employees to form collective organisations to increase their bargaining power when negotiating contracts.

The liberal-collectivist perspective lies behind much academic writing in the USA and UK. It has the support of many British managers and trade unionists and it is the admitted stance of many politicians in the British Conservative, Labour, Liberal and Social Democratic parties.

The ideas behind liberal-collectivist support for collective bargaining are not difficult to unravel. Collective bargaining is the process by which trade unions, representing groups of employees, negotiate with employers or their representatives with the object of reaching collective agreements. Collective agreements specify jointly agreed terms on a range of employment issues like pay, hours and basic conditions of employment. The process requires a political system which allows employees freedom of association so that they can organise into economic pressure groups which are independent of employers or the state. It requires the mutual recognition of divergent interests by employers and employees and their willingness to accept the compromise of jointly agreed terms. Collective bargaining is a power bargaining method in which the negotiating positions of the two sides are backed by economic sanctions. On the employee side this requires the legal right and practical ability to take industrial action like strikes, go-slows or overtime bans. On the employer side it requires the right to act in the last resort without agreement on managerial prerogative, and to lock out or sack employees in dispute. The government's role in this bargaining process is essentially passive. It does not attempt to regulate terms and conditions of employment. It merely provides a limited framework of legislation within which bargaining takes place.

Liberal collectivists argue the case for collective bargaining in terms of industrial and political advantages. They argue that, industrially, collective bargaining creates a form of industrial democracy by allowing employees a voice in the determination of their pay and conditions of employment, while at the same time the employers' freedom to take unilateral decisions on investment, business and the majority of managerial issues is unimpaired. Politically, collective bargaining helps enhance the stability of a society by removing potentially disruptive industrial conflicts from the political arena and providing a set of institutions for the relatively peaceful resolution of employment-based conflicts. As the American, R. Dubin, put it:

> Collective bargaining is the great social invention that has institutionalised industrial conflict. In much the same way that the electoral process and majority rule have institutionalised

political conflict in a democracy, collective bargaining has created a stable means for resolving industrial conflict (in Kornhauser, Dubin and Ross, 1954).

In summary, collective bargaining is seen to be a decentralised, flexible and democratic method for the satisfactory resolution of inevitable, primarily economic conflicts at work. These arguments had wide support among the Western Allies after the Second World War. At that time political theorists in the USA and UK emphasised the need for strong voluntary groups to represent different economic interests in society if democratic, rather than totalitarian, government was to survive. Such functional interest groups were seen to create a balance of power and prevent too great a concentration of power in the hands of employers or the state. For this reason the Allies reintroduced trade unions into the defeated societies of Germany and Japan and advocated collective bargaining as a safeguard against the return of totalitarian regimes.

Some form of collective bargaining has developed in all the democratic mixed economies of the world. The arguments for it have a strong ideological appeal for many. Nevertheless in recent years collective bargaining in the UK has come under attack from a variety of directions, and there have been many prescriptions for change. Although these are usually presented as minor adjustments to the collective bargaining system, they often involve a radical shift from the basic characteristics of collective bargaining outlined above. For example, many of the new prescriptions imply a much more active role for government than is admitted under any form of liberalism.

The criticisms which have been mounted against British collective bargaining take a number of forms. One set of arguments asserts that collective bargaining is too disruptive, either because the level of industrial action is too high and costly for a nation competing in tight markets, or because employers and employees collude to push up wages and prices without due regard to consumers, thereby generating cost-push inflation. Such arguments imply that trade union power is now too strong. Rather different criticisms come from those who assert that the trade union role is too weak and limited under collective bargaining and that the separation of collective bargaining from other political and managerial decision-making processes is misconceived. These argue that employees should not be limited in their influence to basic pay and conditions of employment but should have a voice on a much wider range of economic and political decisions related to work. Employee representatives should be accepted on tripartite decision-making bodies at national government level and should be represented on management boards at company level, in order to ensure genuine industrial democracy and the adequate representation of the labour force's interests.

From such criticisms have come a variety of proposals for government intervention. Some have called simply for government action to reduce the power of trade unions by adopting 'realistic' unemployment policies and anti-trade-union laws. Others have called for new types of decision-making machinery to replace or modify collective bargaining. An assessment of these different proposals is one of the themes of this book. At this stage we need only note that the proposals which call for new types of decision-making machinery imply perspectives on the subject matter which are very different from the traditional and once-dominant liberal collectivism, as we see below. Before turning to these other perspectives we can note that the political controversy over the future of collective bargaining has highlighted theoretical problems with liberal collectivism and shown up weaknesses in the 'systems' model that is widely used by academics working within this perspective.

The systems model of industrial relations
Theoretical analysis within the liberal-collectivist school of thought has been associated with Dunlop's model of an industrial relations system. Dunlop argued that industrial relations should be seen as a social sub-system, parallel to but distinct from the economic system. The industrial relations system consists of actors, contexts, a binding ideology and a body of rules. The actors are the state, employers, employees and any groups they have formed to represent them. These actors establish substantive and procedural rules to govern the employment relationship, by unilateral control, bilateral collective bargaining or tripartite control involving the state. The main external contexts influencing their behaviour are technology, market or budgetary constraints, and the distribution of power in society.

In constructing this model, Dunlop was heavily influenced by the ideas about social systems developed by sociologist and fellow American, C. A. Parsons. Dunlop argued that it was relevant to see industrial relations as a system because a change in one part would have repercussions on other parts, and because relations in the system were, to some extent, self-adjusting. A major upset in one area would lead to adjustments in relations until new rules, and a new stability, were reached. Central to this stabilising process was a binding ideology which all parties shared on the basic need for mutual survival and for procedures for conflict resolution.

This model has been widely used in industrial relations literature because it gives the subject a coherence and identity and has proved a useful framework for description. However, despite over thirty years' use, most comment on the model still takes the form of criticism or attempts at refinement, rather than attempts to use it to explain industrial behaviour. It has generated remarkably few analytical insights and has proved singularly unhelpful in explaining the current political controversy over the reform of British industrial relations.

Within sociology, Parsons' 'structural-functionalist' approach has long been criticised for an inability to explain social conflicts. Systems models rarely give adequate attention to fundamental sources of conflict and instability in society, and they overemphasise the stabilising force of common ideas or ideologies. The analytical device of separating out self-contained, self-adjusting 'systems' from the complex totality of social behaviour obscures the fact that broad-based social divisions can cut across political, economic and industrial relations systems, destabilising them all. By specifying three types of actor and assuming a mutual interest in survival, Dunlop's model discounts the possibility that interest groups may seek to eliminate rivals and in certain circumstances may succeed in doing so.

Most countries' industrial relations are relatively stable year by year, but the conflict generated around employment relations can be sufficiently severe to rupture the 'normal' or pre-existing rules and procedures. Employers have successfully destroyed trade unionism within their companies. Trade unions have sought the elimination of private capital, and governments have outlawed free trade unions and have expropriated employer capital. In such circumstances it makes little sense to talk of self-adjusting social systems. Certainly ideology does not prevent change. If conflicts are severe, then, rather than acting as a unifying force, the ideas that people hold can entrench opposed positions. Ideology can reinforce intransigence as well as collaboration.

There are two traditions within sociology which have generally proved more useful than Parsons' structural functionalism in the analysis of social conflict. These have developed from the work of Karl Marx and Max Weber and we mention both Marxian and Weberian perspectives below.

In what ways does this discussion of sociological theory help us sort out liberal collectivist perspectives? Academics advocating collective bargaining have been closely associated with Dunlop's model. In recent years their analyses have been attacked for theoretical weaknesses that can be blamed, in part, on an overreliance on Dunlop's framework. Free collective bargaining is advocated on the grounds that it satisfactorily resolves conflicts at work and removes economic conflicts from the political arena. For a period after the Second World War these assumptions seemed valid and it was argued that collective bargaining itself provided a stable, self-adjusting system of conflict resolution buttressed by the ideological support of different groups. Now collective bargaining is under attack, the systems-based assumptions that industrial relations can be separated from politics, or that there is consensus support for collective bargaining, are much more suspect. New prescriptions are based on theoretical assumptions which give more attention to the once-neglected questions of the relative power of different interest groups and the role of the state.

CORPORATISM AND AN ACTIVE STATE

Prescriptions which call for active state intervention and for joint decision-making machinery involving government with employer and employee representatives are labelled 'corporatist'. However clear definitions of corporatism are hard to pin down. The label is sometimes used very broadly to refer to any policies which depart from the clear-cut separation of the state and the economy, of governmental agencies from interest groups, which prevailed under old-fashioned liberalism (see the use of Harris, 1972). In more stringent definitions, corporatism is characterised as a system of interest representation in which the state directs the activities of predominantly privately-owned industries in partnership with the representatives of capital and labour. Both employer and employee representatives are able to help the state administer the agreed interventionist policies because their organisations have secure monopoly controls in their respective spheres of influence and because their membership is under authoritarian, well-disciplined control (see Schmitter, 1974, and Panitch, 1977).

Corporatist policies have in practice ranged from the voluntary tripartite participation of free trade unions and employers' associations on a few quasi-governmental agencies, to the highly coercive, regimented, administrative structures of Fascism. Because of this range the concept is usually sub-divided to contrast looser, more voluntary tripartism from more rigidly organised, hierarchically structured, compulsory corporatism (e.g. Harris, pluralist and etatist corporatism; Schmitter, societal and state corporatism; Panitch, liberal and pure corporatism; Crouch, bargained and pure corporatism).

The arguments backing corporatist prescriptions are that unbridled competition and power-based bargaining between groups in society produce results that are socially divisive and unjust, and that more co-ordinated, centrally administered, tripartite decision-making can produce fair and efficient results. The case has moral and pragmatic components.

The moral case for corporatism was put by Emile Durkheim, the French sociologist (1933, 1957, 1962). He argued that the division of labour in modern society had created numerous conflicting interest groups. Competition between these groups was the essence of social life, but a key problem in modern society was keeping this competition within reasonable bounds. With the rapid development of modern industry there was a danger of 'anomie' – a state of unbridled competition in which groups were totally unrestrained in their pursuit of naked sectional interests. Anomie was socially unhealthy. To be socially valuable, pluralist competition must be regulated and restrained by 'social norms' – i.e. agreed rules about fair play, fair rewards, justice and the appropriate means to group ends.

Durkheim briefly discussed how the anomic tendencies of modern industry should be cured and how acceptable regulating norms could be established. He emphasised the need to involve people in the decisions that governed their work. The citizen should be integrated into national government by means of self-government at work. Durkheim prescribed the division of economic activity into functionally distinct corporations which would each be governed democratically by 'a miniature parliament, nominated by election'. The state would be responsible for co-ordinating and planning the activities of the economic corporations and would administer its policies through them. 'In this way economic life would be organised, regulated and defined without losing any of its diversity.' Durkheim envisaged the gradual development of this sytem until the functional corporations replaced Parliament as the main way people participated in national government. He also believed corporatism would develop into a new political and economic system which was neither capitalist or socialist. Private property and private wealth would be eliminated as corporations took over the ownership of their own assets. Society would become meritocratic, there would be no class-based sense of injustice derived from inherited wealth and power, and social inequality would arise from personal merit alone.

This type of moral argument for corporatism has been more readily accepted on the continent than in the UK or USA, where the liberal suspicion of government intervention has had a more dominant impact on political attitudes. The moral case for highly developed corporatism was also discredited by the Fascist regimes of Mussolini's Italy and Nazi Germany where, far from heralding a new and more equal non-capitalist society, corporatist policies were coercively used by powerful groups to reduce opposition and individual freedom in society. Nevertheless, moral arguments for corporatism have been heard in the UK. In the 1930s Harold Macmillan (later a Conservative prime minister) advocated corporatist policies to overcome class conflict and create 'One Nation' in Britain, and from the other side of the class divide, Milne-

Bailey, a leading trade unionist, was advocating a National Economic Council consisting of employers and the Trades Union Congress (TUC) to advise Parliament on economic policy. Milne-Bailey (1934) envisaged a time when the state would direct semi-autonomous nationalised industries with trade unionists on their governing boards, and when unions would have wide responsibilities over the allocation and management of labour.

Since the experience of Fascism both the corporatist label itself, and the moral arguments for corporatism, are less often used within the UK. Corporatist prescriptions are still advocated but the arguments now emphasise pragmatic grounds, and corporatist prescriptions are presented as slight modifications to the existing mixed economy, not as moves to a new and better type of political system. The main argument used now is that the functional interest groups have grown to such a size that free and open power bargaining between them is too disruptive, their unregulated activity too unjust. Business organisations are no longer small, the economy has evolved from the competitive market model to monopoly capitalism in which giant bureaucratic organisations are able to manipulate and regulate markets. On the employee side, trade unions have grown in coverage, and in their attempt to match the power of big business they coerce people into membership and pressure them to support their policies in a way that inevitably reduces their members' freedom of action. The state must take the responsibility for intervening to regulate the activities of these powerful functional groups. In addition it is argued that state policies of non-intervention are premised on fiction. In complex modern economies, state activity inevitably has a major impact on the economy. The state directly employs a large proportion of the labour force. The public sector provides the infrastructure – from education to roads – on which private industry depends. The public sector provides the market for the most advanced technology and sponsors much scientific and technical innovation. Even the traditional fiscal and exchange rate policies crucially affect the distribution of economic resources. The state has very considerable economic responsibilities and once these are openly accepted then it should become apparent that the best way to develop and administer national economic policy is with the co-operation of the functional organisations – the unions and employers' associations – primarily involved.

The arguments backing corporatist prescriptions rest on important assumptions about the distribution of power in society. Moral advocates of corporatism tend to assume that society is subdivided between numerous competing groups, that there is a sufficiently complex balance of power to ensure that no group dominates, and that the state will adopt a neutral 'umpire' role between competing interests. In the UK, the corporatist policies which have been advocated have been at the voluntary, loose or bargained end of the range of corporatism. Advocates of this type of corporatism assume two dominant interests in society – capital and labour. They then assume that there is a sufficient equivalence of power between capital and labour to prevent state intervention degenerating into the totalitarian oppression of one class by the other. Critics of the corporatist perspective believe that capital and labour interests are not matched in power and that therefore state intervention is likely to lead to oppression. However, the critics disagree on whether they see a 'union state' or corporatist capitalism as the likely outcome. Both versions see individual civil liberties and tolerance of opposition sacrificed in the pursuit of dominance by either trade union or capitalist interests.

Corporatism seemed to be the rising perspective on industrial relations in the UK in the 1970's. Academics discussed the inevitable development of corporatist policies and spoke of a growth industry in corporatist analysis. Within politics, the programmes of the Labour party, the Social Democratic party and the left wing of the Conservative party still contain many corporatist prescriptions, and the TUC consistently advocates forms of corporatist state intervention. However, the election in 1979 of the anti-corporatist Conservative government led by Mrs Thatcher brought to prominence a very different perspective on affairs.

LIBERAL INDIVIDUALISM AND NEO-*LAISSEZ-FAIRE*

Liberal individualism recognises conflicts of economic interest between employers and employees, but rejects both collective bargaining and tripartite institutions for handling that conflict. Instead, the prescribed mechanism is the individual contract of employment.

The classical *laissez-faire* economists of the nineteenth century argued that economic conflicts of interest should be resolved by contracts, freely entered into by people operating in perfectly competitive markets. Any combination by the buyers or sellers of any commodity would reduce market competition and this would upset the guiding hand of the free market mechanism which, left to itself, ensured the greatest possible benefit for all.

In the employment field this meant that individual workers should bargain with individual employers to agree contracts of employment for each worker. There would inevitably be conflicts as employees sought the highest price, the best conditions and the least onerous work, and employers wanted the lowest price, the least costly conditions and the most effective and flexible service. However, these conflicts should be resolved in the agreed terms of the employment contract. Thereafter the relationship should be conflict-free. If employees were not prepared to seek other work, renegotiate their contract or challenge their employers' interpretation of the contract in court, they should give the service they were contracted to provide without dispute or grievance. Any combination by trade unions or associations of employers to influence the terms of employment contracts was to be deplored, because it would upset the allocative working of labour supply and demand.

These arguments are liberal because they assume a society composed of an aggregation of relatively equal people capable, if free from state interference, of pursuing their own best interests by freely entering into contracts with others. The arguments are individualist because they follow *laissez-faire* doctrine in deploring pressure groups, monopolies or 'combinations'. Market and moral reasons are given for this. Market reasons we have already mentioned – that, in a competitive market, forces exist which will determine a just, fair price for labour that also ensures the most efficient distribution of labour resources. Combinations, on the employer or employee side, would upset this mechanism by creating too great a concentration of power and enabling some workers and employers to profit at the expense of others. Moral liberalism provides an attack on combinations on political grounds. It argues that the equal right to vote in a parliamentary democracy grants everyone equal power in society. Pressure groups of any kind can coerce their own members or the rest of society. They upset the mechanism of government by elected MPs.

The nineteenth-century assumptions and arguments of liberal individualism fit uneasily into a world where combinations both of employers and of employees have gained unprecedented size and influence and where perfectly competitive markets are a rare feature of the world economy. Nevertheless, the liberal-individualist perspective has long supported an anti-union stance among certain employers, judges and politicians in the UK. Writing in 1977, Moran noted that the Conservative party had always contained a substantial core of market liberals, and 'in recent years the main custodian of moral liberalism has been the judiciary'. The combinations under attack have usually been those of employees rather than employers and the main symbol of oppressive combination has been seen as the trade union practice of the closed shop, on the ground that it takes away individual liberty.

The liberal-individualist perspective has often been presented in industrial relations literature as an outdated hangover from the nineteenth century. It has been seen as barely worthy of consideration in a century which has seen the development of trade unions in every industrial society of the world and the development of giant multinational enterprises with monopolistic or oligopolistic control of many product and labour markets. However the election of President Regan in the USA and of Mrs Thatcher in the UK, both relying on neo-*laissez-faire* economic policies, brought new life to this perspective. The industrial relations policy of the Thatcher government has not attempted to dismantle the old and pervasive collective bargaining machinery, but it exudes a suspicion and distrust of trade unionism often expressed in liberal-individualist terms.

In the USA liberal individualism has never been dead as a source of opposition to trade unions. For many years it has helped fuel employer opposition to trade unionism and it provided the ideology supporting the 'Right to Work' laws which prohibit union shops in many American states. In the UK American multi-nationals have been eloquent in their use of liberal-individualist arguments against trade unionism. For example International Business Machines (IBM) mounted an extensive and expensive campaign putting these views to its employees during a dispute over trade union recognition in 1977.

MARXIST PERSPECTIVES

Marxist prescriptions for revolutionary changes in the economic and political system have few adherents in the UK today. Marxism has always had a weaker influence on British trade union ideology than on most European trade union movements. And in recent years the Marxist assumption that the elimination of private property would remove the fundamental conflicts at work has been discredited by the pervasive evidence that industrial conflict thrives in Poland, the USSR and China. Nevertheless, although Marxist prescriptions for a future conflict-free society are generally treated with scepticism, the Marxist analysis of existing employment relations has a wider following and Marxism provides an important critique of the liberal and corporatist perspectives.

Marxists see the process of control over employment relations as inescapably bound up with antagonistic class relations. Under capitalist modes of production they see a constant and irreducible struggle between capital and labour which extends past economic issues to a political struggle for control. In this process there can be no stable balance of power and any accommodation made by trade union leaders with the forces of capital must be suspect. However Marxists vary on how far they disparage institutions for employee participation under capitalism. Two broad schools of Marxist thought are relevant to our discussion. One view rejects the value of any institutional change as long as the political economy is capitalist. The other argues that institutional reform can be used to weaken gradually the hegemony of capitalist interests in society.

Orthodox or 'hard line' Marxists argue that both collective bargaining and corporatism merely integrate working-class leaders into the existing political structures to the long-term detriment of the working class. Thus Lenin, Trotsky and political theorists like Michels (1915) and C. Wright Mills (1959) have argued that trade unions are hindrances in the process to radical change. Union activities further narrow, small-group or sectional interests, not the interests of the working class as a whole, and the growth of a bureaucratised leadership and of collective bargaining leads unions to adopt bourgeois interests and bourgeois ideology. 'As institutions trade unions do not *challenge* the existence of a society based on a division of classes, they merely express it. . .Trade unions can never be viable vehicles of advance towards socialism. . .They can bargain within the society, but not transform it' (Anderson, 1967). This view of collective bargaining helps explain why collective bargaining has been less developed in France than in the UK, where the largely communist union federation, the Conféderation Générale du Travail (CGT) for many years opposed collaboration with employers over collective bargaining.

Corporatist institutions involving collaboration with government are equally suspect. Current proposals for compulsory planning agreements, extended industrial democracy and public control of the finance industry are attacked for naivety. No government, constrained by the economic power of international finance, could implement such policies unless they were being used to weaken workers' control. There can be no bargained corporatism that benefits working-class interests.

The Marxists who are less dismissive of employee participation within capitalism can quote Marx's support for trade unions as the organisations through which workers would gain the experience and political consciousness which would lead them on to effective struggle for social change and they also cite his support for factory legislation in the UK. With the Italian Marxist, Gramsci (1971), they argue that, in Europe, political change can occur through slow, institutional reforms that gradually increase working-class power.

Both views within Marxism have been heard in the UK, and both added to the controversy surrounding the analysis of the corporatist policies adopted in the 1970s (see Chapter 9). The second, 'eurocommunist', stance has the support of many British Marxists. Richard Hyman, in his *Industrial Relations: A Marxist Introduction* (1975), argues that collective bargaining has benefited British workers, while Will Paynter, the Communist General Secretary of the National Union of Mineworkers (NUM) from 1951 to 1969 believed that bargained corporatism could be used to benefit the working class (Paynter, 1970). However, hard-line arguments about the dangers of government intervention have aided the critics of incomes policy within the British union movement in recent years.

In their analysis of the prescriptions arising from other perspectives Marxists insist that economic and political issues cannot be separated, they place great emphasis on the antagonistic interests of capital and labour, and they focus, in a way that many other perspectives do not, on the importance of assessing the power held by opposing interests.

THE WEBERIAN PERSPECTIVE

This chapter has reviewed a plethora of different types of prescription for British industrial relations. Tangled up with prescription and analysis are different value judgements on the social value of conflict, and on the role of trade unions, management and the state. Table 2.1 summarises the judgements associated with different perspectives. There is much controversy about the analysis and interpretation of industrial relations behaviour, and industrial relations debate is often less concerned with the careful, systematic analysis of evidence than with the search for propaganda to support entrenched value judgements. This is not surprising; few people are indifferent to the social arrangements that regulate work and, as in politics, it would be a very strange person who had no values to express on the issues involved. Nevertheless, we need to recognise that prejudice is rife in discussions on industrial relations and we need to prevent our own value biases from distorting our view of reality. In this context, we can introduce our final perspective, which is derived from a social theorist who gets small mention in industrial relations analysis.

Max Weber was not concerned with prescription, which is, no doubt, why he has no industrial relations following. In his attempt to understand social situations he adopted a value-neutral approach both to conflict and to social institutions. Both conflict and co-operation he saw as inherent in social relations: co-operation because humans are social animals unable to survive, let alone achieve higher objectives, without the collaboration of others; conflict because both within and between social groups there will be competition over resources, values and power.

Weber's approach to the social institutions that develop out of these co-operative, conflictual relations was dispassionate. All societies develop social institutions, i.e. regular patterns of behaviour for dealing with work, family relations, moral values, and so on. However, the fact that these institutions invariably exist in one form or another does not automatically give any particular institution social value. He rejected the common bias – ingrained

Table 2.1 *Value Judgements Associated with Different Perspectives*

Likely Judgement on:	Unitary	Liberal-Collectivist	Corporatist	Liberal-Individualist	Marxist
Conflict at work	Unnecessary and harmful	Group conflicts on economic issues inevitable, beneficial *if* institutionalised through collective bargaining	Group conflicts on economic and political issues inevitable, beneficial *if* institutionalised by incorporating the different interests onto decision-making bodies	Individual conflicts on the economic terms of employment inevitable. Can be resolved in the contract of employment	Class conflict inevitable within capitalism. Cannot be successfully institutionalised unless revolution leads to workers' control
Trade union role	Harmful and unnecessary	Interest groups which can help institutionalise conflict through collective bargaining	Interest groups which can help incorporate workers onto governing bodies	Harmful and unnecessary	Potentially valuable organs of working-class struggle. Harmful if, by accommodation with capital, they dissipate the energy of the working class and prevent change
Management role	Invaluable. Enhances general interests through economic development	Represents employer interests* and can help institutionalise conflict through collective bargaining	Represents employer interests and can help build a unified corporate state	Invaluable. Enhances general interests through economic development	Unnecessary. Servants of power, helping to exploit the workforce. An unwarranted hindrance to workers' self-government
The role of the state	Guardian of the national interest	Potentially coercive. Role in the economy should be minimised	The active guardian of the national interest	Potentially coercive. Role in the economy should be minimised	Under capitalism, the state is the agent of capital

* Some critics have argued that the liberal collectivists are, in practice, more 'managerialist' than this implies, i.e. likely to treat management interests as superior to workers' interests (Goldthorpe, 1974). The same can be said for some versions of corporatism, i.e. management is seen to have a higher, national interest which is not matched by trade union interests.

in the structural-functionalist school of sociology – that assumes that existing social institutions have developed to serve some social purpose and therefore must have social value. Weber argued instead that institutions develop out of the inevitable power battles between conflicting interest groups within society. The form they take therefore depends on the dominant group, and their dominant values.

Total value neutrality is neither possible nor desirable in the analysis of social behaviour, but Weber's views provide a useful caution on the need to be fully aware of prejudice and bias, especially in an area as filled with controversy as is industrial relations in the UK today. Weber was less optimistic than Marx or Durkheim about the potentially egalitarian development of social institutions. He placed an emphasis on the analysis of power, ideology and techniques of control that we shall be referring to again.

CONCLUSION

This chapter has reviewed a complex range of different approaches to industrial relations. Any reader who started without any familiarity with current industrial debates may well be totally baffled by the array of 'isms' and 'ists'. However this categorisation of different perspectives on the subject matter should have demonstrated that the analysis of industrial relations is contentious, and should help explain why there are so many contrasting proposals for reform.

Far from being a descriptive subject, based on common sense, industrial relations is riven with political and theoretical controversy. There are a multitude of ways of interpreting what *is* going on, and a multitude of views about what *should* be happening in the area.

There are no generally accepted global theories in industrial relations. Neither liberal collectivism, corporatism, Marxism nor liberal individualism provide explanations that can account for the main industrial relations trends in the modern world. However these perspectives provide a rich source of ideas that can be used to explain behaviour in particular circumstances at particular times. For example the liberal-collectivist analysis of collective bargaining goes some way to explaining the stability of collective bargaining systems, given certain contexts. The Marxist argument that class conflict exacerbates industrial conflict is crucial in understanding the industrial relations of certain countries at certain times. The industrial relations policies of Japan, Germany and some governments of the UK are illuminated by an understanding of the debate about corporatism.

In the rest of this book we shall look at the raw material around which our abstract perspectives have been drawn. We study employers, employees, the representative institutions that they form, and the activities and role of the state. In this study we will be concerned to assess the types of conflict that seem to predominate, the power available to back up different interests and the social and political consequences of collective bargaining or state intervention in employment relations. These are the issues which need to be clarified if we are to judge between the different assumptions and analyses currently made about British industrial relations.

Chapter 3

Employers and their Strategies

The first of the groups we pick out for analysis are those formed by employers. This choice of starting point needs explanation. The commonsense view is that industrial relations is primarily about trade unions, that unions are the obvious and most important groups involved. Unions are certainly the focus of most public debate in the area and they receive by far the most attention in broadcast and press news. Surveys show that 41 per cent of people quoted or mentioned in newspaper items on industrial issues are from trade unions, whereas only 14 per cent are managers and employers. Employers are similarly absent from television news and have been called the 'invisible heroes' of industrial news stories (McQuail, 1977; Glasgow University Media Group, 1976 and 1980; Palmer and Littler, 1977).

The low profile of employers in the media obscures the importance of employer behaviour for shaping industrial relations. Employers are not powerless or ineffective compared to trade unions, but their power has a different base and its exercise attracts less attention. Employer influence can pass unobserved. Union strength rests largely on the power to strike. This is a very visible weapon and can be powerful if the strikers represent irreplaceable labour, or if the production lost during the strike is of crucial importance to employer's interests: for example, in the newspaper industry, where yesterday's news can never be sold – or anywhere else where demand is high, stocks low and competition fierce. However there are many situations where the strike is a double-edged and dubious weapon. Doubled-edged because strikers risk loss of income during the strike which may take years to recover (Gennard, 1977; Gennard and Lasko, 1975). Dubious because success depends not only on correct tactics against opponents, but also on the strikers' ability to maintain a united stand. If the union membership is divided or loses confidence, then the credibility of the strike as a powerful weapon can vanish overnight.

In contrast to union power, employer power is less visual and newsworthy and can often be used more flexibly. Capital, unlike strike power, can be converted into other profit-generating activities, or even moved out of the country, without the constant need to win the active support of a mass of people. Employer power is not unconstrained but it is considerable. Union power may be considerable, but even where this is the case it is usually so constrained by the problems of mobilising strikes that its use is limited to defensive issues where numbers of people clearly see they have a common interest. British union power has traditionally been directed to the defence of living standards and the improvement of a narrow range of related issues like hours or holidays. Employers are in a better position to take initiatives. They can usually exert a broader influence on the control of employment relations.

Academic work has, for some years, emphasised the importance of employer initiatives in shaping personnel policies and the framework of industrial relations institutions (Turner *et al.,* 1977; Clegg, 1976). The Royal Commission on Trade Unions and Employers' Associations (the Donovan Commission) produced an influential analysis of the problems within the UK's collective bargaining system in 1968 and concluded that the main power and therefore the main responsibility for reform lay with employers. However so far little has been said about these crucial, influential parties. As Thurley and Wood (1983) argue, the importance of the employer is assumed rather than investigated, employers have been almost as invisible in academic studies as in the press.

WHO ARE THE EMPLOYERS?

A stereotyped view of the employer is of a bowler-hatted autocrat, clearly visible at the top of his mine or mill, directly controlling his workforce by issuing personal instructions. This model is too simple even for the nineteenth century, when 'the boss' often related to his workforce through managing sub-contractors. It is even more misleading for modern industry, where 'the employer' is likely to be the board of directors of a public company or nationalised corporation and where the management of the workforce is delegated to a hierarchy of managerial employees.

Roughly fourteen million out of Britain's working population of twenty-four million work for very large employers. The government is the employer for roughly seven million of the country's working population: two million work for central government, the National Health Service, the Post Office or British Telecom; nearly two million work in other nationalised corporations; and rather less than three million in local authorities and education. In the private sector another seven million are employed by large companies with assets of over two million pounds, four and a half million of these in 155 enterprises with ten thousand or more UK employees (Bullock, 1977). One of the most significant trends in the twentieth century has been the concentration of modern industry into fewer, giant companies. At the beginning of the century the hundred largest firms in British manufacturing produced 15 per cent of net output; by 1975 this figure was near 50 per cent. In 1935 there were 136,000 small firms employing less than two hundred people and responsible for 35 per cent of output, but by 1963 their numbers were reduced to 60,000 producing only 16 per cent of net output (Hannah and Kay, 1977). The large employer predominates.

The concentration of business is not just a UK phenomenon although many have suggested it is more pronounced here than elsewhere (Bullock, 1977; Hannay and Kay, 1977). The global concentration of Western business has been accentuated since the Second World War by the rapid development of multinational enterprises (MNEs). Such firms spread their boundaries across nation states and employ people in different countries. Sixteen per cent of the enterprises with over two hundred employees in the UK are controlled from overseas. Large enterprises in the UK employ an additional two million abroad; 51 per cent of enterprises employing over two thousand in the UK have some overseas employees, while 61 per cent of these large employers have more employees overseas than in the UK (Bullock, 1977).

The concentration of business and the growth of MNEs introduces onto the industrial relations scene employers who have the financial resources of small nation states and enough employees to populate large towns. ICI, the UK's biggest manufacturing company, had assets of over £5,000 million and 132,000 employees in 1980. In 1972 there were thirty companies in the UK with over 40,000 employees. The largest private company in the world, the American multinational General Motors, has over 600,000 employees.

The development of giant organisations has not eliminated the medium and small employer, but it has often changed the smaller employers' position in product and labour markets. Many economists and business historians speak of the development of a dual economy. Large monopolistic or oligopolistic corporations operate in the primary economy, surrounded by a secondary economy of smaller, fiercely competitive organisations (A. Friedmann, 1977; Edwards, 1979; Chandler, 1962, 1977; Chandler and Daems, 1980). The employers in the secondary economy often service the core organisations of the primary sector and are likely to feel more vulnerable to market pressures and be pressurised by the primary sector in economic recession.

EMPLOYER OBJECTIVES

Asked about their objectives in industrial relations, employers and their spokesmen rarely say that they wish to achieve maximum subordination to managerial objectives and maximum production and flexibility from their employees, in return for minimum costs. They rarely state that their employees' standard of living or quality of working life must be subordinated to overriding financial objectives. Yet both classical and Marxist theories of capitalist production posit employer objectives in these terms. These economic theories state that if an employer is to succeed, or even survive in the face of competition, he must treat his labour force as a resource, a cost to his business, like his non-human raw materials. Some theorists add the argument that the struggle to contain labour power that has been purchased must be the employers' *main* priority in the search for profit or capital accumulation (Braverman, 1974).

Any employers who do simply seek to minimise labour costs and maximise the exploitation of their labour resources are unlikely to say so in public. The attack on the legitimacy of such objectives from the political left, and from humanitarians who object to the use of other people as a means to one's own end, is sufficient to make discussion of employer objectives a value-laden, smoke-screened topic. Employers have developed a defence against attacks on their objectives towards labour, which emphasises the long-term interest of both employer and employee in a profitable enterprise.

The pressures on employers to treat their labour force as a resource and the problem of legitimising the policies which flow from this are both neatly illustrated by a historical study of Quaker employers, which suggests that market pressures will constrain policy towards employees, even for entrepreneurs whose values and beliefs might favour very different policies. Child (1964) lists four Quaker beliefs that posed serious moral dilemmas for the influential Quaker businessmen of the first half of the twentieth century. These beliefs were: (1) a dislike of exploitation and profit at the expense of others; (2) the importance of service, stressing hard work and personal renunciation in the service of others; (3) egalitarianism and the need for democratic relations between people; and (4) an abhorence of social conflict. From 1902 to 1922 Quaker employers came under considerable pressure from colleagues in the Society of Friends to renounce property rights and the profit motive and establish democratically-run businesses based on moral rather than material objectives. Child charts the response to this pressure and shows that Quaker employers slowly rejected the values of egalitarian and democratic relations and the arguments that employers renounce privileged status or rewards. Instead they emphasised a general notion of service and the abhorence of conflict, i.e. those values that conflicted less with conventional, commerical business objectives. Child suggests that Quaker employers were spurred to produce an articulate defence of management in social terms, which has been widely adopted by other employers. They argued that employers had the moral and social responsibility to lead their organisations effectively and use the most efficient managerial techniques. This would enable them to serve the community – without personal renounciation – by improving the pay and fringe benefits of their employees. It was more socially responsible to be efficient than to be democratic.

Faced with considerable ideological attack from within the Society of Friends, Quaker employers led the way in introducing welfare measures for employees like holidays, sick pay, pensions, even housing, and in providing lighter, brighter working conditions. These benefits would traditionally have seemed harmful to employer interests because they raised labour costs, but Child notes that economic justifications could be, and soon were, found in terms of a reduction in the costs of labour turnover, and increased productivity. Welfare policies did not alter the basic authority relationships at work or represent any radical rejection of the employer objectives posited by classical economic theory.

In competitive markets, owner-managers have usually been forced to minimise labour costs in order to keep the price of their products competitive and make the profits necessary to attract support from financial markets and suppliers. However there is still a debate about the extent to which changes in ownership, or changes in business concentration, have lessened market-based constraints on employer policy towards employees.

Ownership, Control and Objectives

A great deal of industry is no longer run by proprietors. We therefore need to ask whether the separation of ownership from management, or even the nationalisation of industry, has fundamentally altered the constraints that shape employers' objectives in the employment relationship.

The diffusion of ownership in scattered shareholdings and the growth of salaried, professional management has led to an extensive debate in economic, political and sociological literature on the effects of the divorce of ownership from control. Many writers have adopted a 'managerialist' stance. They argue that managers rather than owners now direct business affairs, and that they pursue objectives that differ from those of the owner-entrepreneur. The managerialists can be divided into those who believe managerial interests will be sectional and those who do not.

Non-sectional managerialists take an optimistic view and argue that managers, freed from the controls exercised by the owning elite, are likely to pursue objectives that benefit the community as a whole. They will form a powerful new group acting as a neutral buffer between the warring interests of capital and labour. They will be more concerned with employee and community welfare, or with public opinion, than are shareholders.

Sectional managerialists do not have this rosy view of managers' wider social responsibilities. They also argue that managers are less constrained by shareholders and have more autonomy in running businesses, but they believe this freedom will be used in the pursuit of the managers' own sectional interests. They argue that managers now maximise sales revenue or growth, rather than profits; are concerned with a quiet life or with increasing promotion prospects, rather than financial returns. They are not necessarily more concerned about their employees' welfare, although they will have greater common interest with them in the organisation's survival.

Counter arguments against the managerialist views are put by Marxists and neo-Marxist economists and sociologists. They accept that many large companies are no longer controlled by majority shareholders, but they argue that this does not result in managers pursuing fundamentally different economic or social objectives.

These ideas have stimulated much research and the many strands of detailed argument are best summarised by Child (1969, pp. 36–51). Child assesses the evidence in support of the rival thesis and concludes that, on balance, the evidence supports the Marxist rather than the managerialist view of top management objectives. He notes that owner interests can have a direct impact on managerial decisions even when no majority shareholder exists. Diversified shareholding may simply mean that a minority shareholder, with a significant block of voting shares, can exercise the traditional owners' role on the board. Indeed owner control may be increasing as the growth of institutional shareholding by banks and insurance companies produces 'professional' shareholders more skilled in judging company affairs. Child studies the evidence on how senior managers actually behave and finds they tend to adopt values and objectives very like the traditional shareholder. Nichols (1969) found top managers adopting the same ideology and objectives as shareholders because they tended to come from the same background, share the same social relations and had a high proportion of their own personal wealth in shares. Other studies suggest managerial decisions are constrained by capital markets, even when the direct intervention of shareholders or the shareholder orientation of managers are absent. The threat of takeover, and the need for capital support to finance investment, place considerable constraints on the extent to which any manager can diverge from conventional business objectives.

Child criticises the Marxist view of employer objectives on the grounds that there may be differences between shareholders (for example, differences between national and international or financial and community interests) which can blur the edges of the division of interest between capital and labour. He also notes that the traditional owner-entrepreneur may never have pursued profit maximisation as single-mindedly nor as successfully as either Marxist or classical economists assume, often because of primitive or non-existent accounting techniques. Nevertheless he concludes that the evidence supports the argument that the separation of business ownership and control has not fundamentally altered the objectives pursued by the controllers of business. 'In short the popular managerialist thesis that the separation of business ownership and control is one of the most momentous developments in modern capitalist society fails to remain convincing when placed alongside the available evidence' (Child, 1969, p. 51); a conclusion that is supported by more recent studies of British company directors (Brookes, 1979; Winkler, 1974).

The experience of nationalisation in the UK lends further support to Child's view that in modern capitalist societies 'there are wider economic, social and technological constraints operating on the business enterprise which tend to minimise the behavioural differences between owner-managers and non-propertied managers'. Calls for nationalisation in the first quarter of the twentieth century were based on the belief that public ownership would radically change social relations at work and herald a new era in which employers and workers could work harmoniously for the good of the community. There were different suggestions on how publicly-owned enterprises should be run. Guild Socialists advocated the self-management of industry by democratically-run guilds, who would contract with the employers to produce a certain output, at a given price. The mine workers' union and the National Union of Railwaymen suggested schemes for their industries involving government by councils composed of union officials and technical and administrative experts. A more moderate 'reformist' view was that publicly-owned enterprises should be managed entirely by expert managers free to take decisions on the normal criteria of business efficiency. These managers would be subject to the supervision of a board, appointed by government. It was this last model that was adopted in the Nationalisation Acts of the UK, and experience has shown that the objectives which lie behind nationalised managements' approach to employment relations do not differ very radically from those in private industry.

There is the same concern with labour as a cost, and the same need to maximise the effort and flexibility of labour, and to subordinate labour to managerial authority in order to pursue more dominant objectives of efficiency, low costs and reasonable returns on investment. Government guidelines have placed these managers under increasingly tight economic constraints in relation to their employees. There *are* differences in managerial behaviour between public and private concerns, but these can often be explained as the adoption of different strategies to suit different environments, rather than as evidence of fundamentally different objectives (Thomson in Thurley and Wood, 1983). Public concerns are likely to have to consider social or nationalistic policies, for example requiring support for rural services that normal profit motives would not justify. In the UK, national policy has required nationalised enterprises to support employee representation through trade unions and pay determination by collective bargaining. In many countries national policy gives priority to job security, and some extra concern for public employees' security has been shown by certain governments in the UK. Public concerns in mixed economies are also likely to be monopolies. Monopolistic or oligopolistic market positions may affect the treatment of employees, by widening the choice of strategy available to employers in pursuit of commercial objectives.

There is a broad uniformity in the objectives pursued by employers in the employment field, but the strategies adopted in pursuit of those objectives take many forms. Before we look at the particular strategies that have been adopted towards employees, we need a more general understanding of techniques of managerial control.

TECHNIQUES OF MANAGERIAL CONTROL

The employer's interest in the employment relationship is a by-product of his pursuit of more primary objectives. If these objectives can only be achieved through the efforts of employees, then the employer needs to recruit staff and build an organisation through which employee behaviour can be co-ordinated, monitored and controlled in a way that will ensure that the employer's plans are executed. Simply buying labour power on the labour market will not be enough, for in the market the employer buys hours of work, or labour potential. In order to turn this potential into something of value to the employer, labour needs to be directed, organised and controlled.

What techniques can be used by anyone wanting to organise and co-ordinate employees? Organisation theory has focused on this question and many volumes have been written analysing, for managers, the control techniques that might be most effective. A very simple typology showing the broad range of managerial techniques has been developed by an Imperial College team continuing studies started by Joan Woodward. According to them, there are three basic types of managerial control:

(a) *Personal supervision*   The employer personally allocates work, issues instructions, checks on the methods being used and monitors the standard of results. In organisations of increasing size this function of personal supervision is delegated to managers and a pyramidal hierarchy of 'line management' can ensure that many people are receiving instructions from the top. Hierarchies of supervision are familiar in all organisations of any size. However, most employers no longer rely on direct personnel supervision to express and enforce their demands on organisational behaviour. More impersonal administrative and mechanical controls have replaced personal supervision as the most significant managerial techniques.

(b) *Administrative controls*   Administrative controls are based on rules. Impersonal rules specify desired behaviour, and rules may regulate recruitment, hours, wages, effort, promotion or discipline and may be elaborated to provide complex programmes for production planning, measurement mechanisms or cost control systems. We discuss this type further under the heading 'bureaucracy' below.

(c) *Mechanical controls*   Mechanical controls are a further step towards 'impersonal' control, for the required rules on standards of performance, speed, etc. are planned and built in the design stage of automated machines or process plant. Decisions about the planning and design of work may be taken at a different time and place from where the work is eventually executed. For example, crucial decisions about the pattern of jobs and the work process in a chemical process plant may have been taken by the firm of consultant engineers employed before the plant was built.

This typology has been re-emphasised by the Marxist economist, Edwards (1979), who distinguishes between personal, bureaucratic and technological control on a similar basis.

Many writers have noted a general historical trend away from personal supervision and towards the other methods of control (Kyneston Reeves and Woodward, 1970; Edwards, 1979). Although mechanical controls are increasing, they will not predominate until all production is processed through automated plants and robots replace employees. In order to understand the main employer strategies towards employment, we therefore need to focus on (b), administrative controls. These have been more fully analysed in terms of the concept of bureaucracy.

Bureaucracy and Bureaucratic Managerial Controls

In conventional sterotypes, bureaucracy is often seen as a cumbersome, inefficient form of organisation hampered by red tape and rigidity. Nevertheless much organisation theory revolves around the concept of bureaucracy, and many recent studies of employer strategies towards employees have found the concept of bureaucracy an invaluable guide (Littler, 1982; Clawson, 1980). In modern organisation theory the concept is used in different ways. It is therefore wise to return to the classic analysis of bureaucratic organisation developed at the start of the century by Max Weber.

Weber (1947) saw the widespread development of bureaucratic administration as one of the most significant, far-reaching social changes in the modern world. Bureaucratic techniques gave organisational controllers the potential for unprecedented control over social resources in pursuit of their objectives and enabled them to build organisations that were larger and more complex than ever before. Because these control techniques were so superior to other methods of organisation, they were likely to dominate modern business and political organisations, regardless of the particular political economy in operation. In this analysis Weber took issue with Marx who viewed bureaucracy as a powerful but unnecessary form of government which would be replaced under socialism by more effective and more personal forms of large-scale organisation.

What were the features of this remarkable form of organisation? Weber gave several lists of characteristics, and his analysis needs careful interpretation if it is to be used in the context of modern employer strategies. Here we follow Littler (1982, Ch. 4) in separating Weber's bureaucratic control techniques into two sets. One set consists of the provisions that surround the appointment, promotion, rewarding and disciplining of employees. We can call this the bureaucratic personnel policy. The other set concerns the structure of hierarchical control, the design of jobs and the direction and monitoring of work. We can call this bureaucratic control over task performance. The details are set out in Table 3.1.

Why would such techniques be effective in achieving employer objectives? Weber argued that the impersonal, hierarchical, rule-bound characteristics of bureaucratic organisation gave organisational rulers an unprecedented ability to direct the behaviour of large numbers of people towards organisational ends. They enabled the people at the top of an organisation to plan work, and then allocate tasks throughout the organisation, while specifying the criteria on which any decisions should be based. They also guarded against the danger of senior managers becoming dependent on any particular employee. On the personnel policy side, the much maligned position of bureaucrats with their formal recruitment, job security, careers and incremental pay scales, Weber saw as carefully designed to build loyalty and motivation into the organisation's workforce.

Table 3.1   *Bureaucratic Control Techniques*

Control over task performance	Personnel Policy
A hierarchy of supervision Written rules specify: ● a systematic and detailed division of labour ● the authority and responsibility of each office ● details of how work is to be performed Detailed, written records are kept	Contractual relationship between employer and employee Written rules specify: ● recruitment criteria based on technical or professional qualifications ● discipline procedures Fixed money salaries are graded by rank. Employees have pension rights Employees are given the opportunity of career promotion, based on merit or seniority.

Source: Adapted from Littler (1982), p. 38.

Bureaucratic administrative techniques have become widespread and, as a leading organisational theorist in the USA argues 'the vast majority of large organisations are fairly bureaucratic... Without this form of social organisation, the industrialised countries of the West could not have reached the heights of extravagence, wealth and pollution that they currently enjoy', but '... by its very nature, and particularly because of its superiority as a social tool over other forms of organisation, bureaucracy generates an enormous degree of unregulated and often unperceived social power...in the hands of a very few leaders' (Perrow, 1972).

Virtually all modern organisations use some of the managerial, bureaucratic techniques charted above. However, there are now many forms of bureaucracy. Employers pursue different strategies and different policies towards their employees using different versions of bureaucratic techniques. Employee reactions may themselves force bureaucratic adjustments to managerial controls. We need to look at the different types of bureaucratic strategy that are adopted.

EMPLOYER STRATEGIES ON EMPLOYMENT RELATIONS

Employer strategies towards employees are only now becoming the subject of explicit research in industrial relations (Thurley and Wood, 1983; Gospel and Littler, 1983). A longer tradition of research in this area exists within sociology, where studies of bureaucracy have a long history and where there has been a recent revival of interest in the labour process – i.e. the methods used to manage manual workers in order to convert purchased labour power into valuable work for the employer. Cross-fertilisation of ideas between industrial sociology and industrial relations is long overdue and can help both disciplines improve the study of employer strategies on the employment relationship. The revival of interest in employer strategies started with a vivid and controversial analysis of Taylorism by Braverman (1974). We start our review of employer strategies with this.

Taylorism

Writing as an American ex-craftsman, Braverman argues that work has been degraded during the twentieth century. The dominant strategy employed by American business in relation to its workforce has been to deskill jobs. This has enabled them to hire cheaper, semi-skilled or unskilled labour and exercise tighter control over how work is done.

Central to Braverman's case is the argument that the theories and methods of F. W. Taylor, who worked from 1890 to 1915, were widely adopted by employers, and still provide the criteria used by industrial engineers and work study departments to divide the labour process into jobs. Taylor initiated the 'Scientific Management' movement in the USA and his ideas on work study, job design and individual incentives had a major impact in the USA and Western Europe and, through Lenin's interest, in the USSR. Taylorite schemes have been introduced into many companies over the years, and Braverman's argument is that, despite considerable academic attack and the rise of new fashions like 'Human Relations' or 'Job Enrichment', Taylor's basic principles have not been superseded where it matters most – in job design.

Taylor advocated certain techniques for analysing, measuring, allocating and rewarding work on the grounds that they would greatly increase the efficiency and productivity of labour. However, Braverman sees these techniques not in terms of improvements designed to benefit everyone, but in terms of a strategy designed to improve the employer's position in conflicts over the control and price of labour. Braverman suggests that before Taylor's work study techniques were introduced, workmen themselves could plan and pace their own methods of work; they, rather than the employer, knew the best way of doing a job. Men with skills learnt from years of experience had a valuable asset which they could sell to the employer in the labour market. Taylorism enabled employers to break down this employee-held asset. It taught employers to analyse the work process so that the design and planning stages could be moved from the shop floor to new production engineering and work study departments. These departments could specify the remaining tasks and divide them between simple, repetitive jobs. Such jobs required low grade labour which was available cheaply and easily from the labour market. The jobs required little training and so labour could be seen as a disposable resource, with the employer only needing to employ workers when they could be immediately used. Through work study techniques, the effort required from workers could be precisely calculated and this could be carefully matched to the amount paid by the employer, by Taylor's payment-by-results incentive schemes.

Braverman therefore argues that Taylorism is not a science of work, but a science of the management of others' work. It is not a strategy for scientific workmanship, but a strategy of deskilling, to gain closer control over employee behaviour and cost. He concludes that, having deskilled manual labour, employers now have the administrative and mechanical control techniques necessary to move on and deskill clerical and administrative work.

Braverman's argument can be criticised on the grounds that he exaggerates the universality of this employer strategy, and that he oversimplifies and romanticises the system of work organisation before Taylor (Littler, 1978). However his book has usefully set a spotlight onto a managerial strategy that has had a major impact in shaping many people's work lives – both in Western capitalist and in Soviet-type societies.

Recent studies have traced the significance of Taylor in different societies (Gospel and Littler, 1983; Littler, 1982). Littler contrasts the historical impact of Taylorism in the UK, the USA and Japan, and notes that although Taylor's ideas were significant in the development of modern work organisations they spread unevenly and in competition with other rationalisation movements. Scientific management was adopted but interpreted in slightly different ways in the contrasting economic and social contexts of the USA and UK. In Japan Taylorism had virtually no impact at all. The Japanese development of modern work organisation, based on very different principles, demonstrates that Taylorism is not the only strategy available to capitalist employers.

Littler points out the relationship between Taylorism and bureaucracy. Scientific management gave employers the techniques to tighten the hierarchy of supervision, create a systematic division of labour and elaborate written rules, records and communications about task performance. Taylorism provided techniques to bureaucratise control over task performance (see Table 3.1). However Taylorism did not involve the bureaucratisation of personnel policy. Although Taylor accepted the need for employment contracts and rational recruitment criteria he did not advocate job security or the rewards of career promotion and fixed pay. Instead he sought the complete substitutability of labour. Workers would have a casual relationship with any particular employer and employers should not attempt to induce organisational loyalty. Rather than bureaucratic personnel policies Taylor advocated a minimum interaction policy between employer and employee based on an immediate wage–effort exchange.

Taylorism has been one, but not the only, strategy used by modern employers to manage employees. Writing five years after Braverman, Edwards pointed out that many large American employers have sought to motivate their employees by providing elaborate career ladders, welfare benefits and company unions (Edwards, 1979). As the best examples of this type of policy come from the society where Taylorism has had least impact, we illustrate this second type of employer strategy by looking at the Bureaucratic Paternalism of Japan.

Bureaucratic Paternalism in Japan
Japanese employment policies provide a marked contrast to Taylorism. The most systematic comparison of employment policies in Britain and Japan is that by Dore (1973). He contrasts large companies in the engineering industries of each country in a study in which two factories from English Electric (now GEC) are matched by product and technology with two from Hitachi. Although there have been changes in employment practices in both countries since the case studies were completed, the basic distinctions highlighted by the research remain and have been underlined by more recent analysis (e.g. Clark, 1979).

Dore characterises the broad difference between British and Japanese management by saying that the British are market-oriented, whereas the Japanese are organisation-oriented. British employers and employees relate to a general labour market; there is no permanent commitment between employer and employee. Employees are expected to return to the labour market if their skills are no longer required or if other employers offer higher pay. In contrast, Japanese large-scale companies do not relate to an external labour market for the provision of the core of their workforce. They expect regular employees to be permanently committed to one employer. These employees' future careers, and much

of their non-work activities, depend on their employing organisation.

Dore's study shows that manual employees working on similar
production processes and similar machinery can have radically different employment relations. Three differences arising from the
British/Japanese contrast are worth emphasising:

1   *Lifetime commitment versus minimum interaction*   Many employees in large Japanese companies have a permanent status; they
are recruited straight from the education system and expect, and
are expected, to remain with the company until retirement at
fifty-five. It is only in the most extraordinary circumstances that
these regular employees are dismissed or made redundant and
the strength of the tie between employer and employee is caught
by the term 'lifetime commitment'.

The difference between British and Japanese practice on job
tenure in Dore's study is most marked for manual workers,
because it is for unskilled and semi-skilled operatives that the
British 'minimum interaction' reaches its peak. For British
manual workers the more temporary relationship with the firm is
compounded by the lower provision of holidays, pension rights,
sickness pay, longer and earlier hours, and 'second class' canteens
and toilets. Japanese firms provide more fringe benefits of this
sort, and make them equally available to all regular employees,
whether of manual or managerial status. As Dore writes.

> In English Electric there is a considerable difference between
> managers, skilled men and operatives in the degree to which
> they are given cause to consider themselves 'members of the
> firm' rather than mere employees. This difference is much less
> marked at Hitachi; the official ideology, in fact, holds there to
> be no difference.

In Japan, status distinctions exist but are attached to seniority.
Status graduations are numerous and all regular workers can
increase their seniority and status. In the UK there are much
sharper divisions into two or three 'classes'. The move by British
unions in the late 1960s to negotiate 'staff status' for manual
workers has so far done little to soften the stark differences in
status long symbolised by 'staff' and 'works' canteens.

2   *Group versus individual responsibility for tasks*   In British
factories responsibilities and tasks are allocated to individuals
rather than groups. Again, this is most pronounced for manual
workers who have the most closely prescribed, work-studied jobs.
In Japan the division of labour is less minutely prescribed and

responsibilities are allocated to groups rather than individuals. Associated with the less detailed regulation of tasks by specialised work study or industrial engineering departments, there is far more consultation within the department, section or work group before decisions are taken on how to execute a job. Although the head of the group has formal responsibility for seeing that work is done, there is no suggestion that the results depend on his efforts; the leader can play a figurehead role while more junior and possibly more competent people openly carry the load. The performance of work tasks is therefore not subject to neo-Taylorist bureaucratic controls. Employers rely instead on group working and ideological appeals for group loyalty.

3 *Reward systems; salary scales and career progression versus payments by results* Many British manual workers have two basic components to their pay: a 'basic rate for the job' which depends on going rates for unskilled, semi-skilled or skilled workers, and weekly bonuses from payments by results schemes. If the individual completes work-studied tasks faster than the time allowed, he receives a bonus. British managers and administrative staff do not receive these direct monetary incentives but are paid salaries with annual increments depending on their superiors' discretion.

In Japan all regular workers in large companies are placed on incremental salary scales. There is no attempt to pay 'the market rate' for skills; indeed, the market is irrelevant except at the start of the scales, for the school or graduate intake. Thereafter employees move along their incremental scale and all regular employees, even the most unpromising, are guaranteed gradual upgrading, the high-flyers progressing more quickly. Bonuses are paid but these are group-based, and usually allocated on the same criteria used to place employees to their salary grade – i.e. seniority and merit.

With such stable pay and with employment security, how do Japanese employers motivate their employees? They provide the bureaucratic motivator that Weber believed would be so effective in encouraging obedience to organisational rules, the organisation-based career (see also Stinchcombe, 1974; and Edwards, 1979). Conformity to organisational requirements is rewarded, not just by seniority-based salary increments, but by promotion to higher status and higher paid jobs. Recruitment to the better paid posts in the managerial hierarchy comes from within the organisation and all regular employees can progress up one of the company's promotion lines.

How do employers, operating with a fixed and increasingly costly labour force, respond to market fluctuations and the potential need to cut labour costs? Japan has a dual economy and the regular employee in the primary economy is protected from the vagaries of labour demand by the secondary economy. Large companies sub-contract much work to a myriad of small- to medium-scale sub-contractors whose workers do not enjoy the privileges of the permanent employee, even though they may be employed to work on the premises of the large concern. A secondary labour market also exists in the large companies, operating alongside the internal labour market of the regular employee. Temporary workers are taken on who do not get the tenure or benefits of the regular workforce, and female employees are expected to leave the company on marriage or childbirth. With these policies for support, Japanese 'lifetime commitment' has proved remarkably resilient in the face of economic recessions.

In conclusion, there is more than one way to organise tasks into jobs and to relate to a labour market. It is too easy to take familiar practices for granted and assume they have an inviolate logic. British practices have been heavily influenced by Taylorism; Japan provides a dramatic contrast – the emphasis has been on the construction of bureaucratic personnel policies, not bureaucratic controls over task performance. However, although Japan provides the most highly developed example of Bureaucratic Paternalism, policies designed to bureaucratise personnel policies are by no means unique to Japan.

Bureaucratic Paternalism Elsewhere

In Britain bureaucratic personnel policies with job security, internal promotion and internal labour markets are most evident in the Civil Service and the 'big four' clearing banks. Workers in a small number of large private sector companies, notably ICI, are also managed in this way. Bureaucratic personnel policies have rarely been adopted for British manual workers, although some large nineteenth-century organisations did attempt to create career ladders for key manual workers, and remnants of these are still found in the railway, post office and steel industries. Quaker employers like Rowntree, Cadbury and J. & J. Clarke began to develop paternalistic practices from the 1890s. They emphasised welfare, for example building model factory villages, but could not provide employment tenure or career progression and their welfare model did not spread beyond a minority of employers (Melling in Gospel and Littler, 1983).

Paternalistic policies are more evident in Germany and the USA. In Germany large companies like Seimens and Krupp were highly paternalistic in 1900. In the USA even Ford, adopting Taylorite job design and work study in 1914, sought to reduce the costs of very high labour turnover by instituting a fixed, high day-

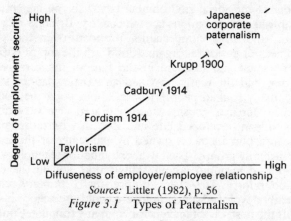

Source: Littler (1982), p. 56
Figure 3.1 Types of Paternalism

wage and creating a 'Sociology Department' to cater for the moral welfare of employees (Flink, 1976). In recent years many large American companies have created elaborate career ladders and put great effort into the generation of organisational loyalty, combined with policies of anti-unionism and 'human relations' techniques for careful communication to and supervision of employees (Edwards, 1979; Littler, 1983). Figure 3.1 charts differences in paternalistic policies.

WHY ARE DIFFERENT POLICIES ADOPTED?

Employer strategies towards employment relations can vary. Why are different policies adopted and to what extent do employers have a free hand in the employment relationships that are created? There are no definitive theories in this area, but plenty of ideas which shed varying degrees of light.

Many people have sought to explain the employment differences between Japan and Britain, described above. After the Second World War it was common for Western observers to assume that Japanese policies were irrational; they represented the unconscious hangover of feudal customs, and in time more rational, market-oriented, Western policies would be adopted. The durability of Japanese practices and their success when introduced in modified form into Britain have discredited this ethnocentric 'convergence theory' and sown doubt about the universal 'rationality' of familiar policies.

More sophisticated explanations recognise the possibility that employers may choose to adopt different policies to suit different circumstances, and that the employers' freedom of choice may be subject to various types and degrees of situational constraint. Dore explained the difference between Britain and Japan in terms of the technological and social environment facing the businessmen who first established organisations in each country. Britain was an early developer and her entrepreneurs presided over the gradual development of industrial organisation from the top of businesses that were small and insecure in the face of market pressures. Agriculture and the crafts provided an existing labour force of free, relatively trained people whose labour could be bought as need arose. Japanese businessmen operated in a very different situation. Japan developed late and the early entrepreneurs ran large, secure bureaucracies owned by the state, or the Zaibatsu merchant-family groups. The advanced modern technology which they imported required labour skills unlike any in the existing adult labour force. However, comprehensive primary schooling had already developed and employers could use school results to cream off the best school-leavers for company training. Contingent factors of this type could mix with cultural preferences to provide rational explanations for the choice of different policies by different employers. Once the framework of employment relations was established, this itself set constraints on the options of those who followed.

Organisation theory provides many studies of present-day constraints or 'contingencies' that influence the employer's adoption of business strategies. Relevant here are the many studies that suggest top management will attempt to centralise planning and decision-making within the organisation in order to achieve maximum control over business operations, but that this desire to gather all control into central hands can meet various obstacles. Centralised decision-making is difficult if there is a need for constant and varying adjustments to behaviour. For example, if there is great unpredictability in the product market or in the production process, then it may be impracticable for the employer to centralise all decisions about how work should be carried out, and too costly to design machines, or administrative systems, that would specify in advance how to cope with all potential variations. The employer will need to accept decentralised decision-making.

For example, Burns and Stalker (1961) contrasted the management of a rayon mill with management in electronic research and development in the UK. The highly predictable market, materials and production process of the rayon mill permitted the development of highly centralised, bureaucratic control over the labour process, with work tasks closely prescribed and all possible contingencies planned for in the reference 'book of rules'. However, the successful electronic R & D organisations were managed in a way that permitted more fluid adjustment to constantly changing tasks by relying, not on centrally defined and controlled work roles, but on 'professional' workers, highly trained to take their own decisions in the light of the circumstances. Similar arguments were produced by Stinchcombe (1959) to explain the different management organisations in the construction and manufacturing industries of the USA. Manufacturing, with its stable production locations and relatively stable workflows, enables management to use modern administrative and mechanical techniques to centralise decision-making and closely prescribe the jobs of those lower in the organisation's hierarchy. In construction these managerial techniqes are used much less, and Stinchcombe suggests that constantly changing work sites and seasonal shifts in demand make it more rational for management to continue to rely on personal supervision and a more decentralised work structure. Many decisions are left to be taken by the workers on site on the basis , not of head office instructions, but of experience and craft training. In the peculiar, unpredictable circumstances of the construction industry 'craft administration' rather than 'bureaucratic administration' can still be the most rational managerial technique.

A final example of organization theory's contribution to the analysis of managerial control comes from a government-owned industrial manufacturing monopoly in France. Crozier noted that a high degree of organisational security and market stability had made possible the development of a highly centralised, tightly controlled, bureaucratic management structure. In only one area did unpredictability cause the failure of centralised managerial controls: machine breakdown could not be predicted in advance and the maintenance department retained considerable autonomy and freedom from administrative regulations (Crozier, 1964).

There is, therefore, an extensive body of work within organisation theory which suggests that the tightness of bureaucratic controls used by employers will depend on the predictability of the work to be controlled. These theories tend to focus on the contingencies which affect employer control over task performance. They say little about bureaucratic personnel policies. Economists studying divided economies and internal labour markets can throw some light on bureaucratic personnel policies, for 'the contemporary idea of internal labour markets is simply Weberian bureaucratic theory transcribed into a different jargon' (Littler, 1982, p. 19). Economists working in this area note an association between large-scale, monopolistic or oligopolistic firms, and the development of internal labour markets (Piore, 1972; Edwards, 1979; A. Friedman, 1977). Why should employers in monopolistic positions adopt bureaucratic personnel policies? Piore and Friedman suggest that employers in control of giant monopolies are able to respond more flexibly to employee demands for job security and career progression. Employers operating under competitive market conditions will be constrained to adopt the direct controls and labour cheapening methods of Taylor. However if an employer can exploit a monopolistic position to raise profits, or use giant size to accumulate capital by tax manoeuvres or currency manipulation, then the containment of labour costs may be less important. In these circumstances employees may be able to win the greater security and better conditions provided by bureaucratic personnel policies. Edwards (1979) and Lazonic (1983) stress advantages to employers rather than employees as the reasons why bureaucratic personnel policies will be adopted. Internal labour markets increase an employee's dependence on his employer. For employers who have the resources to provide these conditions, internal labour markets may represent the most effective strategy of managerial control.

A. Friedman's argument that employer strategies may be modified by pressure from employees highlights the fact that the constraints on an employer's choice of strategy may be social and political. Employers face constraints that are not just technologically or market based (see also Child, 1973, pp. 234–55). The attitudes and power of government and of employees may act as a constraint on the employer's choice of strategies. Where national government is closely associated with the interests of large employers, as in Japan, such employers will gain considerable support for their choice of strategy. In contrast in the USA an early proliferation of welfare policies collapsed in the 1930s, in part because of government hostility to company housing and company unionism in the period of New Deal policies (Littler, 1983).

Employee pressures are analysed later. Here we can note that although employees may press for the rejection of centralised, bureaucratic controls, employees may also advocate certain types of bureaucratic policy and press for the modification rather than the replacement of centralised controls. In this context Littler explains the contrast between British and Japanese personnel policies in terms of the power of key groups of workers during the formative stages of organisational development. The early Japanese gang bosses and subcontractors – the *oyakata* – had greater social prestige than their British counterparts, and Japanese employers felt more vulnerable to militant, socialist trade unionism at the time when their modern, centrally controlled organisations were being built. These factors enhanced the value of internal labour markets for the Japanese, as a means of integrating the *oyakata* into the new organisations and insulating their labour force from external union influences.

In answer to the question, 'Why are different policies adopted?' it would seem that employers choose those policies which give them the greatest control over the work of their employees for the minimum economic cost, but this 'rationality' is bounded by constraints arising from the employers' situation. The practicability of different policies, and their cost, will be subject to contingent factors over which the employers have no control. Many variables influence employers' behaviour, and this complex subject requires more systematic study. From the available literature it is evident that history, the predictability of the environment, the structure of business concentration, the role of the state and countervailing pressures from employees all need to be considered.

For some employers the pressure of contingent factors may seem so great that to talk of choice or deliberate policy may seem absurd. Thurley and Wood (1983) suggest that many British engineering managers and boards feel so buffeted by their environment or workforce that they cope from day to day without any attempt to plan rationally a policy for handling their employees. For some employers options are more restricted than for others, but this does not prevent them from taking decisions on the organisation of work, and their problems may arise from the unintended consequences of past decisions. Employers are important actors on the industrial relations stage, although at different times they may have greater or lesser power to make innovative changes. Any argument that the employer has no choice, and therefore no influence, is as fallacious as the argument, sometimes implied by business consultants or government agencies, that the employer has a total, unrestricted freedom of choice.

THE IMPORTANCE OF EMPLOYER STRATEGY

Obviously the strategies adopted for the organisation of labour have an impact on other aspects of industrial relations. Workers who see themselves as members of an organisation rather than as a commodity on the labour market are likely to form organisation-based rather than market-based, unions. Employees who have job security and career prospects develop different interests and priorities than those without and employees with a 'minimum interaction' relationship with their employer, attached by short-term economic rewards to tightly controlled jobs, are likely to respond by seeking to maximise short-term rewards.

Comparative studies suggest that Britain has a relatively low development of bureaucratic managerial techniques (Littler, 1983). Certainly the bureaucratic techniques used for the management of manual workers have been those that focus on task performance, rather than on the motivators of bureaucratic personnel policy.

Fox (1974) argues that Taylor's policies for controlling work create a vicious spiral of distruct between employer and employee which has served to embitter British industrial relations. Dore

(1973, pp. 73–94) gives a graphic description of the problems associated with individual piecework incentives in the British engineering industry. The scientific management of worker effort and reward can degenerate into a continuous battle between man, foreman and rate-fixers over prices for jobs as each new job becomes the focus for bargaining and every hitch in production or shortage of supplies generates conflicts over compensatory payments for time lost. Conflicts over rewards for effort are, of course, present in all employment relationships but not all management systems stimulate the constant opening of hostilities throughout the day.

CONCLUSION

The employers' role in industrial relations has received remarkably little attention, even though many argue that employers are the dominant influence in shaping employment relations. In spite of changes in the ownership and structure of business organisations, employer objectives in industrial relations must still be seen as dependent on their primary business objectives. Employers are likely to try to maximise their control over employee behaviour at work and minimise the cost of their labour resources in the pursuit of the business's major objectives of making profits or remaining viable in a competitive, capitalist environment.

Modern organisations are bureaucratic but the degree of bureaucracy and the particular set of bureaucratic techniques which are adopted can vary. There is no simple or inevitable way to organise employees' work. We follow Littler in contrasting the bureaucratic strategies of Taylorism and Bureaucratic Paternalism. In the UK Bureaucratic Paternalism is not highly developed, and historical, structural and political explanations are needed for the adoption of different employer strategies towards employees.

Employer strategies towards the labour process are important because they shape the organisation of work and affect the development of employee response and resistance. This chapter has focused on employer strategies at the level of the firm. However employers can act at several levels; at that of the firm, of employers' associations, or of national government and the state. In the next chapter we turn to employers' associations and the factors affecting the co-ordination of employer policies at higher levels.

Chapter 4

Employers' Associations

Employers' associations have had a significant influence on the development of British industrial relations. They were formed by employers who wished to pursue certain strategies requiring action above the level of the individual firm, and they have affected employers' relations with trade unions, as well as the British structure of collective bargaining and the experience of corporatist government in the UK.

Although employers' associations seem similar in structure to trade unions – 'bosses unions' as they are labelled by the media – they are not functionally equivalent as institutions. Employee interests, as we see in Chapters 5 and 6, are primarily represented in groups. Individual employees rarely have the power to influence major issues alone. However individual companies are often in a position to represent their own interests in dealings with government or unions. Indeed multinational enterprises, or companies in a dominant national economic position, may exert more influence than an employers' association.

Employers' associations can also be distinguished from unions on the grounds that their members are likely to see them as more limited representative bodies. Trade unions can be regarded as the main institutions for representing the interests of labour in our society and they adopt broad political, social and industrial objectives. Employers' associations are not equivalent as representatives of capital. Britain's 481 employers' associations primarily represent the labour market interests of the manufacturing industry. There are many other channels for the representation of different industries and different types of interest. There are, for example, about one thousand trade associations which concern themselves with product rather than labour markets and there are specialised associations for the finance industry and commerce. Trade, commercial and financial representative institutions are outside the scope of this book, although their activities, for example in support of particular government policies, may well have an impact on industrial relations.

This chapter reviews the development and functions of British employers' associations. This enables us to take our study of employer strategies above the level of the company, dealt with in

Chapter 3, and gives us some insight into the wider co-ordination of employer interests.

THE DEVELOPMENT OF BRITISH EMPLOYERS' ASSOCIATIONS

Employers form associations for mutual support when they feel a common vulnerability in certain markets, and to seek defence against industrial or political threats from other power-holders. Associations concerned with the employment relationship have been formed to pursue strategies in four broad areas:

1 Labour market regulation
2 Opposition to trade unionism
3 Accommodation with trade unions through multi-employer collective bargaining
4 To influence government policy and legislation

(Jackson and Sisson, 1975, speak in similar terms of defence, procedural/political and market models of employers association.)

Strategies in all four areas have been used in the development of British employers' associations, but it is with the third type of strategy that British associations are most associated.

The history of employers' associations

The history of British employers' associations is as old or older than that of trade unions. In 1776 Adam Smith noted that 'combinations of masters' were widespread and powerful although they attracted less attention and condemnation than combinations of workers. These early employers organisations were specialised and locally based. Because of the prevailing *laissez-faire* ideology any collusion to reduce market competition was unlikely to be broadcast, and the early associations operated quietly and informally. Adam Smith wrote that employer agreements to cut wage rates, or agree maximum rates were always conducted 'with the utmost silence and secrecy' and could pass unnoticed unless the workforce caused an outcry (Smith, 1970, p. 169). As a result there is no precise evidence to tell us how many employers adopted the early strategy of forming associations to regulate their labour market.

We know that some associations of employers were agreeing standard rates for wages or piecework prices before trade unions appeared in their industries. In the early nineteenth century, the coal and iron owners were establishing local agreements on the selling price for their product, and on the wages of their labour, before their workforce was unionised. However we also know there were other employers who determined their own pay policies and collaborated with other employers only on trade or product-market issues, limiting joint activity towards the labour market to the exchange of information, petitioning justices to suppress combinations of workers or petitioning parliament to strengthen the master and servant laws (Jeffries, 1945, p. 10–11).

The main boost to the growth of employers associations was the growth of trade unions. New associations were formed, specifically concerned to co-ordinate responses to the threat of an organised workforce, and existing local organisations were formalised and centralised into stronger, nationally based federations.

A number of policies were chosen by associations adopting the strategy of outright opposition to trade unionism. Clegg describes the spectacularly successful use of lockouts and imported labour by the Shipping Federation. The Shipping Federation was formed in 1890 soon after the establishment of an amalgamated seamen's union (1887) and a major London dock strike (1889).

> Within three years, by a series of strikes and lockouts, it had reduced the seamen's union and the dockers' union to feeble remnants. Thereafter it prevented their recovery for almost twenty years. This it achieved by the organisation of strike-breaking on an unparalleled scale. The federation maintained three vessels to transport and house workers to replace striking seamen and dockers, as well as motor launches on the Mersey and Tyne. Large sums were spent on this and on guarding, feeding and providing beer tokens for these men while they did the work of the strikers. (Clegg, 1972, p. 125)

Similar policies, including the mass importation of non-union labour to break strikes, were adopted by employer associations to defeat the first Miners' National Union in 1844 (Burgess, 1975, p. 180), and to break a seven-month strike by spinners and weavers at Preston in 1853 (Pelling, 1963, p. 47).

Another method to oppose and attempt to destroy trade unions was the use of 'the Document'. This was a signed undertaking in which a worker accepted, as a condition of employment, that he or she would leave, or not join, a trade union. Its use by employers throughout the Midlands, Lancashire and Yorkshire helped crush the 'Grand National Consolidated Trade Union' a utopian socialist union which had a meteoric existence in the 1830s. By July 1834 'The great association of half a million members had been completely routed by the employers' vigorous presentation of "the document" ' (Webb and Webb 1898, p. 137). The document was used again in 1851–2 by the Central Association of Employers of Operative Engineers to enforce a humiliating defeat on the engineers' union, and the Central Association of Master Builders attempted to use it during a lockout of London builders in 1859–60, this time without success. A less publicised but probably longer-lasting policy to prevent the spread of union membership was the use of blacklists of union activists, compiled and circulated by the employers' associations.

Strategies of outright opposition to trade unionism did not succeed in eliminating unions nor stem the gradual growth of union membership from the end of the nineteenth century. Employers therefore moved towards an accommodation with trade union officials, and used employers' associations to develop a system of collective bargaining that limited trade union influence to external, labour market issues and preserved managerial prerogatives within the workplace. There was a marked expansion of new or more visible associations. Whereas there were 336 known employers' associations in 1895, the number had doubled to 675 in 1898 and doubled again to 1,487 by the outbreak of the First World War (Gospel, 1983). Within the general strategy of accommodation with trade unions were four distinct policies, pursued through employers' associations, which had a major impact on the development of British collective bargaining. These were: (a) insistence on multi-employer bargaining; (b) limits on the content of agreements; (c) the insistence that disputes be dealt with by disputes procedures that involved external union and association officials, and (d) industry-wide, 'national' bargaining. We return to these policies again in Chapter 8, but a brief explanation here will show why employers chose to act through associations, and why employers' associations have been called the architects of the British institutions of collective bargaining (Clegg, 1976).

(a) Multi-employer bargaining Employers who decided to respond to union demands for improved conditions often chose to do so collectively, rather than individually, even when the union strength and union attack had been directed at one employer. Initially they signed district, later industry-wide, agreements. Multi-employer bargaining had several advantages for the late-nineteenth-century, early-twentieth-century employers. By combining in negotiations they could pit their united strength against employees in any strike or lockout. They could prevent a union picking off the most vulnerable employer and then using improvements there as the comparative base of leapfrogging wage claims elsewhere. Multi-employer agreements also reduced labour market competition and gave employers the assurance that they all had to pay the same wage rates, that no employer could compete 'unfairly' on wage costs because he was more efficient or more ruthless than his rivals. Finally, companies were still small and

unbureaucratic. They did not possess managerial staff with specialist knowledge or skills in handling trade unions, and they had not adopted bureaucratic personnel policies for managing their employment relations. By delegating responsibility for negotiating with employees to their employers' association officials, employers could handle their new and more complex employee relations without fundamental change to the structure of their organisations.

Collective agreements with employers' associations also had advantages for trade union officials. Although any improvement in terms might not be as favourable as they could expect from the most profitable or most unionised employers, the multi-employer agreements had a much wider coverage than they might otherwise have hoped to achieve.

In some trades the development of multi-employer bargaining with unions occurred as a relatively smooth transition because agreements merely replaced, or made additions to, pre-existing district wage or piece rates. In printing, bookbinding and some building trades district rates had a long history in earlier craft- or guild-based methods of regulating the labour market, whereas in iron and coal, as we have seen, district rates were already set, unilaterally, by the employers. In these industries the transition to collective bargaining merely added new participants to the regulating process; it did not create a new principle of labour market regulation. Elsewhere the transition to multi-employer collective bargaining represented a more radical change in the employers' approach to the labour market.

(b)   Agreements to exclude control of the labour process   When employers moved to recognise trade unions, they were concerned to place firm boundaries around the subjects on which they were prepared to negotiate. Employers came to accept negotiation on external, labour-market related issues, covering basic wage rates, the hours of work for which basic rates were paid, overtime premium rates and piecework prices. However they still resisted any negotiation on internal or 'managerial' issues; on how labour, once bought, should be used. The history of employer–union relations is coloured by large-scale, dramatic confrontations between unions and employers' associations, some on the initial principle of recognising unions at all, but many on the equally intensely felt issue of 'managerial prerogative' and the preservation of non-negotiable subjects. Managerial rights which employers sought to exclude from collective bargaining included hiring and firing, the use and manning of machines, promotions, supervision and discipline, decisions on who did overtime and how much overtime was worked and the techniques of production control.

The protection of managerial prerogative came to dominate employer association policy in the engineering industry and lay behind major confrontations with the unions in 1851–2, 1897–8 and 1922. The skilled engineering workers formed the first central, national union in the UK (see Chapter 6). In the latter half of the nineteenth century the engineers saw their traditional craft status and job control threatened by new technology which enabled once-skilled metal-working jobs to be accomplished by unskilled machine-minders. They used their union to demand that the new machine-tools be manned by apprenticed craftsmen at skilled rates and they resisted the introduction of piecework. On their side, employers were eager to take advantage of the new technology to centralise their control over the labour process and reduce the power and autonomy of the craft groups and of lower supervisory staff. They sought to cheapen the labour process by employing semi-skilled and unskilled labour and to manage the deskilled work by introducing piecework systems. The battles over managerial prerogative did not occur simply because unions were challenging employers' control of the labour process, but because employers themselves were tightening and centralising their control of workplace activity. The engineering union lost the lockouts of 1852, 1897–8 and 1922. The union was not destroyed, but it was forced to sign agreements accepting management's right to man machines and manage labour as management chose.

Using new technology and more bureaucratic control of task performance, many employers were able to shatter the old craft or work-group controls and insist that the management of work should be non-negotiated and managerially determined. However this strategy was not totally successful in eliminating employee control at the place of work. Some crafts, like the print crafts, kept very considerable managerial controls and many strongly-placed work groups within engineering were able to retain an influence on the day-to-day management of their own work. However employee involvement on issues of workplace management took place in the twilight zone of unofficial shopfloor activity and was successfully excluded from the formal system of collective bargaining. Productivity bargaining in the 1960s finally brought these issues within the scope of official collective bargaining but even then this was initially resisted by some employers' associations on the old grounds of not negotiating areas of managerial prerogative.

(c) Disputes procedures to resolve disputes away from the workplace Industry-wide dispute procedures were adopted by many employers' associations in the late nineteenth and early twentieth centuries as a way of helping members handle pressures from trade unions. A typical procedure required that any dispute which

threatened a stoppage of work be referred to a series of meetings of union and employer association officials. The officials heard the case put by the conflicting parties and attempted to conciliate or resolve the dispute. If they failed, the issue was referred to higher regional and central or industry-wide meetings. Only when this procedure had been followed could a constitutional strike or lockout be called.

The advantage of industry disputes procedures for employers was that they brought the full weight of the employers' association into negotiations at local level and they delayed constitutional strike action until the most senior officials had been involved. Industry-wide disputes procedures were agreed between employers' associations and unions in cotton spinning in 1891 after two years of massive lockouts, in footwear after a seven-week lockout in 1895 and in engineering in 1898, after the 1897 lockout. Lockouts of the plasterers and boilermakers ended in central disputes procedures in their industries in 1899 and 1908.

Central procedure agreements spread across the unionised industries. They were not always resisted by unions, for although they acted as a block to the union tactic of concentrating their strength against the most vulnerable employer, they had some advantages for union officials. They provided a channel for resolving disputes, and backward employers might be pressured to provide average terms by their co-employers. They also helped to increase the authority and role of the trade union official and central union executive over local rank and file groups. 'Procedures' provided a major institution through which unions and employers could relate and their significance continues to this day. In 1968 the Donovan Report regarded them as the main benefit provided by employers' associations for most of their members (paragraph 81, p. 22). Central disputes procedures helped establish the emphasis on joint discussion, rather than on formalised legal agreements, that is still a major feature of the British system of collective bargaining.

(d) National or industry-wide agreements Once employers' associations and unions had national level meetings to discuss disputes, it was a small step to the establishment of industry-wide agreements on wage rates, basic hours or overtime premiums. During the First World War the government encouraged employers to take this step by endorsing and approving the spread of industry-wide collective bargaining. The number of employers associations continued to rise and by the 1920s there were 2,403 associations including one major association or federation for each of the main industries. By 1921 national agreements on hours and basic pay rates covered most manual workers in most industries.

Industry-wide bargaining developed further, again with government encouragement, in the Second World War.

For employers, national agreements had the advantages of the multi-employer agreements mentioned earlier and were well suited for the preservation of managerial prerogative. Whereas external, market regulation could easily be extended across a whole industry, managerial, workplace-based issues were too complex and too diverse to be handled on such a wide scale. The scope of national agreements was determined by the membership of employers' associations. On the employers' side, communications and control between members and their negotiating agent was therefore relatively simple. Unions usually had to form alliances if they were to act in a unified way as agents of an industry's workforce.

In conclusion, employers' associations were used by employers to shape the level and content of negotiations with employees and thereby accommodate the growth of trade unionism in a way that enabled employers to protect managerial prerogative at the place of work.

The fourth strategy of using employers' associations to influence government policy and legislation has been less evident than the third, in the history of British employers' associations. Indeed government influence on employers' associations has been more apparent than influence the other way round. The government encouraged the development of employers' associations by advocating industry-wide agreements during and soon after the First World War (see p. 153). This stimulated combination among some initially reluctant employers, and spurred the creation of a central federation of employers' associations, the British Employers' Confederation (BEC), in 1919. During and shortly after the Second World War the government again encouraged employers' associations under a policy of creating comprehensive, industry-wide, management–union regulations capable of surviving the expected postwar recession (Palmer, 1974). The growth of interventionist government economic policies since the 1960s has also stimulated employers' organisations. Largely as a result of government pressure the BEC merged with two national trade associations to form the Confederation of British Industry (CBI) in 1965. Several British governments in the 1960s and 1970s chose to administer economic and social policies through tripartite semi-official institutions, popularly known as quangos (Quasi-Non-Governmental Organisations), which expanded the representative role of both employers associations and trade unions. Tripartite institutions also surround the international governments of the EEC and the UN and have encouraged the development of international employers organisations. British employers' associations are affiliated to the International Organisation of Employers (IOE) formed in 1920 which relates to the UN and its agencies and to the Union des Industries de la Communauté Européene (UICE) formed in 1958 which relates to the EEC. Whether the impetus for tripartite institutions and associated corporatist policies comes from government, employer or employee interests is an issue of hot debate (see Chapters 7 and 9, and also Grant and Marsh, 1977, p. 16) Corporatist institutions and policies require employers' representatives for their implementation, and have acted as a stimulus to the development of British employers associations.

The current functions of employers' associations
Employer organisation for the purpose of unilaterally regulating labour markets is not evident today. Informal wage clubs for the exchange of information on the timing and amount of major changes in pay policy still exist in many areas including those where trade unions do not negotiate. However, for the majority of employers and employees labour markets are now regulated by collective bargaining or by wages councils, established by the government to set legal minimum standards in poorly-organised industries (see page 160). Periodically wage council industries are investigated to see if the legal minima can be abolished, and it is notable that in most cases it is employers rather than unions who argue against abolition, on the grounds that the minimum standards prevent smaller firms undercutting others on wages and prices. 'A cynic might suggest that they preferred to be regulated by the state free of charge rather than go to the trouble and expense of regulating themselves' (Clegg, 1979, p. 298). An employer interest in labour market regulation is therefore still apparent for many small employers, but they no longer rely on association alone to achieve it.

Strategies of using employer associations to oppose trade unions have also declined in the UK. Today unions are well established in most British industries and few employers openly advocate their elimination. Some individual employers still refuse to accept trade union activity within their own companies and can get moral and financial support from organisations like the National Association for Freedom (Rogaly, 1977), and may receive advice from their associations. However many British employers' associations would advise employers to accept, rather than oppose, trade union recognition. The shift from opposition to accommodation with trade unions has been general across western liberal-democratic societies, but it has not been universal or inevitable. In the USA the National Metal Trades Association moved in the reverse direction, from the acceptance of collective bargaining to militant anti-trade unionism (Windmuller, forthcoming). Policies of outright opposition to trade unions are still common among employers in the USA but in the UK, although some politicians and individual industrialists express anti-union views, they are not at present resonated within employers' associations.

The main strategy pursued through British employers' associations has been to accommodate trade union pressure by structuring collective bargaining to determine pay and conditions at industry-wide levels. The relevance of this strategy for employers today is a question of some debate. Industry-wide agreements can set standard terms which are actually applied by all employers, or minima below which employers will not drop. The initial industry agreements generally set standards for both pay and conditions of employment which were then applied across the industry concerned. The Electrical Contracting Association is the best known association which still sets and enforces standard rates in its national agreements. However, in most other industries the control of the national agreements has declined, and on pay, if not conditions, association agreements are treated as minima, or are totally ignored.

Two types of employer policy have weakened association control of collective bargaining. The first is a policy of *strategic independence* (Loveridge, 1982) and is associated with the adoption of bureaucratic personnel policies by large companies who have their own specialist staff departments for managing employment policy. Such companies may prefer to negotiate independently and directly with trade unions, relying on their own strength and expert staff. They openly treat employers' association agreements as minima and in some cases have chosen to leave their associations entirely. Many large American multinationals, e.g. Ford, General Motors, Massey Ferguson and IBM, do not associate as a matter of principle, and Metal Box, Glacier Metal and British Leyland have left the Engineering Employers' Federation in pursuit of strategic independence.

The second policy is that of *federalism*. Loveridge notes that many Midlands engineering companies in the 1960s and early 1970s chose to react to tight labour markets by decentralising control of labour costs to local, lower levels of management. Association-agreed rates were treated as minima but these employers continued to use the national disputes procedures to resolve any disruptive disputes. Federalism avoided the direct involvement of company directors and senior managers with the increased problems of labour management. It preserved traditional strategies of minimum interaction (see Chapter 3) and enabled company directors to continue to be ghosts at the bargaining tables of employment relations (Winkler, 1974).

Changes in employer policy towards national agreements have undoubtedly occurred, but the speed and extent of change are the subject of dispute. Gospel (1983) argues that employer association control of collective bargaining declined from the 1930s as employers responded to greatly increased foreign competition. Small firms undercut the industry rates, although only in coal did the industry-wide negotiations collapse completely. Large firms began to develop self-sufficient, bureaucratic management hierarchies. Gospel notes that ICI established its Central Labour Office in 1927 and withdrew from its employers' association in the mid-1930s, only returning when the Chemical Industry's Association adopted a policy of accepting employers who refused to conform to association-agreed rates. However, although some weakening of association control can be traced back this far, most employers continued to make some use of employers' associations in their accommodation with trade unions. The policy of federalism was widespread in the engineering, construction and shipbuilding industries of the 1960s. In 1968 the Donovan Commission argued that employers' associations acted as a significant bar to the development of specialised management and modern systems of personnel policy in the UK, and it recommended that employers alter their policies to rely less on associations and more on the development of their own company policies at company director level.

How far company-based, bureaucratic personnel policy has succeeded in replacing the traditional British employers' reliance on employers' associations is still the subject of considerable debate. Brown (1981) argues that employer association bargaining is now insignificant and has little impact on the actual terms and conditions of employment of British employees. Elliott and Steele (1976) and Elliott (1981) disagree and argue that changes in nationally-agreed pay rates alter the floor upon which the new company pay structures are built. They also argue that national agreements still determine the length of the working week and holiday provisions, subjects which have an important impact on labour costs and where employers still prefer to establish terms together rather than alone. In the early 1980s, although some industrialists and politicians were calling for the end of industry-wide collective bargaining, the annual process continued, suggesting that it still had relevance for many British employers.

Many associations have adjusted to their lost role as the employers' main negotiating agent by developing general services and providing assistance to company negotiations. The CBI runs a computerised databank of information on pay claims and settlements. Individual associations organise the exchange of information on wage movements and may provide advice and guidelines to help in productivity or other local negotiations. Even companies who feel confident in handling their own relations with unions or with government may decide it is worth their affiliation fee to have access to information collected in confidence by the association from all employers in their industry.

The fourth strategy of using associations to influence government was not as significant in the history of British associations as it was in many other countries. In Germany and Sweden a major stimulus to the creation of strong, centralised employers associations was the threat of significant social or pro-employee legislation. In the UK both employers and trade unions were traditionally reluctant to pursue industrial relations policies through legislation. However there has been a more active interest in industrial relations laws in recent years. British employers' associations sought some of the changes in the controversial laws of 1971, 1980 and 1982 and fought legislative changes from 1974 to 1979 (see Chapters 7 and 9). They now provide expert advice for members on the increasingly complex British labour laws. They have also reacted to threats from international legislatures, and in the late 1970s and early 1980s helped co-ordinate the successful opposition to European Directives and changes in Euro-company law which would have required the adoption of the continental system of industrial democracy, with elected employees on company boards.

If governments adopt corporatist policies, then employers' associations are likely to become involved in the associated tripartite institutions. The CBI was created at a time when corporatist policies were gaining strength in the UK and there have been times when CBI officials have become heavily involved in corporatist policies. However employers themselves have been ambivalent to this development. Association officials have often faced hesitancy and resistance from their 'rank and file' membership to association involvement in the administration of corporatist policies. We return to the complex relationship between employers and the state in more detail in Chapter 7.

THEIR STRUCTURE AND GOVERNMENT

Employers' associations present a complex structure based on a mix of organising principles; industry, territory, size and type of ownership being most important in the UK. Although the government listed 481 employers' associations in 1979, precise figures must be treated carefully, for associations may be informal or transient. One of the few surveys of employers associations in the UK found 118 national and about seven hundred local associations. Some of the local associations were independent, some were affiliated to, and some were branches of the national associations (CIR Study 1, 1972).

British employers' associations range from complex, giant organisations employing several hundred staff, to tiny specialist associations whose main service is the provision of an annual members' dinner. At one end of the scale is the Engineering Employers' Federation (EEF) with 5,000 to 6,000 'establishment' members covering nearly two million employees in 1979 and itself employing 300 people; or the equally well-staffed National Federation of Building Trade Employers (NFBTE) with 11,500 UK company members covering 325,000 employees, besides its foreign affiliates. At the other end of the scale are many small organisations – like the British Felt Hat Manufacturers' Federation (11 members, 1,520 employees in 1972) or the China and Glass Retailers' Association (150 member companies) – often operating without any full-time staff. Details of the membership affiliation and government structure of individual associations can be found in Marsh (1979). Here some general points will be made about employers' associations, noting in particular the contrasts with trade unions.

The governing structure of employers' associations varies according to their size and the extent of regional, trade or company-based divisions of interest. Some have no complex constitutions, for example the Newspaper Publishers' Association (NPA) has only nine member companies, all based on Fleet Street, and members meet as and when necessary, and day to day industrial relations issues are discussed in weekly meetings of an Industrial Relations Executive. However, associations with larger memberships usually have constitutions in which members have ultimate control over policy decisions through a structure of representative committees. The central policy-making body is usually a general council composed of regional or specialised trade representatives. Where this is too large for effective decision-taking (for example the EEF's has 90 members, the NFBTE 120), there is a management board or executive committee which meets more frequently. Sub-committees of the council or the management board may be advisory or may be delegated to act within a general mandate.

Although employers' associations and trade unions have somewhat similar formal structures of representative government, in practice their decision-taking processes are very different. Decision-making within employers' associations is centralised and often occurs through informal channels in which firms of very large size, or with particular interests, can have more weight than is formally allotted to them in the committee and council structure. In the formal committees a consensus of opinion is sought and differences are not publicly aired. When balloting occurs votes are apportioned by numbers of employees, total payroll or dues paid, not one member one vote, and balloting invariably serves to ratify decisions and compromises worked out informally beforehand, or to confirm candidates for offices already agreed on, rather than to establish majority opinion. Elections to association offices are rarely contested, indeed there is often a reluctance by members to give time to running associations. Employers and senior managers do not compete to display oratorial or political skills at association meetings, for their personal careers are more likely to benefit from efforts spent running their own companies, not their associations. Gaps on committees are filled, and informal power centres within the membership accommodated, by the frequent use of co-option onto representative committees. In all these respects, as Windmuller (forthcoming) notes, the political cultures of employers' associations and trade unions are worlds apart and 'participatory democracy, as a form of internal government, is not characteristic of employers' associations'.

There is little evidence that the government structure of employers' associations leads association officials to act against the wishes of association members. Criticisms of employer association government and structure are made, but usually come from people critical of policy decisions which do, in fact, have broad membership support. The EEF is subject to most criticism. An increasingly acute difference of interest between large-scale and smaller employers has stimulated criticism of the EEF's governing structure because the EEF affiliates separate plants or establishments into eighteen local associations, thereby giving small employers more weight than giant multi-plant companies on the EEF council. Suggestions that large companies be allowed direct affiliation have been consistently rejected by the 'backwoodsmen' on EEF council whose only accommodation to considerable pressure has been the co-option of twenty representatives of large companies onto the EEF management board – now eighty people strong. The type of policy conflict between large and small members which leads to criticism of the EEF is well illustrated by the EEF's difficulties in agreeing a policy for large construction sites.

The EEF includes in its membership many companies which operate both in factories and on construction sites. They make and erect equipment like boilers, turbines and generators. Engineering site work has traditionally been covered by the same range of national agreements that operate within the factories, but in the late 1960s and the 1970s attacks on these agreements became intense. Industrial construction sites made great advances in size and complexity and large sites, especially those built for the petro-chemical industry, became increasingly difficult to manage.

Severe industrial disputes became a common feature of large site construction and investigations, by government and the parties involved, concluded that the continued use of the national engineering agreements on large sites served to exacerbate both employee grievances and management's inability to solve them (NEDO, 1970; CIR Report no. 29, 1970). The major clients for large site construction formed a new employers association – the Oil and Chemical Plant Constructors' Association (OPCA) – which argued for a new national engineering agreement specifically for large site construction, to be supplemented at each site by a co-ordinated site agreement. These proposals were supported by large engineering companies, by the EEF central officials and specialist staff, by government agencies and by the unions involved. Proposals for a new national agreement for large sites were submitted to the EEF's managing board on several occasions. They were repeatedly rejected on the board by the many smaller firms who only occasionally worked on large sites and who feared that new, higher, national rates for large site work would unsettle their employees' acceptance of the factory national rates. Attempts to resolve the different interests within the EEF continued for over ten years despite considerable pressure from outside, and the much heralded new national agreement for large sites was not signed until 1981.

More general criticisms of employer association structure can also be traced back to disagreements on policy, or employer unwillingness to adopt common policies. In many industries employer representation is highly fragmented. For example, in 1974 clothing had twenty-one different employers' organisations with an interest in employment relations, seven catering solely for the hat sector. Together they represented only 21 per cent of clothing establishments, employing only 43 per cent of the industry's manual workforce. The eleven largest associations between them employed seven full-time staff. The CBI sponsored an inquiry which was highly critical of the generally diversified structure and poor resources of British employers' organisations (the Devlin Report, 1972). It estimated that whereas large British companies paid 0.014 per cent to 0.0396 per cent of turnover for their industrial representation, figures for Europe could rise to 0.25 per cent (France), 0.21 per cent (Italy) and 0.22 per cent (West Germany). Devlin called for radical restructuring to merge small organisations into institutions that could provide more expert staff, with sophisticated information and advice services. The Report advocated a more unified, centralised system of representation in which employer co-ordination would be more effective and disciplined. This package of reforms was roundly rejected by British employers, most of whom were not prepared to exchange their existing institutions for the Devlin Report's vision of rationally centralised, united employer action.

THE CONFEDERATION OF BRITISH INDUSTRY

The CBI was formed in July 1965 to act as a central voice for all employers. Initially created by the merger of three previous federations that acted in the manufacturing industry, the CBI now claims to recruit in all sectors of business including the nationalised industries. It has over one hundred employers organisations and over twelve thousand individual firms in membership. About ten million of Britain's twenty-one million employees work for employers affiliated to the CBI.

The CBI is organised into thirteen regions and members elect representatives to regional councils. However, past this stage the organisation does not attempt to be democratic in the sense of having elected policy-makers. The governing body of the CBI is a central council of about four hundred people, meeting monthly. The council selects its own members to reflect the highly diverse interests within the CBI. There are numerous committees and sub-committees of the national and regional councils actively involving many hundreds of directors and managers. For industrial relations there is the Employment Policy committee which formulates broad policy and co-ordinates the more technical studies of policy carried out by the Industrial Relations committee, the Safety Health and Welfare committee, the Social Security committee and a number of specialist study groups. There is also a Labour and Social Affairs committee with 130 members representing the employers associations, the nationalised industries and large non-federated firms. Confidential discussions between companies engaged in collective bargaining take place in the Wages and Conditions committee. An International Labour committee co-ordinates CBI work at the International Labour Organisation in Geneva, and there are a varying number of working parties and panels on such matters as labour statistics or equal pay.

In 1977 the CBI instituted a national conference of regional representatives, held each November. This is designed to test member opinion and act as a showpiece to attract publicity in the media; it is neither a governing nor a decision-taking body and motions for discussion are selected for their publicity value. Nevertheless this move to copy the annual decision-making conferences of trade unions may have had an impact on CBI policy-making. Booth (1982) suggests that the strength of support for neo-classical, *laissez-faire* economic policies at the CBI's first public conference in 1977 helped to deflect the CBI leadership away from its previous support of corporatist policies.

The CBI's director-general heads a staff of about 250 in offices in London, the regions and Brussels. Its annual income in 1981 was £7.7 million, a relatively small amount for a national organisation of this type.

The CBI's activities are restricted by the unwillingness of its large and disparate membership to agree common policy or fund an extended role for the CBI. The conflicts of interest within the EEF mentioned above pale by comparison with those in the CBI, spanning as it does large and small firms in different industries and in the public and private sector. Since its formation in 1965, the CBI has rarely been able to co-ordinate employers to present united policies towards trade unions. Proposals that are totally acceptable to their nationalised or large-sized members may be bitterly resisted by others. The CBI has never negotiated directly with unions but in 1980 CBI officials finalised a draft technology agreement with the TUC, containing provisions for consultation and the disclosure of information about the introduction of new technology. The proposals were elementary by the standards of those CBI members with established negotiating relationships with trade unions. Yet these terms were rejected in council by members who still preferred to resist trade unions, rather than develop working relationships with them.

Conflicts of interest between the nationalised and large-scale companies (who provide half the CBI subscriptions) and small independent companies with under two hundred employees (who provide half the membership) are very apparent, and fundamental differences of policy and philosophy hinder most of the CBI's attempts to 'lead' employers on industrial relations policy and restrict its activities to representation to government, and the provision of services like the databank of pay claims. CBI members rejected the proposals of the CBI-sponsored Devlin Report that the CBI be given funds and powers of co-ordination equivalent to the more centralised organisations abroad like the German DBA and DBI, the French Patronat or the Swedish SAF.

The CBI is not totally representative of British industry. Important sectors remain outside the CBI, for example the Retail Consortium discourages CBI membership and City financial institutions have preferred to rely on their long-established contacts with the Treasury. The CBI is influential as the one voice speaking for British employers; but it competes in this role with the Institute of Directors and the trade-based Chamber of Commerce. The CBI's actions are circumscribed by the need to represent a highly diversified membership and it is not a body with authority to act on its own.

Nevertheless, despite the divisions of interest within the CBI, on issues where members are united the CBI can present a powerful front. The CBI was totally united in 1977 when it helped to crush the recommendations of the Committee of Inquiry on Industrial Democracy for Employee Directors on Company Boards, and its threats to mount a major campaign of non-co-operation if the government passed the recommendations into law were taken seriously. Case studies of CBI attempts to influence government also show that, on technical matters like pollution legislation or sick-pay deductions the CBI presents not only a united, but a powerful voice for British employers (Grant and Marsh, 1977.)

THE POWER OF EMPLOYERS' ASSOCIATIONS

The main determinant of an employers' association's significance is the extent to which its members choose to act together rather than handle their employment policies alone. If employers do choose to collaborate on policy, then their power will depend on the unity they can maintain and the sanctions they can use against other power groups.

Problems in establishing common policy

Employers do not necessarily act together in their employment policies. Windmuller (forthcoming) lists the centrifugal forces which may operate against united action as: trade union pressure to break ranks; employers' quest for competitve advantage over rivals of labour or product markets; managerial attempts to keep marginal enterprises afloat; and principled differences over policy.

Recent studies have tried to explain why employers form strong and united associations in some situations but not in others. The first survey of British employers' associations found that homogeneous, distinctive labour or product markets were associated with high degrees of employer solidarity, but that the relationship did not always hold, for the NPA, with its nine members all operating in Fleet Street, has been outstanding in its inability to submerge internal differences in united action (CIR Study 1, 1972).

Gennard (1976) distinguishes shipping, footwear, building (especially electrical contracting), furniture and the docks as the industries where employers' associations have had the most prominent and permanent influence over employer policy and where association agreements still effectively regulate employer policy on pay and conditions. He highlights three factors that appear to increase the need for united employer policies: casual labour, small company size and, associated with these, a low level of bureaucratic management control.

There was a tradition of casual labour in most of the industries Gennard studied; in building, electrical contracting, shipping and, until 1967, the docks. Employers in these industries did not maintain permanent workforces but offered employment on short contracts, coping with variations in workload by a policy of temporary hirings, and by firing when work was slack. Casual labour moves constantly between employers and the use of standard, industry-wide rates of pay is convenient for employers because it prevents the need to negotiate terms at the start of each new job or contract. Effective industry agreements create stability in a situation in which employers would otherwise by vulnerable to the constant poaching of labour, to haggling and disputes at the start of each job, to 'leapfrog' tactics by unions and a resulting inability to predict labour costs.

Small company size applied to all the strongly united industries except the docks. Small firms lack specialist managerial resources and may feel more vulnerable to competition and trade union pressure than larger companies. Strong associations which establish standard employment conditions and can act for the employer in negotiations are therefore likely to be attractive.

Finally, Gennard notes that both small size and the use of casual or sub-contract labour suggest a very low level of bureaucratic managerial control. If an employer does not possess the administrative control techniques of modern bureaucratic organisation then one way of handling inevitable labour problems is to 'contract out' the labour relations policy. The employers' association plays the role of professional agent, handling labour problems for the employer without the advantages of internal bureaucratic resources and techniques. We can add to Gennard's analysis the argument that an organisation which has bureaucratised its personnel policy by offering internal careers and permanent employment is less likely to need to collaborate with other employers, because it does not share a labour market with them. Firms with internal labour markets are less concerned about the regulation of external labour markets (see Chapter 3).

Factors affecting employer unity are thrown into relief by cross-cultural comparisons. Ingham (1974) contrasted the extraordinarily high employer solidarity in Sweden with the more disunited UK. In Sweden the central employers association, the SAF, was formed as early as 1902 with wide powers to act on behalf of Swedish employers. It dominates and determines employers' policy on labour relations, backed by a strike insurance scheme, started in 1920 and worth £130 million in 1979, and by powerful sanctions to discipline disruptive members. In contrast British employers' associations are divided and weak, and the CBI has none of the SAF's bargaining or disciplining powers.

Ingham suggests that a country's industrial infrastructure determines the degree of employer unity. Sweden industrialised late, industry is concentrated into a few, highly specialised industries, and within these industries a few firms dominate production. There are only a handful of major firms in the economy and they see their main competition as coming from outside Sweden's boundaries, not from within. In contrast the UK industrialised early and has a highly diverse, fragmented industrial base with a high degree of internal competition. Ingham's analysis is illuminating but has been found wanting in application to other societies (von Beyme, 1980). A crucial factor ignored by Ingham's analysis is the influence of other power groups on employer action. Employers are usually stimulated to submerge their differences and act together in response to some threat. This may be the threat of intense competition in product or labour markets. However employer unity has arisen more often as a response to threats by employees acting through trade unions, or through labour or working-class political parties. As Jackson & Sisson (1976), and Shalev (1980) note in criticism of Ingham's work, it was the shock of a major strike for manhood suffrage in 1902 and the decisive victory of the Social Democratic party in 1936 which enhanced Swedish employer solidarity. Political threats demonstrated the employers' need for strong, central co-ordination of policy and pushed employers towards the advocacy of central, nationwide collective bargaining. Such threats were not seen to exist in the UK.

Employer association unity in response to political rather than industrial threats is significant in Crawcour's (1978) discussion of the origins of Japan's permanent employment system. Riots, strikes and the beginnings of a radical labour movement combined with exceptional shortages of skilled labour to stimulate the creation of united employer policies. As a result of pressures from labour, the Industrial Club of Japan was founded in 1916 to co-ordinate the development of employment policies that would segregate large companies' employees into internal labour markets. The National Federation of Industrial Organisations (Zensanren) was formed in 1931 in response to the threat of legislation which would have legitimated craft and industrial unionism. Employers enhanced their solidarity and developed a powerful ideology to legitimise their preferred employment practices in the face of political, rather than strictly economic pressures. Now that the political threat has receded in Japan the current central employers' association, Nikkeiren, has lost some of its former significance and employer co-ordination is most maked on trade policies, through the central trade association, the Keidanren. This contrasts with Germany where the superiority of the employers' association, DGB, over the trade association, DBI, suggests that employers feel more need to co-ordinate policies towards employees than towards trade.

In the UK employer solidarity on employment policy towards trade unions was at its peak in the late nineteenth/early twentieth centuries when relatively small, non-bureaucratic employers faced the threat of widespread unionisation among manual workers. Employer unity on the strategy to be adopted towards unions has declined as companies have become more disparate in size and as more large-scale employers have adopted strategies of strategic independence.

British employers' reluctance to give their associations the authority or power to ensure united employer action is still illustrated by their lack of interest in formal strike insurance schemes. Strike insurance is used by associations in Sweden, Germany and the USA to underwrite employer solidarity against trade union pressures. In the UK employers have been less willing to establish formal procedures for bailing out competitors in industrial relations crises. The EEF has a scheme which was used with great success in 1972 (*Financial Times* 19.9.1979) and schemes exist in the Electrical Contracting Association, the Footwear and the Road Haulage Associations. However when the CBI investigated the possibility of establishing a central strike insurance fund in the late 1970s, they found members unwilling to contemplate a formal, centralised fund on the grounds that it would give the CBI control over members' policies. Even the idea of a mutual insurance scheme, not controlled by the CBI, was resoundingly rejected in 1980. British employers club together on an *ad hoc* basis to finance particular causes, but will not establish formal, association-controlled procedures for the purpose. In accordance with this reluctance to create highly centralised or powerful associations, most associations in the UK do not discipline or expel members who chose to act alone and break agreed association policies. Members of some early associations contributed a deposit to be forfeited if they broke agreed policy, and building employers once used inter-trading boycotts to pressure non-conformers, but such practices appear to have been abandoned. The expulsion of members for paying above agreed rates, for breaking lockouts or for breaking ranks during a strike does still occur, but it is not common.

Power in relation to other groups
If employers *do* choose to act together through their associations, there are various sanctions they can mobilise in pursuit of common policies.

(a)   Power vis à vis employees   In industrial disputes with trade unions employers' associations have the usual sanctions available to individual employers: of unilateral decision-taking to enforce

the conditions they want and of lockouts, threats of closure, suspensions and dismissals against employees resisting such conditions. Associations can co-ordinate employers' use of such sanctions. They can provide moral or financial support on a formal and an *ad hoc* basis for members engaged in industrial action with unions. More secretly they may organise blacklists against individuals who have caused trouble for employers.

Employers' and employers' associations' power against employees will be heavily affected by the results of political, rather than simply industrial contests. We discuss the political side of industrial relations in more detail in Chapter 7, but here we can note that employers' associations are not necessarily strong under Conservative and weak under Labour party governments. Political reality is more complex than conventional wisdom and the evidence of party affiliation might allow:

(b) Power vis à vis government: Employers' main power in relation to government derives from the close interaction between government and business in the implementation of day-to-day economic and industrial policy. Governments need information from, and the support of, industry for the implementation of most government policies and there is likely to be constant consultation between government departments and relevant interested employers. This close contact may take place between ministers and the directors or chief executives of powerful companies, but it also forms the staple work of many employers' associations. Constant access to, and influence on government may appear to be strongest under Conservative governments, when personal friendships and careers which span industry and politics help strengthen the pressure that can be brought to bear. However *any* government which is concerned to intervene in the running of the economy will find employer support or lack of support a powerful constraint. In recent years this has been most evident under Labour administrations. Organised employer non-co-operation effectively nullified the 1975 Industry Acts' proposals for planning agreements between large companies and governments. In 1977 the CBI warned that it would consider organising non-co-operation in the collection of government statistics, refusal to consult with any government department and the mass withdrawal of employers' association nominees on statutory bodies, all to demonstrate its opposition to proposals for worker directors and industrial democracy, proposals which were later withdrawn.

Employer association influence on Conservative governments is affected by the fact that the Conservative party is an alliance between manufacturing and business interests and financial and landowning groups. The alliance is not always united and the balance of power with the Party does not necessarily work in the employers' associations' favour. Kumar (1978) argues that the middle class or bourgeoisie in Britain has traditionally been weaker *vis à vis* other groups in the ruling class, compared with France or Germany. In Britain there is 'a fundamental tension' between industrial and financial capital which arose because the original landed class transformed itself into a capitalist class well before the rise of industry, and put its money into trading ventures. There was therefore a pre-industrial commercial elite based on the City of London and international trade and, as Francis (1980) points out, the landowners and merchants within this elite were *not* interested in financing industry as the industrial revolution gained momentum.

Early British businessmen had to rely on self financing more than in countries where the interests of commerce and industry developed together and a distinction between the interests of industrial and financial capital emerged. When the interests of industrialists and financiers conflict, employers' organisations are visibly weakened. In the 1920s the major employers' organisation, the Federation of British Industry (FBI), was incapable of reconciling the divisions within its ranks between free-trade exporters and protectionist home-marketeers. It therefore had no influence over policy as financial interests achieved the restoration of the gold standard to protect the exchange rate, effectively depressing the economy, especially in the export sector (Booth, 1982); '. . . matters which were likely to raise controversy within the organisation were studiously avoided, and this included almost every one of the crucial issues which affected industry during this period' (Blank, 1973). Similar problems have arisen for employers' associations in the 1980s. CBI pressure on Mrs Thatcher's Conservative government to modify its monetarist, neo-*laissez-faire* policies to protect the home manufacturing industry are not only rejected by financial interests, but have provoked the disaffiliation of CBI members as well.

The weakness of the manufacturing-based employers associations can be contrasted with the far smoother and more effective influence on government exerted by the farming industry. The National Farmers' Union (NFU) has extensive and detailed links with the various government departments involved in agriculture policy, so close that it is essentially a partner with government in the administration of a highly protectionist agricultural policy of farm subsidies, grants and intervention prices. The NFU's influence with governments, of both parties, cannot be explained in terms of parliamentary weight, for the NFU represents a relatively minor industry in the UK economy, and cannot threaten politicians with the loss of major, or marginal political votes. Its power derives from the absence of any organised anti-farmer lobby to represent the consumer or taxpayer in consultations with government and the historically close association of farming with the commercial elite.

Employers' associations' influence on government is weakened when capitalist interests are divided, but where those interests are united employers can mount strong and co-ordinated campaigns. If governments remain obdurate in the face of non-co-operation, then employers' associations can attempt to mobilise public opinion against government policy by advertising and by organising events to attract media attention, like running opinion polls and surveys, techniques which have been used with success against threats to nationalise the construction and insurance industries and against national and international threats to legislate for workers on company boards.

CONCLUSION

Employers' associations are complex representative institutions. They are not functionally equivalent to trade unions because their individual members may be as powerful as or more powerful than their representatives, and because the interests they represent are narrowly defined. British associations are less concerned with the maintenance of unity and use their representative structures of internal government in a more centralised way than do British trade unions.

In the UK employers combined together on an industry by industry basis in the nineteenth and early twentieth centuries primarily in response to the growth of trade unions. The basic industrial structure of employers' associations created at that time still exists, as do the arrangements the associations developed for handling trade unions by industry-wide collective bargaining arrangements on basic pay and hours of work.

Since the Second World War many employers have placed less reliance on their associations in negotiations with unions, preferring to decide on or negotiate employment policies within their own companies. Some large-scale companies have adopted modes of strategic independence whereby managerial control over pay and personnel policy is tightened and centralised through the adoption of bureaucratic personnel policies. The growth of multinational conglomerates who have powerful organisational resources and who do not fit neatly within industrial boundaries has spurred this type of development. Other companies have retained traditional non-bureaucratic personnel policies but have adopted strategies of federalism, allowing local managers to negotiate increases in pay and conditions but continuing to use their employers' association dispute procedures. Public policy in recent years has been to pressure firms away from 'federal' and towards 'strategic independence' strategies (see Chapter 9).

With the decline in the relative importance of industry-level negotiations, employers' associations have developed their provision of services to members, and their role as representatives of employer interests to government. Representation to government increases and becomes more detailed as more government policies – including 'non interventionist', monetarist policies – have an impact on business affairs. With the growth of international government, international employers' associations have been strengthened.

Employer association power rests on the extent to which employers choose to unite to establish common policies, and on the sanctions the associations can muster. Studies of employer solidarity suggest that co-ordinated policies are likely to develop where employers share a sense of vulnerability within a common labour market or see common interests in the face of political threats from employees. British employers have so far formed less centralised, united employers' associations than exist in some continental countries. Employer association sanctions towards employees and towards government are more effective when divisions of interest within industry, and divisions between industrial and finance capital are overcome.

Chapter 5

Employees and Workgroups

The United Kingdom has a working population of about twenty-six million. Nearly two million people are self-employed, and there are 20.5 million employees in employment, and well over three million (or about 12 per cent) registered as unemployed and looking for employment (*Department of Employment Gazette* figures for June 1982). What can we say about the demands these people make of work, and what influence do employees have on their own terms of employment?

EMPLOYEE OBJECTIVES AND EXPECTATIONS

There have been many attempts to understand what employees want from work. Clearly, most people work to earn a living, but beyond the basic need for income lie more complex issues. Do employees limit their interest to the economic rewards of work, or do they have a wide range of expectations and demands? Are they, for instance, concerned about job design and job content, do they want to exercise skill or judgement at work? If they have an interest in the content and control of work do they want radical changes and workers' control, or do they accept managerial authority but want some constraints on its use? Different answers to these questions lead on to very different predictions about how employees will behave and debates here centre on the concept of the 'work ethic' and on the prevalence of different value systems among employees.

Employees and the work ethic
The work ethic can be defined as a set of assumptions and beliefs that give work a very central place in our society. According to the work ethic, work is a major source of value: good work is associated with social success and moral worth. Work integrates the worker into the community, giving the worker his or her wider social significance. Through work, people define their identity and achieve their life goals.

In *The Protestant Ethic and the Spirit of Capitalism* (1930) Weber argued that the values of the work ethic linked with Protestant ideas about individual salvation to help motivate and sustain the merchants and entrepreneurs of Britain, Holland and Germany, who started the industrial revolution. The question now is how far the values of the work ethic permeate society and act as a motivator and source of expectations for employees.

The assumption that workers *do* operate in terms of the work ethic runs through theories as diverse as the managerial Human Relations School, Marxism and Corporatism (Anthony, 1977a). Human Relations theorists argue that workers demand and need interesting, stimulating work where judgement can be exercised and there are rewarding social contacts. Without such work, employees will be alienated and unco-operative and managerial objectives difficult to achieve. If, however, management can provide work with these features, then employees will be motivated and satisfied and will not press further demands. Marxists also assume that workers need self-fulfilling, interesting work but add the contention that there must be industrial democracy and workers' control of management, if the ills of alienation are to be avoided. Marxists therefore assume extensive employee expectations including demands for radical political changes. Corporatists make similar assumptions about employees' need of, and demand for, some form of industrial democracy. These three sets of theories all assume that employee demands will stretch beyond an interest in economic rewards and will cover some managerial issues on how work is organised and how business organisations are run. In contrast, management theorists like F. W. Taylor give work a high priority but argue that employee aspirations only relate to direct and immediate economic rewards. If employees are to achieve their life goals through work they should do so by maximising income, and the moral assumption is made that employees should not challenge managerial prerogatives by concerning themselves with political and managerial controls at work.

There is no absence of theoretical and moral arguments about what people want from work. Empirical evidence suggests that work is valued in different ways by British employees and that no simple set of assumptions can be seen to hold.

Survey evidence on employee expectations
Early empirical research threw some doubt on the widespread theoretical assumption that employees make a range of demands of work.

In 1968 Goldthorpe *et al.* surveyed about three hundred male, married, manual workers in Luton and concluded that they had economic, instrumental orientations to work. Their only interest was pay, they did not demand interesting or self-fulfilling work – indeed, several had given up more intrinsically satisfying work for the higher pay of their monotonous, dead-end jobs. Goldthorpe *et al*. did not assume their sample represented the approach to work of all manual workers. Instead they suggested that different types of orientation to work might be associated with the community in which people lived. 'Solidaristic orientations', placing high value on social relations with colleagues at work, would be found among miners, dockers or craftsmen. 'Bureaucratic orientations', valuing job security and prospects for promotion, would be held by salaried middle-class workers. For both categories, work was of central importance and aspects of the work ethic might be held to apply. However, for the relatively affluent workers on new housing estates, like their Luton sample, work was not given much value. It was merely seen as the means to achieve the money needed for more valued leisure or family activities. Workers with 'instrumental orientations' were not likely to make demands for interesting work, for rewarding social contacts, or for participation in job control or management. Instead they would concentrate all efforts to achieve the maximum financial returns from work.

Later studies have pointed to more varied orientations. Beynon and Blackburn (1972) found different orientations to work to be associated with particular family roles. In one factory they found the night-shift men, who were older and had heavy family responsibilities, primarily concerned about job security and pension rights. The day-shift men were younger, less concerned about these aspects of employment but had higher expectations for interesting work, good pay and promotion prospects. Full-time women valued their social relations with colleagues, and expected considerate supervision. Part-time women had low expectations in all areas and made low demands on pay, security, social relations or interesting work. The demands made of work can vary with family commitments and constraints.

The experience of different types of work also influences what people want from work. Manual workers with skilled work or rewarding relationships with colleagues usually value such advantages and expect to maintain them (Wedderburn and Crompton, 1972). The same is true of the advantages of professional work in white-collar bureaucracies (P. Child, 1981). People learn from experience what can be asked of work. They use their own past experience and the experience of others in 'similar' jobs to define what they see as reasonable, legitimate demands. Past experience and the experience of others in comparable work also affects the straightforward economic demands made of work. Most employees can make an assessment of the state of supply and demand in their labour market, and the affect this has on pay (Blackburn and Mann, 1979). However they also make an assessment of how other workers in similar work are rewarded. These comparisons with reference groups have a powerful impact on the expectations people have of their rewards (Wootton, 1955), and so do prevailing social ideas about 'fair wages' or a 'fair day's work' (Hyman and Brough, 1975). Simple economic models based on labour supply and demand cannot be used to predict what employees will see as their legitimate expectations.

Finally, employees make different demands in different contexts. Daniels (1973) studied worker attitudes during union–management negotiations to link changes in pay with changing work methods. He distinguishes between 'bargaining contexts' and 'work contexts'. When the workers were bargaining with their employer, they emphasised the economic rewards of work, apparently placing little value on job interest, freedom from close supervision or other offered advantages. However, in the context of daily work they expressed more interest in non-financial rewards. Instead of the oppositional stance towards management expressed during negotiations, they were more likely to emphasise teamwork and mutual co-operation with management to solve production problems.

People's expressed preferences alter with the constraints they see operating in different situations and with what they think they can achieve. The spread of 'realistic', low pay claims at times of high unemployment demonstrates this point. The sharp increase in unemployment from 6 per cent in 1980 to 12 per cent by 1982 caused a significant reduction in employee expectations and demands compared with the 1960s and early 1970s, when unemployment was under 4 per cent and when there were growing demands for industrial democracy and worker participation. However, it would be an unwise manager or politician who assumed that recession-depressed expectations would survive changed circumstances. High unemployment highlights the fact that some kind of work ethic is held by many employees in society. The depression, the sense of worthlessness and the associated ill-health that accompanies long-term unemployment, derives from the ethic that sees work as the way of achieving adult status and a worthwhile citizenship in society and not simply from the absence of earned income.

Employee ideology and value systems
Evidence suggests that three distinct types of value system can be found within the British working class: (a) a *dominant* value system which asserts the value of work and insists that issues of the managerial or political control of work are outside employees' legitimate sphere of interest – employees should be primarily con-

cerned with pay; (b) a *radical* value system which argues for workers' control; and (c) a *subordinate* value system which does not reject the major tenets of the dominant ideology but which stretches or seeks to manipulate them (Parkin, 1972). Radical values are now expressed by a very small minority. They had some influence in the 1880s and among the shop stewards movement of the First World War, but they are no longer a significant force in Britain, where the relevant values now are a mixture of (a) and (c). The dominant value system is widely disseminated but its total acceptance presents problems for employees. The employment relationship does not involve a simple exchange of a certain quantity of labour for a certain price. It is an exchange of labour potential or service which thereafter needs to be managed to extract its value. It is difficult, therefore, for employees to ignore managerial questions and most have some interest in how they are managed, if only in preserving any elements of discretion and self-determination that they may have. Subordinate values do not challenge managerial control of the hierarchical structure of authority at work, but assert the employees' right to fair treatment under that authority. The subordinate value system is probably widespread among the British working classes. Employees operating with such values do not make demands for radical or fundamental changes. In claiming fair treatment within existing social structures they exploit bureaucratic notions about the basis of rational administration by arguing that precedent, comparability or seniority be used as criteria in decision-making (see Chapter 10, pp. 227–8).

In summary, there are many theories about what people *ought* to want from their employment. The evidence presents a complex picture of a wide range of potential demands whose expression varies with the constraints that are seen to be operating. The total rejection of managerial authority is not widespread in the UK today. However, many employees cannot totally accept dominant managerial values and their activities need to be seen in terms of a subordinate value system which seeks to extract maximum advantage from the work provided within existing political and management systems.

INDIVIDUAL EMPLOYEE ACTION

Can employees achieve what they want from their employment, by their own actions? The individual can, theoretically, choose the type of job he applies for, negotiate terms with his employer and press his own interests once he is employed. However, for most employees individual power in all these areas is slight.

Blackburn and Mann (1979) studied the choice of jobs available to manual workers in the Peterborough labour market in the late 1970s. They concluded that manual workers had little scope for choice even at a time of nearly full employment. The jobs available to external recruits were at the bottom of the heap in terms of job interest, financial or other rewards. Eighty-five per cent of manual jobs required less skill than would be involved in driving to work. Differences in pay or conditions were slight. No matter what individual preferences might be, the labour market gave the unskilled manual worker little choice, even in the 1970s. The contraction of labour demand since then has greatly reduced the choice of more skilled workers.

In the initial negotiations on terms of employment, most prospective employees are in a weak position compared to the employer. Competition for jobs is usually greater than competition for workers. The employee usually requires a job more urgently than the employer requires one more employee, and so time works to the employer's advantage in negotiations. For the employer, vacancies can often be covered by rearranging the workforce and lost production can be made up later. In contrast, the employee often needs an immediate sale because accumulated savings are small compared with family outgoings and labour is a perishable product: it cannot be 'stored' and each day's unsold labour is a loss of part of the asset. Finally, the employer or his agent conduct more negotiations with employees than vice versa. This experience, coupled with higher social status and an accustomed position of authority, gives the employer an advantage in the 'art' of negotiating. The employer will also find it easier to get to know the other employers in the area, in order to exchange information or agree maximum rates. Employees are less likely to know their competitors. For all these reasons, most individual employees are at a disadvantage in negotiating their contract of employment, for few are in the happy position of possessing essential, rare and desperately needed skills (Burkett and Bowers, 1979).

Once in employment, can the individual act by himself or herself to improve his position at work? He or she may try to evade or manipulate managerially-determined rules and regulations. Case studies have found employees evading rules they believed to be restrictive, manipulating payment systems to their own advantage and generally attempting to expand their zone of discretion on the effort they put into work (see Brown, 1973, Lupton, 1963, and Roy, 1952 and 1954, for case studies involving manual workers; and Dalton, 1959, and Crozier, 1964, for white-collar examples.) Individual manipulation of rules is, of course essentially evasive and usually does little to change the basic, employer-determined features of the employment relationship.

Individual action can have more influence for the employee if the employer provides, or employees can create, an internal labour market so that existing employees have privileged access to the more interesting, better paid jobs within the organisation. If clear promotion hierarchies are created by management as part of their personnel policy, then individual action to gain the favourable attention of superiors is expected and encouraged. Even where management does not consciously develop career ladders, employees may be able to manoeuvre to get privileged access to better jobs, and Blackburn and Mann's Peterborough study found the better-rewarded, most interesting manual jobs were not available to external recruits but went to existing employees who used the 'discretion' inherent in their jobs to demonstrate reliability, compliance to supervisory demands, and a willingness to adopt managerial values and orientations.

Where the chances of promotion up the managerial hierarchy are slight or non-existent, then the scope for individual action to improve one's position at work is limited. Even with promotion opportunities, the individual can do little, alone, to alter the employer-determined rules of employment. For example, employees acting alone can rarely prevent unfair dismissals, alter the criteria for recruitment, promotion or disciplinary action, or achieve major changes in the allocation of reward or in methods of work. We need to turn from individual to group action, to see the most powerful methods used to achieve employee objectives at work.

GROUP ACTION BY EMPLOYEES

Employees form groups to protect and further their interests at work. These groups are so common that their absence, rather than their presence, should be seen as unusual. Employee groups come in many disguises and range from transient, face-to-face alliances to major organisations with millions of members and international staffs.

Traditional studies of employee groups in the UK have focused on trade unions. However, in the 1960s the significance of less formal employee workgroups became more apparent (Hill, 1974) and studies in occupational sociology have emphasised the importance of other formal groupings, like professional associations. If we can see when different types of group form, and note the factors which affect their strategies and power, then conventional trade unionism can be understood as one particular form of the wider phenomenon of pressure group formation at work. In the rest of this chapter we review the various types of small group that develop at the workplace. Chapter 6 surveys the larger and more formalised institutions created by employees.

SMALL GROUP ACTION

Small groups of people acting together to improve their employment conditions are widespread at work. There will always be isolated individuals who do not collaborate with their colleagues, and some work situations appear to discourage group formation. For example casual building navvies in the UK are unusually individualistic, reluctant to make any group commitments to either management or their mates, and react to grievances by quitting rather than forming groups to pressure for change (Sykes, 1969a, b). However, such situations are unusual: group formation is as common as friendship and friendship groups at work can often be used to further the employment interests of their members.

There are many studies of the small group activity of manual workers in the UK and USA. In the UK in the 1960s the activity of manual workgroups and the control they appeared to exercise over recruitment, job security, work methods and the working of incentive payment schemes caused considerable managerial and government concern. Many of the radical shifts in government policy which we discuss in Chapter 9 have been concerned to solve the 'problem' of manual workgroup power. Although manual workgroups have atracted most attention, it is important to realise that small groups with an interest in improving employment conditions are *not* confined to manual workers. Workgroups active in their own self-interest can be found throughout most organisational structures.

On the rare occasions when research penetrates the protective barriers of management, then managerial workers can be found pursuing their interests through informal, face-to-face 'cliques' and 'cabals'. Dalton studied non-union managers in three American organisations for thirteen years to produce his classic study *Men Who Manage* (1953). He found managers creating informal groups to provide mutual aid in their pursuit of promotion and, their attempts to empire-build their departments, and to protect their interests against attack. The operation of these groups was covert, and difficult for a stranger to detect, but cliques and cabals had a major impact on organisational and individual behaviour. Employee groups operate more openly in Japan, where the *ringi-cho* system of extensive group consultation throughout the permanent workforce of large companies gives small pressure groups an open and recognised channel through which to press their claims. Before we turn to the extensive literature on manual workgroups in the UK and USA, it is worth asking why small group activity among managers has attracted so little interest and why manual workgroup activity is not seen as a problem in Japan. Such ques-

domestic bargaining

tions highlight one of the themes of this book: that managerial control techniques and employee behaviour at work interrelate. Employee behaviour cannot be isolated from the organisational context or from the managerial strategies adopted by employers.

Workgroups vis à vis management structures and strategies

Small group activity, and the development of manual employee workgroups as a present-day managerial problem, can be related to the strategies adopted by employers for the construction of their business organisations. In *The Development of the Labour Process in Capitalist Societies* (1982), Littler argues that before modern, bureaucratic organisations developed, businessmen in Britain, Japan and the USA were reliant on the operation of largely autonomous, self-managing workgroups. Nineteenth-century merchants and entrepreneurs did not possess their own managerial resources. They controlled production by using work gangs, organised on a craft, family or gang-boss basis, as subcontractors or as internal contractors within the first factories. Slowly employers moved to gain more direct control over these workgroups and in Chapter 3 we noted the contrasting policies associated with Taylorism (influential in the USA and UK) and bureaucratic paternalism (influential in Japan). Policies associated with Taylorism were designed to break up the pre-existing workgroup ties. Employees were seen as isolated individuals with temporary commitments to their employer and were subject to highly centralised, bureaucratic controls over task performance. The managerial pressure to break or prevent workgroup ties is illustrated by comments about Ford's (USA) in the 1920s and 1930s: 'There was no association with other men. Any association with other workers in the department, line or bench where you were working was frowned upon' and 'chatting or fraternising with workmates during the lunch hour was taboo' (quoted in Beynon, 1973).

In contrast, Japanese policy was to incorporate workgroups as units into the new managerial structures. Many of the old subcontract group's functions on the allocation of work, work methods and quality control were retained, workgroup leaders were given a clear managerial status, and group members guaranteed job security and prospects of seniority-based promotion. Under these policies workgroup activity continued to have a legitimate role to play within the managerial structure, and workgroups did not become the focus of an alienated opposition to managerial controls. However, in those societies which relied on Taylor-type policies, workgroup activity was either successfully crushed, or continued to survive as the unofficial side of organisational life, often acting as a source of resistance to managerial control. Littler suggests that such resistance was more prevalent in the UK than USA. The UK had longer traditions of workgroup activity, and the transition to direct control occurred during recession. In the USA the transition to modern organisation and direct managerial control occurred in expansionary periods which softened the impact of change on employees, and the later adoption of bureaucratic personnel policies by many large-scale American employers also helped lessen opposition to the new managerial structures by providing more long-term rewards for employee loyalty. With a more bitter transition to direct controls and the long absence of bureaucratic personnel policy, the UK was left with severe managerial problems for the control of large-scale production. Workgroups continued a well organised but unofficial existence on British shopfloors, often in opposition to managerial controls, and British managers are still notable for their lack of success in the management of large-scale plants (Prais, 1982).

In the UK workgroups have survived for many years in engineering, shipbuilding and construction. In the 1960s growing concern about workgroup activity occurred at a time when tight labour markets were enhancing workgroup power and when extended, highly competitive product markets were squeezing profits (Hill, 1974). Employers sought to cut labour costs by mounting a new challenge to the workgroups' remaining areas of control and it was in this context that workgroup power came to be seen as a national problem.

The analysis of workgroup power
Most studies of employee workgroups are of manual workgroups in the USA and UK operating outside, and largely in opposition to, the normal managerial structures of control. An early study by Sayles (1958) investigated three hundred workgroups in the US manufacturing industry and classified workgroups according to the type of pressure they exerted in grievance activity against management, as shown in Figure 5.1.

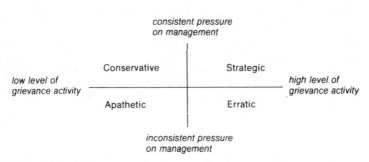

Figure 5.1 Sayles' Typology of Workgroup Grievance Activity

Apathetic groups rarely mobilised themselves to act together in their own interests. Conservative groups were strongly united and had high morale, but they were not seen by managers or unions as a source of grievance activity; instead, they were accepted as significant groups within the management structure. Strategic groups were consistently active on local disputes. Erratic groups were unpredictable – they could erupt in protest over minor issues and fail to react to major worsening of conditions

Sayles argued that he could predict the classification of particular workgroups according to (a) whether the division of labour isolated workers or welded them into integrated teams, and (b) whether they occupied a strategically powerful position in the production process. Apathetic groups were common in noisy, heavy metal-sanding or hammershop work in the car industry, where working conditions militated against the formation of friendship networks and where the groups had little strategic power to stop production. Erratic groups were found among small assembly lines and packers. Their cohesion and power was also weak but they could occasionally be mobilised by strong or militant leadership. Strategic groups did not need powerful leadership; they always coalesced into strong social units with sufficient power to build confidence in their own negotiating abilities, and they were found among welders or internal truck drivers in engineering and among the pressers in clothing manufacturing. The conservative groups were found among the skilled cutters in clothing or the general repairmen in car plants. They were highly skilled, played a crucial role in the production process, and were accepted as a group with legitimate interests by management; they did not need to use oppositional tactics and wild-cat strikes to achieve their ends.

Sayles' analysis is useful but incomplete, for his structural factors do not entirely determine workgroup behaviour. Nevertheless his study shows how the division of labour within a factory can facilitate or hinder the development of strong group ties and can affect the extent to which workgroups adopt oppositional or managerial tactics. His work also demonstrates that group action by employees is not inevitable. In some situations even face to face groups may not see sufficient common interest or have sufficient confidence to overcome barriers of apathy and the pressures towards individualism.

A major recent study of workgroups in a British plant of a multinational vehicle manufacturer outlined a number of factors influencing workgroup activity and power. (Batstone, Boraston and Frenkel, 1977 and 1978). The study found a marked contrast in the strength of workgroup organisation between manual production workers and the white-collar or manual service workers.

On the shopfloor the strongest groups exercised an influence over many managerial issues. These workgroups had bargained to establish and maintain a sectional system of management that made decisions on job allocation, manning levels, methods of work and piecework earnings accessible to workgroup pressure. Men were recruited through the workers' trade union and obtained transfers to amenable jobs through the union. Each section had a shop steward who worked out the rotas for overtime working, night-shift working and lay-off, with or without pay. As part of a decentralised union structure the workgroup was responsible for ratifying agreements made between union officials and their management on basic rates of pay and conditions. Most of the sectional workgroups on the shopfloor had also developed their own rules to relieve the sick, the elderly or those with domestic problems from night work and to relieve men over 60 from assembly-line work. They collected for the long-term sick and on one occasion a workgroup had 'carried' a blind man at significant loss of earnings to themselves. In contrast to the strong workgroups formed by production workers on the shopfloor, workgroups among the white-collar workforce exerted much less influence on the day to day management of their own work. These white-collar groups were linked into white-collar trade union branches, but they did not have the protective functions of the shopfloor workgroups, their pay and conditions of work were determined at central, not workgroup level, and they were not active in pursuit of day to day improvements in employment conditions.

Batstone *et al.* found many variables were needed to explain this contrast. The difference between shopfloor and white-collar workgroups could not be explained by any significant differences in the orientations of the workers themselves, for they all appeared to have similar objectives for employment. The researchers therefore analysed the contrast in terms of a basket of factors, some arising from organisational structure, some from the centralisation of management's personnel policies and the distribution of power between managers, and some from the organisation and leadership of the workgroups themselves.

Some of the differences in workgroup activity and power related to the workgroup's position in organisational structure and to the extent to which it occupied an important position in the production process (see Sayles' second factor above). Batstone *et al.* used strategic contingency theory (originally developed by organisational theorists to analyse the power of different *management* departments) to isolate four sources of power that may be available to any sub-group within an organisation. These power resources depended on:

1　The extent to which group members have skills which cannot be easily replaced or substituted
2　The extent to which group members occupy a crucial position or bottleneck in the organisation's workflow
3　The immediacy with which group action can affect or disrupt production
4　The extent to which the group can create or cope with uncertainty in the production process (Batstone *et al.*, 1978, p. 28)

Therefore skilled men maintaining irreplaceable production machinery or technicians operating a central computer could be expected to exert more powerful pressure than storemen or canteen workers, just as finance departments usually carry more weight than the safety or works departments. In the case study, many of the shopfloor production workgroups appeared to have a higher rating on these variables than did the staff departments.

Batstone *et al.* recognised that the four power resources derived from organisational structure were not outside the scope of human influence but could be affected by the strategies pursued by managers or workgroups. The researchers did not consider the wider aspects of managerial strategy and workgroup control discussed above (pages 84–5), but they did look at the impact of present workgroup and local management strategy on the structural sources of power. They found unskilled men, who could easily be replaced by others, acting to increase management's dependence on their labour (resource 1 above) by preventing substitutes from 'blacklegging' when they were in dispute. At the time of the study, management rarely attempting to 'man-up' manual strikers' jobs because workgroup leaders could organise widespread manual worker opposition to such provocative attacks on union principles. By applying the 'no blackleg' principle flexibly, shop stewards were able to influence the power of different workgroups and, by threatening to 'man up' jobs of certain strikers, had effectively weakened groups whose claims they did not support. Workgroups also acted to increase their power in relation to the other power resources listed above. They attempted to increase the force of any industrial action by picketing, sit-ins or requests for sympathetic action in order to create a more crucial impact on production. The immediacy of a production group's action depended upon management's stocks in their product; workgroups therefore attempted to reduce stocks by overtime bans, or working to rule if a dispute seemed imminent. In these ways the manual shopfloor workgroups acted to increase their power resources. Management also manipulated the structural power resources, for example by building up certain stocks. Finally, the power derived from a crucial position in the production process could be turned against a group by other parties. Some assembly-line workers could have such an immediate impact on production that both management and other workers sought to curb their use of strike action. Batstone notes that if a group like this is very important in the production process, it is possible for management to stir them to strike action to avoid having to pay those laid off when markets slump, supplies run short or breakdowns occur.

In this case study the strongest and most active shopfloor workgroups had a strong sense that their interests were opposed to those of management. Batstone *et al.* note the importance of employee values that represented a strong version of the subordinate value system, with traces of radical values (see page 80 above). Workgroup leaders acted to sustain this counter-ideology and develop workgroup strategies consistent with it. Focusing on workgroup leadership the authors classified workgroup shop stewards into 'leaders' who saw themselves as responsible for guiding their members and upholding trade union principles in opposition to hostile managerial objectives, and 'populists' who simply saw themselves as delegates responsible to their members alone. They noted how a higher proportion of 'leaders' on the shopfloor formed themselves into a tight network, headed by a 'quasi-elite' capable of mobilising considerable ideological and practical support and of developing and executing long-term strategies to increase workgroup power. The study shows the leadership and internal government of shop-steward-led workgroups to be a fascinating area for research.

Another British case study of shopfloor activity in the 1970s provides an interesting contrast to the Batstone study, because it describes a situation where the threat of oppositional workgroups had been defused by careful managerial strategies on job design and trade union relations. 'Chemco' is the pseudonym given to a chemical company with a modern plant in the West Country. The researchers suggest that Chemco's managers had adopted a number of policies to prevent the development of oppositional groups among their unskilled and semi-skilled workforce at the case study plant. The workforce was divided spacially and by means of a continental shift system, which meant that workers on one shift rarely met their colleagues on another. A trade union had been invited in by management and given a closed shop, so that no workgroup ties had formed around demands for union recognition. Managers aided the appointment of moderate shop stewards and the negotiation of company-wide collective agreements helped to ensure that strongly organised, oppositional workgroups did not emerge to create managerial problems on the shop floor (Nichols and Armstrong, 1976; Nichols and Beynon, 1977).

The extent of workgroup activity
The Batstone and Chemco studies discussed above follow a tradition of industrial relations research. They are concerned with
workgroup activity which is clearly seen, by workers, managers
and researchers alike, to be opposed to managerial controls. However, studies within industrial sociology show that workgroup
activity is not always an industrial relations issue, for many workgroups are sufficiently incorporated into organisational structure
to further their group's interests by using managerial rather than
oppositional tactics. Dalton (1959) showed this process operating
within American management. He referred to managerial groups
as cliques and cabals, and noted that the strategies available to
such groups were affected by the way the groups related to the
organisational structure. *Vertical* cliques formed up and down the
authority pyramid, while *horizontal* cliques formed across single
grades in the hierarchy. Dalton argued that vertical symbiotic
cliques were most powerful. They were small groups formed by a
senior officer and a few subordinates who were in constant contact
and whose job required teamwork. With access to organisational
resources and decision-making procedures, a cohesive vertical
symbiotic clique could initiate major policy changes which would
help increase the group's power and aid members' chances of
promotion. In contrast, horizontal cliques – for example all foremen, or all departmental superintendents – were more difficult to
mobilise. They were not in constant contact and had separated,
disparate jobs. They could usually be organised to resist clearly
perceived attacks on group interests, but once the immediate
threat had passed, problems of communications and differences in
immediate interests would cause the 'action group' to lapse. Horizontal management groups could be organised on defensive issues
and could resist change by policies of non-co-operation, but they
were not as powerful as the more integrated vertical groups
because they could not initiate major changes in management
structure.

Dalton's study reminds us that confrontational tactics are not
necessarily an indication of the greatest workgroup power, and
that groups which can protect or enhance their interests without
the need to openly oppose managerial controls may be in a more
powerful position than those which cannot. Other studies within
organisation theory also demonstrate that high levels of workgroup activity can exist in a managerial rather than an industrial
relations context, and that such activity among professional or
managerial groups may well be defined as part of the normal established process of managerial decision-making (see Strauss *et al.*
1971; or Tugendhat, 1973, pp. 129–32).

Accurate estimates of the extent of employee workgroup activity are not available. The fact that workgroup activity can be part of the normal administration of an organisation, and that pressure on employment issues may be transitory or covert, all make it difficult to gauge the number of active workgroups in the UK. The only attempts at measurement have been associated with studies of shop steward activity and these measures have been noted for a tendency to understimate. In 1968 a Royal Commission estimated that there were 175,000 British shop stewards. A survey in the manufacturing industry a few years later revised the estimate to between 250,000 to 300,000 (CIR, 1971). In the late 1970s the TUC suggested there were 300,000 shop stewards, 200,000 safety representatives and 100,000 union pension trustees, all with some representative functions at the workplace who might conceivably be in a position to mobilise workgroup pressures. To these estimates must be added the workgroup activity which is not linked to trade unionism. There are no measures of this, although the survey of British manufacturing produced an estimated 45,000 shopfloor workgroup leaders who represented their colleagues' interests on pay, discipline, work methods or grading, but had no apparent trade union affiliation. Clear measures of workgroup activity and detailed studies of the range of possible types of activity have yet to emerge. Nevertheless it is clear that the most visible, oppositional activity fluctuates with economic constraints. In the 1920s Goodrich saw the shopfloor as the 'frontier of control' between managerial and workgroup interests, and noted that the frontier shifted as the strength of the embattled parties was affected by the external economic and political context. This has become very apparent in the 1980s for, with the return of mass unemployment, the powerful workgroup controls of the type examined by Batstone *et al*. have come under concerted attack. Although no academic studies have charted the effects of this renewed battle, it would seem that strong shopfloor workgroups have been greatly weakened since the 1970s (*Financial Times*, 16/8/82; Francis *et al*., 1982, p. 14). The more confident managerial attack on workgroup controls was symbolised by the dismissal of the senior steward or convenor of British Leyland's Longbridge plant (Mr Derek Robinson) in 1981. The collapse of the strike to reinstate Mr Robinson heralded a managerial roll-back of workgroup controls, across those parts of the British manufacturing industry where oppositional workgroups had been at their strongest.

CONCLUSION

There has been much debate about employee objectives at work. Some people argue that employees have limited, short-term and strictly economic objectives. Others contend that most employees hold some form of work ethic and are likely to demand interesting work, self-determination and possibly self-government at work. Evidence suggests that employees have a wide range of objectives and that the demands made of work vary with individual circumstances and the perceived distribution of power at the workplace. Studies of employee values conclude that a radical and fundamental rejection of employer authority is rare in the UK, but that there is widespread support for subordinate ideologies which seek to protect employees by limiting and constraining the exercise of managerial authority.

Whatever their objectives, employees rarely have the opportunity to achieve major changes in the conditions of employment provided by their employer by themselves. If their organisation has an internal labour market so that employees can gain promotion to more interesting, better-paid jobs, then an employee may be able to achieve some of his objectives by individual effort and promotion. However, in most situations individual efforts have only limited results and it is common for employees to further their interests by acting with others in various types of group.

In this chapter we looked at the small, face-to-face groups formed by employees. Much managerial anxiety and industrial relations research has focused on workgroups formed by manual workers on factory shopfloors. The power of manual workgroups has been blamed for low levels of productivity in the UK, and for the British reputation for problematic industrial relations. However literature within organisational and industrial sociology demonstrates that small groups of workers acting to further their members' interests are not unique to manual shopfloors, but pervade organisations in most societies from the level of the boardroom downwards. It is not the existence of workgroups active in their own self-interest, but the way that such groups relate to managerial structure, that should be seen as significant for industrial relations.

Some employee workgroups are incorporated into managerial structures of control and their activities are not regarded as an industrial relations issue. Strong and self-confident workgroups may operate to protect and enhance members' interests, but because they act by manipulating managerial resources, information flows and arguments, they do not attract much attention. Sayles' 'conservative groups', Dalton's managerial cliques and cabals, and the workgroups within the permanent workforce of Japan's large companies are of this type. If these group members are involved in confrontational opposition to management, then this takes place above the level of their workgroup. Other employee workgroups are active in opposition to management in their day to day activities at the place of work. They operate with values which emphasise differences of interest between employer and employee and see workplace activity as the 'frontier of control' between opposing interests (Goodrich, 1975). Studies of such groups show that the frontier shifts as the balance of power between employer and employee swings with economic and political changes (W. Brown, 1973 and 1981; H. Beynon, 1973; Batstone *et al*., 1977 and 1978; Armstrong *et al*., 1981).

Workgroup activity needs to be analysed in terms of different types of organisation structure and managerial control. Research in this area is underdeveloped but it would seem that whereas incorporated workgroups tend to be associated with bureaucratic personnel policies, the most alienated, oppositional workgroups have emerged as the unintended consequence of Taylorite policies designed to atomise the workforce and break workgroup ties.

Workgroup activity reached a recent peak in the late 1960s and 1970s in the UK. The recession and mass unemployment of the 1980s have taken their toll of the more visible, oppositional workgroup activities.

Face to face workgroups are not the only, or the most significant, groups formed by employees to further their interests at work. Most oppositional workgroups and many of those which are incorporated into management structures are linked to the larger, more formally instituted groups for the protection of employees which form the subject of Chapter 6.

Chapter 6

Trade Unions – Employee Institutions

Face-to-face employee pressure groups can operate without complex institutional arrangements. However if local employee groups link up across workplaces and organise on a wider scale, then formal organisations or institutions are needed. All industrialised societies develop institutions for the representation of large groups of employees at work, but the form that these take can vary. Most call themselves trade unions but, as we shall see below, there is no logical or clear distinction between employee institutions labelled unions and those labelled staff or professional associations.

In this chapter we look at the different types of employee institutions that exist. We review the historical development of large-scale employee organisation in the United Kingdom and we note the impact that different bases of organisation have on the objectives, tactics and internal government of employee institutions.

TYPES OF EMPLOYEE INSTITUTION

Unions Structured by External Interests

In several societies employee institutions have been established or reshaped by government action. Where this is the case, unions usually follow the regional or industrial administrative structures of government. Such unions provide governments with channels of communication and consultation with employees and may be used by government in attempts to mobilise worker support for government policy. Lesser degrees of government influence may occur if, rather than forming or reshaping unions, legislation is passed to licence or permit only those unions that conform to certain specifications in terms of their objectives or methods of operation.

No government in the UK has ever attempted to form or reconstruct employee institutions in the way that occurred, for example in Nazi Germany, Fascist Spain or in the communist countries of USSR, Poland or China. In the UK there have been few government attempts to legislate on the form that employee institutions should take. However government policy in the 1970s and early 1980s did stimulate a debate on the extent to which the state could or should influence the forms of employee institutions in the UK (see Chapters 7 and 9).

Employee institutions may also be established by employers. In the USA and UK some large companies have formed staff associations or company unions to act as a channel of representation for their staff. In staff associations all company employees are usually members, they elect representatives who have rights to sit on various consultative committees with management, and have a role in employee welfare. They are rarely intended to do more than inform management of staff views before decisions are taken and the typical staff association does not have the right or the sanctions to challenge seriously managerial decisions. Institutions of this type are usually resented by the surrounding trade unions on the grounds that they are formed as part of managerial strategy to prevent the spread of independent trade unionism and to thereby protect managerial prerogatives. Such suspicions have been encouraged by the widespread use of company-sponsored 'sweetheart unions' in the USA. In 1926 company unions had about half as many members as the main union federation and were a significant factor in the failure of independent unionism to spread in the USA. In the UK staff associations are now mainly found in the finance sector. The UK banks responded to the sharply rising membership of the independent Bank Officers Guild (BOG) in the 1920s by forming rival, company-based staff associations which effectively blocked the BOG's attempts to gain recognition. As a result industry-wide collective bargaining was not established in banking until 1968. In insurance, staff associations helped weaken the appeal of independent trade unionism until the 1970s. However, outside the finance sector the impact of company-sponsored institutions has been slight in the UK.

With the exception of the finance industry British employers have had little success in establishing staff associations and until very recently British governments have not followed the strategy, common elsewhere, of attempting to shape or at least licence approved trade unions. Employee institutions in the UK have essentially developed 'from the grass-roots' – created by employees themselves. Not only have they developed independently of governments and employers, but neither churches nor political parties have had much impact on their development. This contrasts with most other European countries where communist and socialist political parties and the Catholic church have fostered trade unions. For example in France, the Netherlands, Belgium and Italy, union structure has been heavily influenced by the existence of communist, socialist or Catholic-sponsored unions.

In the UK employees themselves have formed the major employee institutions and in order to understand the type of institution formed we need to focus on the factors which aid employee organisation. The formation of independent employee institutions is never simple. It requires the development of communication networks, leadership or administrative roles and ideological and material incentives to member loyalty. Nevertheless, there have been many attempts to create independent employee institutions and the first institutions to achieve any lasting success were organised around the possession of an occupational, market-based skill.

Market-Based Skill: Occupational Institutions

The earliest institutions to be formed by employees were organised around clearly defined skills which could attract many buyers on an open market. The formation of institutions to protect and enhance a marketable skill pre-dates industrialisation. The feudal guilds were powerful economic, social and political institutions in the cities of Europe from the twelfth to the fourteenth centuries. The guilds were not employee organisations in a strict sense, for they covered masters as well as journeymen, but their organisations were based around the possession of an occupational skill and their economic objective was to preserve and increase the value of that skill. To achieve this they attempted to monopolise the supply of their skill on the market. Using Weber's terminology we can say they adopted policies of *closure* (Weber, 1947, pp. 10–143). They attempted to close social and economic opportunities to outsiders in order to maximise the advantages their skill could bring group members. They sought to close access to their advantageous market position by restricting numbers of apprentices taken on to learn their trade and by requiring long training and possibly the completion of a 'masterpiece' before potential recruits were allowed entry to the occupation. The guilds then attempted to stop any outsiders from breaking their monopoly over the supply of their skills on the market. They prevented the dilution of their skills and forbade competition between guild members on the market by laying down a network of rules, determined in guild parliaments, which regulated the apprentice system, methods of work, tools, manning levels, the pay of apprentices and journeymen, and the prices at which supplies should be bought and goods sold.

Many guilds were politically active and were able to gain charters from the crown or from national or city governments to protect and legitimise their market monopolies. At their height they were powerful self-regulating groups, able to maintain tight internal discipline and to dictate terms to their suppliers and their customers (Schneider, 1969; Weber, 1974). Guild controls decayed with the growth of capitalism, but their closure policies have been copied by other occupational groups, notably by professional associations and craft trade unions.

1 *Professional Associations* The ancient professions sought autonomy and self-regulation in their work and like the guilds used policies of occupational monopoly and closure (Caplow, 1954, and Johnson, 1972). The most powerful skill-based organisations in the UK today are still those for doctors and lawyers. Both the British Medical Association and the Law Society have wide-ranging self-regulatory powers backed by charters issued by the Privy Council to the Crown. The associations attempt to control or influence recruitment to training; the length and content of training; qualification as a practitioner: standards of work and the disciplining of sub-standard work. They prevent competition by advertising among their members and have, in the past, established scale fees. Political lobbying has resulted in state backing for some of these professional controls. Acts of Parliament may restrict certain key professional activities – such as signing death certificates in medicine, or representation by barristers not solicitors in the High Court – to practitioners whose names are included on the register kept by the professional association. As a result of these practices the ancient professions of the UK and USA can, as Caplow notes, exercise an extraordinary degree of occupational control over recruitment, work methods, discipline and the rewards received for work (Caplow, 1954, Chapter 5).

The ancient professions' extensive control over the terms and conditions of work of their own members has been the envy of many other groups. Today there are over one hundred and fifty professional associations, ranging from the ancient Inns of Court and Royal College of Physicians to more recent institutes for travel agents, municipal building managers or nuclear engineers. All are concerned to establish training systems and examinations to be used to register professionals as competent to undertake particular areas of work. Many of these qualifying associations also attempt to raise their group's status and increase their autonomy by the elaboration of codes of ethics and the disqualification of members who break these codes. Many take part in publicity and pressure-group activity directed towards government, major employers and the public at large (Millerson, 1964). Professional controls are supported and professional association activities justified by ideologies which emphasise the importance of the group's skill for society as a whole and the need for the occupation itself to act as the best and only custodian of standards.

Attempts to form professional associations by new occupational groups continue and show no sign of decreasing. However, no new occupation is likely to achieve the very extensive self-regulation and unilateral control exercised by the ancient professions, for reasons we will discuss below (page 99). Before that discussion, however, we turn to the other modern form of occupational organisation oriented around market-based skill: craft trade unions.

2   *Craft Trade Unions*   Skilled craftsmen were the first manual workers to form organisations capable of operating beyond a single workshop. Evidence of trade societies of skilled men, organising on a district or town basis, can be traced back to the seventeenth century, and by the end of the eighteenth century we know that local trade societies had been established for many workers, including printers, shoemakers, weavers, spinners, hatters, coopers and building tradesmen. The earliest craft societies attempted to achieve unilateral control of their wages and work methods. For example, members of the Shipwrights Provident Union Society, which flourished in the Thames shipyards, drew up stringent rules for the employment of their members, for their pay and conditions of work, and insisted on a high standard of professional knowledge on the part of foremen (Pelling, 1963). Millwright societies circularised employers in their districts with their rates of pay and enforced craft methods and practices. Direct strike action was occasionally threatened and used against recalcitrant employers, but industrial action was generally less important than the policies of closure adopted to monopolise and limit the craft's labour supply. Societies attempted to organise all apprenticed craftsmen, to limit the numbers of apprentices taken on by employers, and to insist on long (often seven-year) apprenticeships. They tried to ensure that their traditional areas of work were undertaken only by their own members and that traditional craft methods, work practices and standards, were maintained. The solidarity of the craftsmen in maintaining these practices was supported by policies of mutual insurance. The societies organised insurance for sickness and death benefit among their members. Unemployment benefit and the system of 'tramp relief' (whereby skilled craftsmen travelling in search of work would be helped by the appropriate trade society in each town) served not only as an insurance benefit to members but also acted to prevent the undercutting of the society's wage rates through competition from unemployed craftsmen.

The success of the craftsmen's policies depended not only on the coverage and discipline of the craftsmen's organisation but also on employers' demand for their skills. Craft bargaining power was rarely sufficient to dictate to employers all the terms on which craftsmen would work, but in times of economic prosperity, for example when the engineering industry faced relatively soft markets, or building faced a construction boom during the second half of the nineteenth century, craftsmen found many employers willing to accept, or at least bargain on, the trade societies' preferred terms of employment (Burgess, 1975). The local societies of artisans developed in the mid nineteenth century to become the first national trade unions in the UK. In 1851 the Amalgamated Society of Engineers was established, followed in 1860 by the Amalgamated Society of Carpenters and Joiners and in 1866 by an amalgamated society for tailors. These amalgamated societies centralised their administration and the control of their funds and employed some full-time staff. Their bureaucratic institutional structure earned them the label 'New Model Unions' from the Webbs (Webb and Webb, 1898, p. 16).

Craft unionism reached its height with the New Model Unions and was to be significant in the historical development of unionism in the UK. Craft unions were the first stable manual-worker unions. They operated horizontally, following their members across firms and industries. Their objectives were sectional, designed to preserve the privileges of the 'aristocracy' of labour. At times their policies were explicitly justified by reference to the old professionals and, like the professions, their ideology was generally elitist. The craft unions were therefore based on very different principles from those of the often vertically organised, more socialist unions that were later to develop alongside them.

The occupational control of the ancient professions and the self-regulation and autonomy of the old crafts have been envied by many other occupations. However few have been able to match the old professions and most craftsmen have seen their old, unilateral controls whittled away. We need to explain why certain occupations have been able to achieve unilateral controls over their own working conditions.

Factors Affecting the Success of Occupational Institutions
There are variations in the success with which different occupations have been able to control their own working conditions, through policies of monopolistic closure. An occupation's success will depend on the power resources available to the occupational group and the countervailing power of any rivals (Turner and Hodge, 1970). The power resources available to the occupation itself centre on their position in the labour market and factors which facilitate group organisation.

1 *Power Resources Held by an Occupational Group* The *sine qua non* of occupational organisation is marketable skill. If the occupation is to achieve any monopoly control over the supply of its labour, then it needs to provide a form of labour which em-

ployers will find difficult to replace or substitute from the general labour market. As Braverman noted, deskilling work, so that unskilled labour can be substituted for skilled, has been a powerful employer strategy in reducing the power and control of once-skilled groups (see Chapter 3). It will be more difficult for employers to find easy substitutes for certain skills if those skills include diagnostic expertise only gained after long practice, or if the knowledge base of the skill is not understood or available to anyone outside the skilled group itself.

If a group possesses a non-substitutable skill, then the extent to which they can bargain to achieve good rewards and a high degree of self-determination in their work, will depend on the buyer's need for the skills they offer. If their skills are essential to their employer, having a pervasive and immediate impact on his ability to achieve his objectives, then the occupation has a potentially powerful resource.

In order to protect and take advantage of the labour-market power provided by skill, an occupational group needs to build occupational institutions capable of enforcing the necessary closure policies. It is not easy to build long lasting organisations, and organisation is facilitated if an occupation's members are concentrated geographically, are literate and are brought together by long periods of training when they can develop strong social ties and a sense of occupational identity. The earliest professional associates and craft unions – the Inns of Court lawyers and the London printers – were favourably placed in these respects. Once a group forms to protect and enhance a marketable skill, its success in imposing its terms on the buyers of its skill will depend not only on the market demand for its labour but also on the group's political success in its conflicts with rivals. Leadership, effective strategic planning and the development of ideologies to legitimate group claims will play a part in this. In battles for control the group's links with other power-holders may also be significant. As Turner and Hodge (1970) note, if a group can guarantee recruits of high social status so that its members have family and social contacts in, for example, the courts or government, then it is less likely to find its occupational claims successfully challenged.

2 *Power Resources Held by Rivals to the Occupation* There will always be other parties interested in challenging occupational controls. The most powerful rivals are employers and the government.

The countervailing power of an employer depends on the employer's position in the labour market and on the organisational and political resources which he commands. If an employer monopolises the demand for labour in his labour market, then his bargaining position is obviously greater than if he does not. Clients buying the skilled labour of medical doctors or lawyers are usually scattered individuals, often in a personally vulnerable position which makes them highly dependent on the skills they seek. Such employers are much less powerful than the large company with monopsony control of its local labour market.

Occupational controls flourished in the nineteenth century in the UK, when employers were small and competitive. The growth of modern, large-scale organisation has threatened occupational control in two ways. First, the concentration of business activity makes it more likely that there will be employers who dominate their local labour markets. Secondly, the growth in the size of companies has been accompanied by the development of bureaucratic management structures and specialised staff. These enable an employer to develop policies to make him less dependent on externally generated, market-based skills. Two types of policy may be used. Jobs may be redesigned in order to deskill the labour process and enable the employer to substitute unskilled labour for skilled (see the discussion of Taylorism in Chapter 3). Or the employer may develop an internal labour market within his company such that any necessary skills are created within the organisation itself and are not easily sold on the open market (see the discussion of bureaucratic employment policies in Chapter 3). Labour in this instance is not unskilled, but the skills are learnt by company training and experience and are likely to be company-specific because they derive in part from an understanding of company policies and procedures. An employee with this background may find it difficult to find another market for his skill. Under either the deskilling or the bureaucratic personnel policy, the conditions for the development of occupational, market-related employee groups are no longer met.

Occupational controls are most likely to flourish under a passive government. If governments take an active interest in the regulation of employment affairs, then an occupation is unlikely to find itself with a free hand in occupational regulation. For example, the teaching profession, developing in conjunction with the modern state, has never achieved the self-determination of the medical profession, developing before it. Even when the National Health Service was introduced in 1944, doctors bargained to maintain many of their advantages. The British Medical Association insisted that the relationship between government as employer and the occupation be kept at arm's length, and general practitioners, unlike teachers, are not direct employees of the state.

Varying Success of Market-Based Occupational Controls
With so many factors affecting the formation of occupational institutions and the power that they can exert, it is not surprising

that there are marked differences in the occupational institutions of different societies. On the other hand, groups like medical doctors, lawyers or craft printers have succeeded in forming occupational institutions with relatively high degrees of self-regulation in many societies, the success of less powerful groups is very varied. For example, midwives have survived on as a coherent and separate occupational group within the medical profession in the UK. A similar group lost the battle for survival in the USA (Donnison, 1973; Ehreneich and English, 1974). Occupational groups of both the professional and the craft type are more firmly entrenched in the UK and USA than in societies where government or state agencies have always intervened in the regulation of economic affairs or where industrial management has traditionally been highly centralised and bureaucratic.

Within the UK lawyers still show a remarkable resistance to any challenge to their traditional professional self-regulation, their restrictive practices and their demarcation rules (Zander, 1968). However, for most skilled groups the twentieth century has brought growing threats to occupational autonomy and self-determination.

Even well-entrenched occupations like the medical doctors face challenges to their occupational controls. As NHS administration has grown, doctors are challenged by administrators within the hospital service. The knowledge base of the doctor's skill has become accessible to outsiders with the growth of the study of biochemistry, and sophistication in diagnostic machinery. Centralised government control of the NHS also presents a continuing challenge. Reflecting such changes, the BMA is increasingly adopting direct bargaining tactics in attempts to reinforce its traditional use of the political lobby to protect its interests.

Challenges to occupational controls can be seen most clearly in the case of manual craftsmen. Craft controls which flourished in the second half of the nineteenth century were attacked as employers were able to use new technology to deskill jobs. The pioneering ASE suffered major defeats soon after it was formed, on the 'machine question' and the replacement of apprenticed engineers by unskilled or semi-skilled labour and machine tools. After losing major strikes and lockouts in 1898 and 1922, the ASE was forced to abandon its original skill-based policies of closure and self-determination. The national union lost its powers of craft protection, although craft controls survived in some local districts amongst powerful workgroups (Burgess, 1975). A similar decline in craft controls can be traced in many industries. Shipwrights lost influence with prefabricated ships; vehicle builders were able to carry the hand skills of coach building into the railway workshops but were finally by-passed by the assembly-line technology of the car industry. Today printing is often regarded as the last bastion of craft controls, but the skill base of the printers has been destroyed by offset lithography technology and is further threatened by computerised print-setting.

Monopoly control over jobs has become increasingly difficult to maintain in the face of managements' use of both technology and scientific management policies to reduce its dependence on externally-generated skills. Nevertheless, well-organised groups who have tight member-discipline and who retain some vestiges of non-substitutable skill have sometimes been able to cling to their monopoly of certain work and demand a high price for the buying-out of their traditional job-rights.

The problems facing new groups who wish to establish professional self-regulation can be illustrated by the fate of the United Kingdom Association of Professional Engineers. UKAPE was formed in 1969 and abjured strike action and limited its membership to professionally qualified engineers. It devised codes of professionally approved behaviour, espoused a 'responsible', pro-management ideology and sought recognition by engineering employers as the body with which they should agree the employment conditions of their professionally qualified staff. UKAPE provoked hostile reactions not only from the trade unions already in the area, but from employers who argued that the category of 'professional staff' did not fit in their bureaucratically-organised staff-grading structures. UKAPE could not muster the resources even with a favourable government in power, to overcome this opposition (see CIR Reports 32, 55 and 66, and L. Dickens, 1975).

In conclusion, occupational institutions protect and enhance the value of market-based skill. In the UK they grew to strength in the nineteenth century when governments did not actively intervene in the regulation of work or employment and when employers were small and non-bureaucratic. However, many employees do not have non-substitutable skills and many of the old skills have been undermined by developments in technology and in managerial controls over the labour process. What types of employee institutions are formed by those without a clear market-based skill? We turn first to look at the institutions that were formed in the late nineteenth and early twentieth centuries to cater for the unskilled or semi-skilled manual worker without a high level of non-substitutable skill.

Unskilled Trade Unionism

Most workers in the developing industries of the nineteenth century had no clearly defined skill which could be used to support policies of closure and monopoly control. Many attempts were made to mobilise workers in local areas to try to improve their working conditions, but these faced constant difficulties because unskilled, low-paid and ill-educated workers had few resources with which to build effective organisation. Employers could use the generally anti-union laws particularly successfully against such groups (see Chapter 7), and employers could all too easily replace protesting employees with new recruits. In the face of these barriers to organisation, ideologies developed to help underpin the mobilisation of the hard-to-organise employee. Ideas spread that the difficulties facing employee organisation were worth surmounting, that risks were worth taking because radical improvements could be achieved. For employees with few power resources in the existing structure of society, the prospect of a radically changed, socialist society became one of the anchorages of employee organisation.

1 *General Trade Unionism* The ideology of General Unionism developed to help counter the fact that unskilled workers had no significant labour-market power as long as employers could replace dissidents from the mass of the unemployed. It declared that all workers could and should unite to form a single, general union. In a single union the united class of workers would have the power to demand major industrial and political concessions.

The ideology of General Unionism had its greatest appeal during the 1830s (the Webbs marked 1829–42 as the 'revolutionary period' of British trade unionism). The most spectacular general union was the Grand National Consolidated Trades Union, created by Robert Owen in 1834. Formed initially to support workers in dispute at Derby, it quickly expanded its aims and membership. It proposed to rationalise the sectional, splintered craft unions into a united structure that would include agricultural and other labourers. It advocated production through co-operatives and aimed to provide assistance for any worker on strike. It attracted a probable membership of half a million people, but its organisation could not be maintained. It was persecuted by employers and the government – the deportation of six Dorset labourers, the Tolpuddle Martyrs, being the best known case. It was unable to provide the level of assistance that strikers expected and the treasurer finally absconded with its funds.

Similar problems dogged the many more localised attempts to establish unions for unskilled labourers in the nineteenth century. Organisation would appear to make progress in periods of rising prices and strong markets only to be broken in the next economic recession. It was not until the 1880s that general unions achieved any permanent success. In London a strike by women at Bryant and May's match company in 1888 attracted considerable public sympathy, and in conditions of unusually full employment general unionism spread to the gas industry and to the docks. The high point of this development was the dockers' strike in 1889 when a five-week strike achieved six pence an hour and eight pence for overtime after a colourful march through London and donations of £30,000 from trade unionists in Australia. Unskilled workers were beginning to make an impact through organisation, but the ideal of a single, general union had faded. The organisation of the entire working class was too difficult, common interests seemed too insubstantial and, given continuing competition from the general labour market, general organisations were too weak. The general union organisers retreated to concentrate on areas that could be highly organised, like the new gas industry or the docks, where a highly united labour force could use strike tactics to exact concessions from the most profitable employers.

The UK today has two general unions which trace their origins to the general unionism of the nineteenth century. The General, Municipal and Boilermakers' Union (GMBU) developed from the organisation among the gas workers, the Transport and General Workers Union (TGWU) from that of the dockers. The illogicality of having *two* general unions has often been noted but with the decline of the general union ideal they remain distinct and separate institutions.

2 *Industrial Trade Unionism* As the hopes for a single general union faded, the idea of one union for each industry developed as a way of achieving working-class organisations with sufficient common interest, and sufficient control over their labour markets, to achieve industrial and political objectives. The most radical advocates of industrial unionism were the Syndicalists. Syndicalist ideas developed in the USA and France and spread to the UK from 1910. Syndicalists argued for the merger of sectional union interests into industrial groups capable of revolutionary action against employers and government. Sorel, in France, advocated the use of strikes as a political weapon to win control of the state. After the revolution and the destruction of private ownership, industrial unions would govern industry. Syndicalist ideas were not widespread or long-lasting within the UK but Tom Mann, an engineer, started a monthly syndicalist journal in 1910 and an articulate expression of syndicalist thought was published in 1912 by the Unofficial Reform Committee of the South Wales Miners' Federation. *The Miners' Next Step* called for the end of private ownership and the administration of the economy by industrial unions co-ordinated by a Central Productivity Board.

Syndicalist ideas horrified many of the skill-based trade union officials who were attached to the more respectable notion that any political action should be processed through Parliament. Such officials were more receptive to the moderate, non-revolutionary philosophy of workers' control through industrial unions which was developed by some British journalists and intellectuals under the label 'Guild Socialism'. This sought to accommodate worker and capitalist class interests by leaving ownership in the hands of capital, but putting the government of industry in the hands of industrial unions or 'guilds'. 'Collective contracts' between owners and 'worker guilds' would establish the output and price of an industry's goods (Cole, 1923).

The advocates of industrial unions, like their general union predecessors, were therefore hoping for various types of radical, socialist political change. Unlike the craftsmen their members were not the 'aristocracy of the working class', able to afford high subscriptions and with the skill base to use monopoly and closure tactics rather than strikes to achieve job control. Instead their organisations were fragile, they needed to support mass membership on very low funds and their industrial muscle seemed slight. The problems facing the organisers of the 'New Unionism', as it was termed by the Webbs, and the way that they were gradually brought to adopt and accept collective bargaining as their dominant method, are well illustrated with the case of the miners.

Unskilled Unionism – The Case of the Miners   The classic example of unskilled, industry-based trade unionism comes from the mines. Organisations of miners formed in the isolated mining villages and local miners' societies gradually linked together to form regional and national bodies. The mining industry grew in size and national importance throughout the nineteenth century, but despite this the early miners' unions proved extraordinarily difficult to maintain. Organisations claiming thousands of members arose in boom periods, only to be destroyed when the trade cycle brought falling prices and the fragile unions were unable to resist employers' wage cuts. There were many difficulties. In any confrontation with employers, unionists could easily be replaced by the mass importation of 'blackleg' labour from the large numbers of unemployed agricultural or Irish labourers. Miners were highly dependent on their employers' goodwill, not only for wages but also for housing and food in what were often company-run towns and villages. Local magistrates could be relied upon to favour the mine owners rather than their men in any dispute that reached the courts. Low pay entailed low subscriptions, low funds and limited organisational resources. Differences in regional interests and a tendency for miners' leaders to become respectably distanced from their dishevelled, militant members all worked against the establishment of organisations able to maintain their unity or build up reserves to carry them over recessions. Before 1850 miners typically alternated between outbursts of militancy, often associated with riots, and a despairing apathy (compare the behaviour of Sayles' erratic workgroups, discussed in Chapter 5). It was not until after 1850, when the industry became a major exporter and rising prices and profits bought more prosperity, that any stable district or industry-wide association developed.

Even when miners' organisations became more established, the occupational strategy of reducing labour supply by closing jobs to outsiders was untenable. There was a ready army of unemployed always available to take their jobs. The first national miners' association, formed in 1842, therefore adopted a policy designed to increase the value of coal, and hence miners' labour, by restricting output. To support this policy a legal fund was created to defend miners prosecuted by employers for breach of contract. However the Miners Association of Great Britain and Ireland did not survive a bitter four-month strike in 1844, and with its defeat its policies were discredited. Thereafter most miners' leaders sought to achieve their objectives not by unilateral action, but by extracting concessions from government or the employers. They formulated demands for higher wages or improved conditions and addressed them to whoever was thought to have the power to take decisions. Demands for wage increases were sent to local employers, backed by the threat of strikes. Demand for shorter hours, improved safety and the abolition of abuses related to truck (payment in kind) or the measurement of coal mined, were addressed to the government, backed by lobbying and the funding of Liberal miners' MPs.

Slowly these bargaining and political tactics achieved success which lasted beyond immediately favourable market conditions. Employers moved cautiously towards an accommodation with union officials as a means of controlling the miners intermittent 'guerrilla war' (Burgess, 1975). First, they accepted a system of 'sliding scales' which linked coal-price changes to wage changes, the scales to be administered by independent committees of lawyers, JPs, etc. Then, when the unions became strong enough to resist the wage reductions often derived from this system, employers accepted direct negotiations with trade union officials on wage issues through District Conciliation Boards. Collective bargaining had been established.

Achievements in the political sphere started with Acts on pit safety, checkweighmen (to measure the coal dug) and limits on the working hours of boys underground. The miners retained their interest in direct political solutions, calling for the nationalisation of the mines, and in 1919 putting forward proposals for the control of their industry by a Council on which the Miners Federation (forerunner of today's National Union of Mineworkers) would have controlled half the seats.

The NUM today is probably the UK's nearest approach to a 'pure' industrial union, recruiting only within one industry and attempting to recruit all employees in that industry. Even in the mines, however, the vertical principle of organisation is not total, for supervisory grades, colliery managers and some other white-collar employees have separate unions.

In other industries there were attempts to create industrial unions by mergers or membership exchanges between existing unions, but the prior existence of craft and general unions hindered success. The major result of the syndicalist and guild socialist call for industrial unionism was the merger of three unions in 1913 to form the National Union of Railwaymen (NUR).

The new unionism of the unskilled, non-craft workers therefore developed on both general and industrial lines. The hopes of the early organisers were not met, for the new unions did not sweep all before them, uniting the working class into rationally structured organisations capable of revolutionary challenges to existing employer or government controls. The new unions did not herald the development of worker control of production nor of revolutionary political change. Nevertheless they survived, despite many early failures, based on pockets of strength and areas of sectional interest. They became heavily reliant for their achievements on bargaining with their existing employers. Collective bargaining could occur with a multitude of unions organised on different lines and so, with the development of this method, pressures for the rationalisation of employee organisation on general or industry lines lost their importance.

Contrasts Between Market-Skilled and Unskilled Unions

The contrasting power resources of the market-skilled and unskilled workers is reflected in the organisation and tactics of the institutions they formed. Even when the craftsmen could no longer retain unilateral control over their wages or work methods, they still sought to enhance their bargaining power by closure policies, trying to close access to their skill to enhance its market value. The new unions, with few skills to protect, adopted different tactics.

Policies towards recruitment, union security and the closed shop, provide the most obvious contrast. Many craft-based unions still limit their membership to qualified, skilled workers and seek to close access to their traditional job territories to all but their own members by *pre-entry* closed shops. They insist that their employers only employ people who are already members of their union for their traditional areas of work. In contrast, the new unions are more open in their recruitment of members and do not seek pre-entry closed shops. If they wish to consolidate a high union membership at a particular place they try to establish *post-entry* closed shops or one hundred per cent union membership agreements. Under these the employer agrees to make it a condition of employment that a new employee must join an appropriate trade union once he or she has started work. The basis of this policy is not the exploitation of skill, but simple resentment of 'free riders' who both benefit from union members' negotiating activity and corrode united employee action. A Department of Employment (DE) survey published in 1980 found 5.2 million employees or 23 per cent of the workforce were working in closed shops, but only 16 per cent of these, or about 837,000 were in *pre-entry* closed shops. Closed shops had spread to new areas in the 1970s, but this extension occurred in the non-craft areas and with the acquiescence of employers who saw advantages in supporting disciplined, simple union structures. A comparative study of closed shops in Britain, the USA and West Germany found certain groups of workers, especially the old crafts, to be 'closed-shop prone'. The extent to which the less skilled groups were able to gain union security agreements was significantly influenced by employer attitudes – such groups usually did not have the resources to impose closed shops by themselves (Hanson, Jackson and Miller, 1982).

Skill-based and non-skilled unions also differ in their policies towards the management of their own work. Craft unions, with their continuing desire to maximise the relevance and value of scarce skills, have traditionally taken a close interest in the details of how their work is organised. The leaders of other unions have often found it difficult to formulate bargaining objectives on the complex issue of the management of detailed work. The craftsmen's interest in work methods and their pressure to retain traditional working rules are derogatively labelled 'restrictive practices', and their concern to preserve a division of labour which maintains their skill base lies behind demarcation disputes. Both restrictive practices and demarcation issues are less likely to arise with less skilled workers. Although the new unions originated with the most revolutionary, anti-managerial ideologies, they are the most passive towards the managerial use of their own labour because of the limits of their negotiating resources (Turner, 1962). They have focused instead on the collective bargaining of basic pay and conditions.

The distinction between skilled and non-skilled unions is analytically useful because it highlights the importance of varied power bases. The type of membership organised by a union also affected the methods of internal government adopted, with the craftsmen exercising a more confident control over their paid officials, and adopting methods of government which decentralised power to levels which could be related to local labour markets. However, the distinctions between craft and unskilled unionism have never represented a rigid division. The new unions' socialist ideology influenced many of the leading craftsmen and helped integrate the different types of trade union into a common movement. Over time the methods of the different unions have blurred together. Many craft unions have seen the value of their skill eroded and have adopted more open recruitment policies and more direct confrontational tactics toward employers. For example the Amalgamated Union of Engineering Workers now often acts as a general or industrial union. On the other hand, some sections of the unskilled unions have been able to develop such a cohesive and united organisation that they have been able to gain a form of group monopoly over their jobs. For example, with the legislation to decasualise the docks, the dockers' section of the TGWU achieved the dockers' register, which closed employment in the docks to their own members.

The slow, historical development of employee organisation based on craft, general and industrial unionism created a complex network of intermeshing organisation across the manual workforce. The multi-union picture of employee organisation was to be made more complex by the separate development of trade unions for the non-manual, white-collar employees. Before we turn to the remarkable recent growth of white-collar trade unionism in the UK, we need to consider the type of institution formed by employees who have skills which are needed by their employer, but which are gained through employment rather than by apprenticeship or professional training.

Organisation-Based Skills

Some workers possess a form of skill derived entirely from work experience rather than craft or professional training. The institutions developed to exploit and protect such skills have been called 'promotion-line unions' by Clegg, and he notes that in iron, steel and cotton-spinning there were no apprenticeships but that the top manual workers were skilled by experience. They formed unions to systematise the rules governing the size of work teams, and to regulate the promotion from labourer to the top man in the team (Clegg, 1979, p. 26). The top men of these unions did not use them to exclude all unskilled men, instead they sought to recruit anyone placed at any stage of their promotion ladder. Junior workers who could potentially act as substitutes for the skilled men were therefore joined into unions with them, although usually in a subordinate position, for the top men dominated the government of promotion-line unions.

With the growth of large-scale business organisations, some employers built promotion ladders into the structure of their organisations. Rather than deskilling the labour process or buying in skills from outside, employers controlled the development and transmission of the skills they required. Necessary skills were learned through work experience and company-sponsored training, and employees were appointed to the more highly skilled and rewarded jobs by internal recruitment. Employees entered the organisation at the bottom of the career ladders and not in mid-career. Such policies were usually accompanied by an emphasis on the importance of company loyalty (see Chapter 3). In the nineteenth century the civil service, the post office and many of the steel and railway companies adopted such policies.

What type of institutions are formed by employees in these conditions? Generally it would seem that when careers are shaped within single organisations, then employee institutions follow the structures established by management and shape themselves around promotion ladders. If the employer endorses or encourages employee organisations, then enterprise trade unions or staff associations are a likely development. If the employer resists employee organisations, then the institutions which form will start with a more confrontational ideology, but will still be patterned in part to follow the career interests of their members. Civil Service and Post Office unions have from the start been structured around their members' organisational grades and career lines. The early railway companies were paternalistic but stridently anti-union. The railway industry eventually developed a radical industrial union in the NUR, but this did not attract the footplatemen who established in the Association of Steam Locomotive Engineers and Firemen (ASLEF) a promotion-line union assertively protecting the organisation-based skill of the train driver.

Employees with organisation-based skills are likely to be highly dependent on their employer for their career prospects. Job security is likely to be of crucial importance for such people, and they can be expected to be particularly concerned with the regulation of promotion criteria and promotion procedures. In achieving their ends they will not have the market-based power to use craft or professional policies of 'closure'. Their methods are therefore likely to involve some mix of confrontational collective bargaining and attempts to become part of, or at least to influence, normal managerial decision-making. In the twentieth century private employers in the UK have rarely provided career ladders for manual employees. However, such policies are common for white-collar workers and help explain the character of some of the white-collar trade unions.

The Growth of White-Collar Trade Unionism
The extension of British trade unionism since the Second World War has largely occurred because white-collar workers – i.e. office and managerial workers, technicians and scientists – have increasingly joined trade unions. White-collar trade unions like the National and Local Government Officers' Association (NALGO) or the Association of Scientific, Technical and Managerial Staffs (ASTMS) have shown phenomenal growth, and white-collar workers have been recruited into the manual unions, often in special sections like the Managerial, Administrative, Technical and Supervisory Association (MATSA) of the GMBU, or the Association of Clerical, Technical and Supervisory Staffs (ACTS) of the TGWU. Although no official data distinguishes white-collar from manual union membership, Bain and Price have estimated that white collar membership increased by 79 per cent from 1949 to 1970, at a time when manual membership was static. From 1948 to 1964 the growth of white-collar membership barely kept pace with the growth of the white-collar labour force, but from 1964 to 1974 the density of union membership spread from 29.6 per cent to 39.4 per cent of the white-collar workforce (Bain, 1970; Bain and Price, 1972; Price and Bain, 1976; Bain and Elsheik, 1976).

White-collar workers are still less likely to join trade unions than their manual colleagues, but this expansion of white-collar trade unionism in the late 1960s and 1970s saved the British trade union movement from the membership consequences of heavy job loss in the traditionally well-unionised industries of coal mining, railways and the docks.

There has been a considerable debate about the reasons for this white-collar growth. Before it occurred it was confidently assumed that the generally more conservative political orientation and more privileged work situations of the white-collar worker would prejudice him or her against trade unionism. In 1966 Lockwood first noted that the unionisation of white-collar workers was closely associated with bureaucratisation. He suggested that as business organisations grew and became more bureaucratic, white-collar workers felt impelled to create their own separate and formal representation to affect the growing regulations. However, white-collar workers might have chosen to express their interests through professional or staff associations. It has been estimated that if this type of institution is included, the density of organisation by white-collar and manual workers is roughly the same (Lumley, 1973, p. 25). The tendency to join trade unions rather than other types of institution has been affected by the limited power resources of most white-collar workers and by managerial and government policies. Bain's studies have pointed to several variables affecting white-collar union growth: employment concentration; employer policy on union recognition; government action; and economic conditions causing inflation and falling pay differentials. Government policies encouraged unionisation through two channels. The recurrent income policies of the 1960s and 1970s made it apparent that employees benefited from national-level representation backed by industrial sanctions, for only such representation could guarantee a place in the new, highly centralised negotiations on incomes policy. Secondly, from 1971 to 1980 governments endorsed collective bargaining and actively supported the recognition of trade unions. Unions could call for inquiries or ballots in companies where they sought recognition and if the government agency – the Commission on Industrial Relations (CIR) or the Advisory, Conciliation and Arbitration Service (ACAS) – found support adequate then recognition was endorsed. The CIR and ACAS had a marked impact on the spread of white-collar trade unionism to new areas, and actively discouraged staff associations and the further development of professional associations. Staff associations were subject to the demand that they prove themselves independent of management. Faced with this, many staff associations in the finance sector merged with conventional unions and the formation of new associations was discouraged. Professional associations found their desire to separate off their membership on the basis of their professional qualifications met hostility from management and other unions, which brought the decisions of the government agencies down against them.

A final factor in the growth of white-collar trade unionism can be attributed to the union members and officers who took advantage of the managerial and government policies and seized the opportunity to spread trade unionism. The flamboyant, expansionist style of Clive Jenkins, General Secretary of ASTMS, is an often-quoted example.

Given the rising importance of white-collar unions, what form do they take? Some are structured around a marketable skill, for example the British Airline Pilots' Association (BALPA) regards itself as a professional association as well as a trade union. Many white-collar workers aspire to the occupational controls of the professions, but few have the market-based skill to make professionalism meaningful. In recent years several white-collar employee organisations have abandoned their professional aspirations to move nearer traditional trade unionism. An important development here was when NALGO decided to affiliate to the TUC in 1964. NALGO claims to be the largest white-collar union in the world and this affiliation ended the possibility that white-collar unions would split the British union movement by creating different types of employee institution. In 1981 NALGO moved a step nearer to the old trade unions and their methods by establishing a strike fund.

The strong desire for occupational identification and the existence of white-collar workers with organisation-based skill create pressures for the representation of sectional interests within white-collar unions. Where organisation-based skill is significant white-collar unions are usually based on enterprise branches, and have company sections or sub-groups, often with considerable autonomy in deciding the policies they will adopt. In one respect, white-collar unions remain clearly distinct from most manual unions – few affiliate to the Labour Party. The long-term impact of this on the politics of industrial relations remains to be seen.

TRADE UNION STRUCTURE AND MEMBERSHIP

The slow, organic growth of trade unionism based on a number of organising principles created a complex multi-unionism. Many unions compete for members in the same job territory and many employers are faced with the need to deal with several different unions. This complex structure has long been criticised for being unwieldy, involving much duplication of effort. At one time the TUC strove to rationalise British union structure to create the industrial unionism the TUC recommended to the postwar German union movement. However, the many resolutions passed by TUC Congress on rationalisation have always foundered on the practical impossibility of equitable exchanges of membership for the old craft and general unions. More recently, the value of industrial unionism has been questioned as industrial unions have been shown to be relatively powerless in the face of their industry's decline, as industrial boundaries have shifted and as conglomerate companies develop across the old industrial divisions.

Despite multi-unionism, British trade unions have proved able to operate together in national or establishment-level collective bargaining by jointly working on negotiating committees, or by forming federations – like the Confederation of Shipbuilding and Engineering Unions (CSEU) – to co-ordinate bargaining tactics with common employers. Multi-unionism complicated union representation at the place of work but may have contributed towards the stronger development of employee workplace organisation, because local management preferred to solve industrial problems with shop stewards on site, rather than attempt to contact several full-time officers (Brown *et al.*, 1981).

The TUC acts to regulate membership disputes arising from multi-unionism through the Bridlington Agreement of 1939. It also encourages mergers as a means of reducing the numbers of unions and enabling unions to benefit from economies of scale.

Some unions have always pursued a policy of growth by merger. The TGWU absorbed eighty-four unions from 1922 to 1978; ASTMS absorbed twenty-nine from 1968 to 1979. In 1964 legislation was passed to simplify the legal procedure for mergers and this encouraged a new spurt of union amalgamations, reducing the number of unions from 622 in 1966 to 438 in 1980. Amalgamations have sometimes sought to bring together unions with similar craft or industrial interests but have often been based as much on expediency, with the results determined by the chance that a particular union seeking expansion happened to be near at hand at a time when a weaker union was floundering.

Processes of union expansion and amalgamation have acted to concentrate the bulk of union membership into a few large unions, many of whom represent a complex mix of different interests (see Table 6.1). Sixty per cent of trade unionists in the UK are now members of ten trade unions each with over a quarter of a million members (these are the TGWU, AUEW, GMBU, NALGO, NUPE, USDAW, ASTMS, EEPTU, NUT and NUM). There are many smaller unions with long histories of sectional representation, but the weight of numbers of trade unionists is concentrated in giants which are best regarded as conglomerates, spanning many different labour markets and types of skill.

Table 6.1 *The Concentration of Trade Union Membership (1980)*

| | | Percentage of: | |
Number of members	Number of unions	number of unions	membership of all unions
Under 100	69	15.8	0.0
100– 499	118	26.9	0.2
500– 999	45	10.3	0.2
1,000– 2,499	56	12.8	0.7
2,500– 4,999	39	8.9	1.1
5,000– 9,999	25	5.7	1.3
10,000– 14,999	7	1.6	0.6
15,000– 24,999	21	4.8	3.0
25,000– 49,999	19	4.3	5.6
50,000– 99,999	14	3.2	7.9
100,000–249,999	15	3.4	19.5
250,000 and more	10	2.3	59.9
All members	438	100.0	100.0

Source: Department of Employment Gazette, February 1982.

The Membership of Employee Institutions

Employee institutions have developed to become an important influence at work and in national politics. The total membership of all employee institutions is hard to gauge, for there are no national figures combining trade union and professional and staff association membership. Lumley estimated that about 2.25 million people were members of the principal staff associations and professional associations in 1972. However, far more detailed, time-series data is available on the membership of trade unions. In 1980 there were 12.9 million union members, a fall from the peak of 13.4 million in 1979.

Figure 6.1 charts the growth of trade union membership in the UK from 1900 to 1980. The slow growth of union membership can be seen and also the way the major economic recessions of the 1920s, 1930s and 1980s caused the loss of members through high unemployment. Bain and Price have compared union membership with the size of the workforce to calculate union density, i.e. union coverage of potential membership. The density of union membership rose from 11.2 per cent in 1892 to 23 per cent just before the First World War. In 1920 it was 45.2 per cent, but fell to 22.6 per cent by 1933. Union density then increased steadily to about 45 per cent after the Second World War. It then hovered between 42 and 44 per cent for many years before rising from the late 1960s to a peak of 59 per cent in 1979–80. Average figures of union density disguise many variations. Contrasts between white-collar, manual, male and female densities are shown in Table 6.2.

Table 6.2   *Union Density, 1974*

	Men	Women
White-collar	44.5	32.6
Manual	64.7	42.1
Total	59.6	36.7

Source: Price and Bain (1976).

The lower organisation of women relates in part to many women's more casual relationship to the labour market and in part to their tendency to be concentrated in smaller establishments and in the less well-organised service industries. Industry differences in union organisation are illustrated in Table 6.3.

One major factor which helps place industries at the top or bottom of Table 6.3 is establishment size. If employment is concentrated, then it is very much easier for employee institutions to become established and to maintain their organisation. The traditionally well-organised mines and docks have heavily concentrated work-

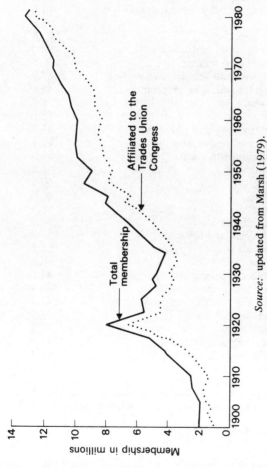

Membership in millions

Total membership

Affiliated to the Trades Union Congress

Source: updated from Marsh (1979).

Figure 6.1 Trade Union Membership, 1900–80

Table 6.3 *Union Density by Industry, 1974*

	Density
Sea transport	99.6
Railways	96.9
Coal-mining	96.2
Road transport	95.1*
Port and inland water transport	94.7
Pottery	93.8
Air transport	93.6
Gas, electricity and water	92.0
National government	90.5
Post Office and Telecommunications	87.9
Education and local government	85.6
Footwear	79.0
Glass	78.5
Paper, printing and publishing	71.6
Metals and engineering	69.4
Entertainments, media	64.9
Health	60.9
Fishing	60.5
Clothing	60.0
Rubber	55.9
Other mining	51.8
Food, drink and tobacco	51.2
Chemicals	51.2
Leather	46.6
Insurance, banking and finance	44.8
Cotton and manmade fibres	40.9
Bricks and building materials	40.4
Wood and furniture	35.2
Construction	27.2
Agriculture and forestry	22.2
Distribution	11.4
Hotels and catering	5.2
Other professional services	3.7

* Substantially overstated because membership categories could not be disentangled.
Source: Price and Bain (1976).

forces, whereas in construction, agriculture, distribution and catering, employees are scattered and harder to mobilise. Price and Bain estimated the impact of establishment size on all manufacturing industries in 1974. They calculated that the overall density of trade union membership was 62.2 per cent, but that if establishments employing less than 100 workers were excluded it rose to 76.9 per cent and excluding less than two hundred workers, to 89.2 per cent.

The return of mass unemployment in the 1980s, and the reduction of the total workforce which accompanied it, has obvious implications for trade union membership. The trends in trade union density are less clear. The growing concentration of business activity presents an underlying pressure for the increased membership of employee institutions. On the other hand, trade unions have seen and are seeing the decline of many of their traditionally organised industries and the shift in economic activity to the less well-organised insurance, banking, finance, professional and scientific services and distribution industries. If the industrial distribution of employment had not changed between 1948 and 1974, union membership and density would have been greater by about 81 per cent. Nevertheless, unions cover a substantial proportion of the working population in the UK. Overall trade union density in the UK is not as high as it is in Sweden, Belgium, Denmark, Italy or Australia, but it is higher than is found in West Germany, France or the USA.

INTERNAL UNION GOVERNMENT

How are employee institutions managed and governed? All the problems surrounding the maintenance of formal organisations mentioned in Chapter 3 apply, but with the added complication that the organisations' members are both the rulers and the main resource. In order to survive, independent employee institutions must gain their members' loyalty and subscriptions by acting on their behalf. However, to achieve any success against rival interests the institutions need to unite and co-ordinate their members' behaviour in a way that will require some member sacrifices and will curtail individual freedom. Some coercion lies behind the maintenance of any formal organisation. In self-governing institutions the question of who has the power to call for member sacrifices, and in pursuit of what policies, is likely to be a live and hotly-debated issue.

Like most self-governing institutions, those for employees have constitutions designed to make the executive responsive to members' wishes. A broad model is that members are grouped into branches and elect their own branch committee. Through their branches members elect delegates who are sent to the annual conference chaired by the president. This determines policy by debating and voting on policy resolutions submitted through the branches. To implement policy and act for the institution between conferences there is an executive committee, which operates through a staff of full-time officers headed by the general secretary. Different employee institutions vary in their detailed interpretation of this broad model, for example some conferences are biannual and large unions are usually subdivided into specialised regional, trade or company groups with conferences and executives of their own, but all adopt some constitution of this form.

There has been little interest in, or study of, the constitutions of professional or staff associations, but there is a vast literature on the government of trade unions. Trade unions are seen by many people as one of the principal sources of challenge to dominant power groups in society. Many who view trade unions in this light have strong beliefs about how trade unions ought to behave, and look to changes in union government as the handle to shift trade union behaviour away from the representation of sectional interests and towards the social role they favour. Those on the left call for the decentralisation of power within trade unions and the greater accountability of union executives to delegate conference. This is seen as a way to reduce the influence of full-time officers who often operate through accommodation with business interests, and instead increase the influence of lay activists who are less likely to be committed to established methods and might be more likely to espouse radical working-class policies. Those on the right call for 'responsible' trade unionism which will support rather than challenge management decisions. They call for postal ballots to be used both for the election of senior officials and for decisions to strike. This is in the belief that secret ballots will give conservative union leaders the backing of the less active, more conservative members, by-passing more radical lay activists. Altogether, the political debate about how trade unions should act in society directs an attention to the technicalities of trade union government which we cannot cover in depth in this volume. (For useful summaries see Coates and Topham, 1980, Chapter 3, and Clegg, 1979, Chapter 5; see also Edelstein and Warner, 1975; Undy *et al.*, 1981; Hemingway, 1978; Martin, 1968.)

Some variations in existing trade union constitutions relate to the varying bases of organisation discussed earlier in this chapter. The governing structure of the craft unions reflects the craftsmen's old control of local labour markets and a self-confident control of their own officials. Craft unions are more likely to decentralise many decision-making powers to local or district levels, and full-time officials are likely to be elected and subject to periodic re-election by the membership. The AUEW is often held up as the union with the most democratic constitution: it has an elaborate separation of powers between a powerful president, the national executive committee, district committees, a final appeals court, and all-elected officials. Clegg notes that this parallels the structure of USA federal and state government. It is no coincidence that the more elaborate attempts to decentralise union government and place checks on the growth of oligarchic central control is found in an old craft union.

In contrast, power in the unskilled unions tends to be more centralised. The members of the old general and industrial unions did not have the skill to regulate their local labour markets. In addition the high labour turnover of unskilled members and their mix of different job interests made strong branch life much less likely for them than for the craftsmen. Their unions developed centralised structures of government, relying heavily on a staff of paid officials who were more likely to be selected rather than elected and, if elected, were less likely to be subject to re-election. The staff-based general secretary was likely to be more powerful than the conference-based president. Nevertheless, to cope with the large and sprawling membership of such unions, trade-group sub-divisions were usually added to branch and regional structures to give more channels through which members could influence policy-making. Thus the TGWU takes decisions about union rules and general union government at region and national level but decisions about collective bargaining are decentralised to eleven trade groups. The unions' elected, lay-member executive reflects this dual structure.

The general and industrial unions are all democratic in that their constitutions attempt to give members a voice in government, even though effective power is often centralised. Some of the promotion-line unions were less careful with the formalities of democracy. In the Iron and Steel Trades Confederation (ISTC) there was little chance for the less skilled members to determine policy. ISTC did not even have provisions for the usual annual delegate conference until 1976.

In recent years enterprise and company level structures have developed more prominence within union government. Unionists with organisation-based skills relate best to enterprise or company groupings. Most white-collar unions have workplace branches and ASTMS, pursuing its policy of growth by merger, attracted many recruits by guaranteeing considerable autonomy to company sections or groups within the union. With the development of more formal workplace and enterprise bargaining for manual workers in the 1970s, many manual unions also adjusted their structures to give enterprise-based shop stewards a more prominent role in their unions' constitutional committees. These developments have served to make British unions more responsive to their workplace-based membership (Clegg, 1979, p. 209).

To summarise, the structures of union government vary. The differences can often be linked to the original bases of organisation but union constitutions have also adjusted over time to reflect changing power-bases within the unions. As constitutions not only reflect, but help to entrench the distribution of power in institutions; as trade unions usually contain a complex mix of pressures towards different policies, and as many within and without the trade union movement take an acute interest in the policies which are finally adopted, we can confidently predict that trade union constitutions will continue to attract attention. Much of the debate on union government is conducted in terms of the emotive word 'democracy'. However, democracy is a concept that can mean many things. For some, union democracy requires a two-party system or some degree of factionalism among the minority who take an active interest in the details of union affairs, so that full-time officials are subject to constant challenge and the membership has a clear choice between different policies at elections. For others, democracy requires the use of individual, postal ballots rather than votes taken at branch metings, even if this voting technique serves to reduce the influence of active trade unionists and entrench the hegemony of union officials. For yet others the debates about democracy are sterile. These argue that all union officials are accountable to, and constrained by, their membership to some degree. They argue that unions operate within constitutions that are as democratic as are found in most institutions in British society and that, because unions are only as strong as their members' support, union officials cannot in practice pursue wildly unpopular policies for very long.

A study which broadly adopts this third perspective contrasted the development of twelve major unions between 1960 and 1980 and assessed each union's government on the basis of effective adaptation to environmental change, rather than some formal model of democracy. It is interesting to note that, using this criterion, the very formally democratic, faction-ridden AUEW rated lower than the centralised, more authoritatively-led TGWU (Undy *et al.*, 1981).

THE TUC AND INTERNATIONAL FEDERATIONS

The existence of union federations and joint working to co-ordinate trade unions in industry or local-level collective bargaining has already been mentioned. Employee institutions may also form national federations for mutual services, and to co-ordinate approaches to government. In the UK there are no formal federations for professional associations. The Confederation of Employee Organisations had in membership 47 staff associations with a membership of about 62,300 in 1979. The TUC in 1979 had 112 trade unions with a membership of 12,128,000. The TUC therefore covered all but half a million trade unionists and could be said to represent about half the working population of Britain.

The TUC was initially formed in 1868 by trade unions who wanted an annual meeting for the discussion of union affairs and the co-ordination of lobbies of Parliament to press for changes in law to protect trade unions. The TUC has remained essentially a service organisation to its membership of autonomous trade unions ever since. As the trade union movement grew, the TUC slowly adjusted to include the newer unions. The new general and industrial unions affiliated as they developed, and from the mid twentieth century the TUC has recruited significant numbers of the white-collar unions. The TUC now gives British trade unions a unity within one central national federation that is matched in few other countries.

Member unions send delegates to the annual Congress each September. A general council of 54 acts as the executive committee of the TUC. Its composition attempts to reflect the TUC's diverse membership: 6 seats are reserved for women, elected by congress as a whole; unions with less than 100,000 members together elect 11 councillors, and larger unions are automatically allotted the remaining 37 seats, distributed according to union size. The administration of TUC business is led by a general secretary, elected by congress 'for life', and an appointed staff of about 145. The TUC staff at Congress House are organised into departments to service the various sub-committees of the general council.

Although there were attempts in the 1920s to give the TUC a strong, co-ordinating role in trade union affairs, with the failure of the General Strike in 1926 the TUC reverted to the servicing role it has held for most of its history. It has never succeeded in acting for its members in direct bargaining with employers. Even attempts to sign a guideline agreement with the Confederation of British Industry on the introduction of new technology failed to overcome employer opposition. Instead it administers the Bridlington principles, regulating inter-union membership disputes through a TUC disputes procedure, it services a network of inter-union committees, liaises with locally based inter-union Trades Councils and acts in consultations with or lobbies government.

In recent years the growth of government intervention in the economy and in employment affairs has increased the significance of the TUC. In 1962 the government established the tripartite National Economic Development Council. The TUC provided the employee side of this and all subsequent tripartite institutions. Since 1968 the TUC has produced an annual economic review, detailing and forecasting national economic trends and advocating detailed government economic policies of an expansionary, protective and interventionist nature. As governments moved to intervene in wage determination through incomes policies, the

TUC at times supported and at times opposed incomes restraint. TUC reaction to changes in trade union legislation has been less equivocal and in the 1970s it greatly strengthened the TUC's authority. In 1969 it demanded the withdrawal of legislation proposed by the Labour government and, to help fend off unwanted legislation, altered its own rules to increase its power to intervene in inter-union disputes and unofficial strikes. It led a campaign against the legislation of the Conservative government of 1970–4 with spectacular success (see page 197) and played a prominent part in the highly interventionist government policies of the Labour government of 1974–9. At the time of writing, the TUC is mounting a mass education and publicity campaign against the industrial relations legislation of the Conservative government elected in 1979. Governments are becoming more active in employment relations but whether this will continue to act as a pressure to give the TUC a stronger co-ordinating role in the unions' responses remains to be seen.

International Federations

International federations were first formed at the end of the nineteenth century by unions seeking to exchange information, and stop strike-breaking by employers who were importing workers or exporting jobs. The first international federation was formed by printers in 1889, followed by one for miners in 1890. Karl Marx was instrumental in forming the first International Working Mens' Association, and later Socialist Internationals advocated the establishment of International Trade Secretariats for different trades and an International Federation of Trade Unions. These international federations suffered many reverses as national trade union movements became divided by war and Cold War. In 1949 the unity of the international federations was broken when the non-communist unions formed the International Confederation of Free Trade Unions (ICFTU), leaving communist unions in the World Federation of Trade Unions (WFTU). Today the ICFTU has 120 trade union bodies from 88 countries with a membership approaching 56 million. There are 16 international trade secretariats, catering for different industries, working within the ICFTU. The prestige of the ICFTU in union circles was weakened in the 1970s by allegations that it had been used by the Central Intelligence Agency, through the American unions, as an agent of American foreign policy. In response to this, regional federations have been strengthened. In 1973 a European Trades Union Congress was formed from two previous groupings. By 1974 the ETUC co-ordinated thirty national federations from seventeen European countries and was establishing industry committees for the European unions. These obviously cause some 'multi-unionism' in conflict with the international trade sec-retariats, but the European groupings achieved some successes in 1978–80 when they campaigned for shorter hours of work in the form of a thirty-five-hour week and five weeks annual holiday.

The British TUC now spends vast sums on international affilia-tions. In 1977, 29.4 per cent of the TUC's total budget went on delegations and affiliations to the ICFTU, the ETUC and to the Trade Union Advisory Committee to the OECD. It has been esti-mated that the true figure, including the work of the TUC's inter-national department, represented 34 per cent of the TUC's annual expenditure (Coates and Topham, 1980). The results of these large figures are difficult to see. Although unions exchange infor-mation, they have rarely been able to use their international links for more direct assistance in bargaining with employers. Despite the growth of multinational enterprises and the increasing inter-nationalisation of much business activity, unions so far have failed to achieve any permanent negotiations with employers on an international basis. International federations concentrate on lob-bying international government.

CONCLUSION

Employee institutions in the UK developed slowly and organically as different groups found ways of establishing permanent institu-tions for their own protection. The process started when occupa-tional groups built institutions to protect scarce, marketable skills. Professional associations and craft unions adopted closure policies, restricting entry to occupational training and closing access to jobs to untrained men in order to monopolise skilled labour supply. They aimed to use this monopoly control to dictate their employment terms to their employers. Later, mass general and industrial organisations developed to cater for the less skilled worker. With much less labour-market power to exploit, these adopted a more confrontational stance and called for radical, socialist changes. With their more openly political objectives they were instrumental in the formation of the Labour party, but at the level of the workplace radical demands gave way to the acceptance of collective bargaining on limited issues with employers. Workers who are skilled but whose skills are based on work experience rather than apprentice or professional training tend to develop institutions that relate to the structure of their employing organisa-tions. Such company- and enterprise-based trade union structures have become more common in the UK, with the growth of white-collar trade unionism.

Slow, organic growth created a complex multi-unionism in the UK. This has been modified to some extent by waves of mergers, such that 60 per cent of the UK's twelve million trade unionists belong to ten unions. Many of the large unions are now conglomerates, spanning different occupational, industrial and company interests. The differences in tactics and organisational structure derived from different organisational bases have been blurred.

Trade union government attracts far more attention than that of professional or staff associations. Trade unions have formally representative constitutions within which internal power battles are fought out. In most unions there will be tensions about policy between lay activists and full time officials. Many also need to accommodate sectional interests within the membership. Virtually all union officials are sufficiently under the control of their members to find themselves running institutions on the basis of scant financial reserves. Union subscriptions in the UK are low compared with those of many other countries and the unions rely heavily on the unpaid work of activists.

Virtually all trade unions of any size in the UK are now affiliated to the TUC. The TUC role has traditionally been a limited, service role towards its affiliates. However government intervention to regulate employment relations serves to push the TUC into a more active and visible position.

Chapter 7

The Politics of Industrial Relations

For a period, between the late 1920s and 1965, industrial relations appeared to have little to do with politics in the United Kingdom. Employment relations were sorted out between employers and employees without obvious political activity, and without much intervention by politicians or government agencies.

Since 1965 industrial relations has moved into the centre of the political arena. All recent governments have been concerned to introduce major changes in industrial relations law. Both the Trades Union Congress and the Confederation of British Industry have proposed legislative changes that have provoked outraged protest from the other side. And fundamental differences in policy towards unions have been at the centre of all the recent election debates.

This change in the level of political activity in industrial relations has stimulated an academic debate on the role of the state in employment relations. The state can be described as the institutional system of political government with a monopoly over taxation and the legitimate use of violence in a society (Hill, 1981). The set of state institutions comprise the legislature (Parliament), the executive (government ministers), central administration (the Civil Service), the judiciary, the police and army, local government and specialist agencies like industrial tribunals, pay boards, conciliation and arbitration services, and equal opportunities or health and safety executives and inspectorates. What role do these complex institutions play in employment relations? Are they a background, neutral force merely setting the scene within which employers and employees govern their own affairs, or do they play a more positive role? To what extent are the powers of the state used by employers or by employees in pursuit of their own objectives? Why has public policy on industrial relations become so controversial within the UK?

Details of public policy since 1965 are discussed in Chapters 8 and 9. This chapter begins the analysis of the role of the state in industrial relations by reviewing the early development of public policy in the UK, and by looking at the political activities of employers and employees and the impact they have on the behaviour of state institutions.

THE EARLY DEVELOPMENT OF LABOUR LAW

A review of the early development of British labour law shows the state varying its approach to the regulation of employment relationships. The approach adopted in the nineteenth century, when unions were developing, was important in establishing a peculiar 'voluntary' form of industrial relations in the UK and in helping to ingrain a suspicion and distrust between unions and certain state institutions which still exists today and is more evident in the UK than in many societies abroad.

In pre-industrial Britain, occupational groups which combined the functions of capital and labour were often able to gain state support. As we saw in Chapter 6, the guilds and early professional associations sought and gained political protection for their organisations and for their economic functions of price, wage and apprenticeship control. When the medieval guilds declined, their detailed regulation of employment and trade was increasingly taken over by the state. A series of enactments, starting from the Ordinance of Labourers of 1349, empowered local magistrates to fix wages and regulate labour markets by specifying numbers of apprentices, limitations on the use of machines, etc. Indeed, 'the dominant industrial policy of the sixteenth century was the establishment of some regulatory authority to perform, for the trade of the time, the services formerly rendered by the Craft Guilds' (Webb and Webb, 1898). The policy of state regulation of labour and product markets did not imply support for organisations formed solely by workers, nor did it give equivalent treatment to masters and men. A succession of acts from the Statute of Labourers in 1351 prohibited the formation of organisations by employees and subjected workmen who failed to fulfil their duties to their masters to criminal penalties including imprisonment. Many thousands of workers were imprisoned under the various Master and Servant Acts for crimes such as leaving or neglecting their work, and the legislation was widely used in periods of social stress.

Paternalistic, state intervention in employment and trade came under attack in the UK with the rise of the new entrepreneurial class of the industrial revolution. Petitions from workers for the enforcement or updating of the regulatory laws were met by arguments from the new masters that they needed freedom to use new methods and machines, freedom to recruit cheaper 'illegal' or unapprenticed labour and freedom to pay and sell at market rates if they, and the economy, were to prosper. The state, in the form of magistrates and Parliament, responded by dismantling the old regulatory laws. By the late eighteenth century, state regulation had been replaced by *laissez-faire* and the state refused direct intervention in the regulation of the labour or goods markets. In place of the old paternalistic policies of state regulation was put the doctrine of freedom of contract and the notion that free and equal individuals should regulate their own affairs by concluding voluntary contracts. In the employment field, even when no contract had been written down or verbally agreed, it was argued that the courts could interpret the terms of any individual's employment contract in the light of normal custom, and could therefore resolve, by litigation, any dispute between employer and employee.

The shift in public policy from state regulation to *laissez-faire* had a profound effect on the development of trade unions. The Webbs argue that this shift in policy, stimulated by employer pressure, had the direct though unintended consequence of first stimulating trade union consciousness:

> So long as each section of workers believed in the intention of the governing class to protect their trade from the results of unrestricted competition, no community of interest arose. It was a change of industrial policy on the part of the Government that brought all trades into line, and for the first time produced what can properly be called a trade union movement. (Webb and Webb, 1898, p. 41)

Employees, faced with employer-dictated terms of employment, did not readily accept the doctrine of freedom of contract. The doctrine represented an advance from feudal ideas of servitude, but the assumption that the employment contract expressed a free bargain between equally powerful parties was a legal fiction. Inequality between employer and employee was embedded into contract law because the service sold by an employee was thereafter regarded as his employer's property, to be protected as such by the full weight of the law (K. Wedderburn, 1980). Employees, therefore, still sought protection against employer-dictated terms of employment, but were now deprived of their old channel of protest to the state. They turned to develop more independent forms of trade union activity, but they found their attempts to mobilise group pressure attacked through the courts. Between 1858 and 1875, ten thousand employees were prosecuted under the Master and Servant Acts and thousands of trade unionists were imprisoned (Simon, 1954). The old criminal sanctions against groups of employees had been strengthened by the Anti-Combination Acts (1799 and 1800) but even when these had been repealed unions were still liable for conspiracy and action in restraint of trade.

Trade unions continued to develop, despite the hostile legal climate. With their continued existence and pressure, the most repressive anti-union legislation was gradually removed. However, the methods used to grant trade unions scope to operate within the law took a unique form in Britain compared with other countries. As trade unions developed, the first reforming step, throughout Europe, was to make the formation of employee organisations lawful. Legislation in the UK (1824 and 1825), in France (1884), Germany (1869); Sweden (1864) and Italy (1889) granted some freedom of association. Unions henceforward were free to exist, although their activities were severely restricted.

The next step was to legalise trade union activities and permit the industrial bargaining or political pressure needed if unions were to regulate employment conditions. In most countries this was achieved through laws which clearly specified trade union rights. For example, in European countries where the old feudal or paternalistic policies had not been completely dismantled, union rights were incorporated in constitutional provisions or in laws granting unions a clear legal status. Codes of positive labour law can be found in most countries of the New and Third Worlds. In the UK there was no legislation to codify union rights to organise, strike or participate in decisions affecting employment. In the absence of positive legislation specifying trade union rights and the trade union role, British unions operate lawfully because Parliament has enacted immunities designed to protect them from the prevailing judge-made laws. The development of British labour law has been more fully described elsewhere (Lewis, 1976 and 1981). Here we can note that there has been a pattern, in which periodic attempts have been made by the judiciary to impose penalties on certain types of union activity through their interpretation of the law. These judicial challenges have been followed by union pressure on Parliament to grant statutory immunity to protect unions from the new, judge-made liabilities.

The battle between unions and the judiciary over the scope of trade union activities started with the famous case of *Hornby v. Close* in 1867. The judgement in this case found that, although the repeal of the Combination Acts had made unions technically lawful, unions could not prosecute officials who embezzled their funds, because union objectives were illegal under common law; they were in 'restraint of trade'. *Hornby v. Close* occurred at a time when there were widespread calls from the press and Conservative politicians that 'something be done' about growing trade union influence, and the first Royal Commission to investigate trade unions was set up in the same year in 1867, in the wake of the 'Sheffield Outrages' of machine-breaking and violence. Unions responded by mobilising a political defence. A group of union leaders from the skilled, craft unions presented liberal collectivist arguments to the Royal Commission, emphasising the respectability of their unions and the social value of collective bargaining. In 1868 the first Trades Union Congress was held to organise joint representation of the union case to Parliament. The unions' political lobby was aided by the extension of the right to vote to most urban male workers in 1867. The campaign achieved the Trade Union Act of 1871 which gave trade unions protection from the 'restraint of trade' doctrine. In 1875 two other major, reforming acts were passed. The Employers and Workmen Act finally removed the threat of imprisonment from employees in breach of contract of employment, and the Conspiracy and Protection of Property Act gave unions immunity from the crime of conspiracy when the combination was 'in contemplation or furtherance of a trade dispute'. This creation of immunities set a precedent for future labour law.

The growth of new unionism from the 1880s increased the concern of business and propertied classes about union activities and provoked a new wave of judgements against trade unions based on civil, rather than criminal, liability. Judges found that strike action could be construed as a *civil* wrong, on the grounds that union objectives were unlawful; the injured party could therefore claim damages. The most famous case was the *Taff Vale* judgement of 1901 which awarded the TV Railway Company damages and costs against the Amalgamated Society of Railway Servants of £42,000, a prodigious sum at the time. This award against a trade union, rather than against an individual union official, undermined the apparent legal status granted to unions over the previous forty years. The new legal threat served as a considerable stimulus to the formation of the Labour Representation Committee in 1901 (designed to promote the election of independent labour-sponsored Members of Parliament), and the formation of the Labour party in 1906. Twenty-six labour candidates were elected to Parliament in the elections of 1906, and the Liberal government was persuaded to pass the 1906 Trades Disputes Act which gave unions immunity against judge-made civil liability, especially over breaches of the contract of employment. However, as unions succeeded, by political lobbying, to re-establish their ability to act in industrial bargaining, the courts struck a blow against their political activities. In the *Osborne* judgement (1909) the Law Lords decided that trade unions could not use their funds to support the new Labour party. It was four years before the unions could again fund the political party they had helped create. The Trade Union Act (1913) legalised the creation of political funds by trade unions, but only after the approval of a ballot of union members and as long as individual members had the right to contract out of paying to the political levy. In 1927 a restrictive Trade Disputes and Trade Union Act, passed in the wake of the General Strike, again reduced Labour party funds by introducing the need for union members to 'contract in' to the political levy.

The conflicts between unions and the courts were followed by a long period of torpor in which both the courts and parliament essentially left trade unions and industrial relations alone. The 1927 measures against sympathetic strikes and political action were not used and from the late 1920s until the judges again responded to business pressure to act against trade unions in the *Rookes* v. *Barnard* case of 1965, public policy supported a system of industrial relations that was remarkably unencumbered by law. Kahn-Freund, the founder of labour law study in the UK, was to argue: 'there is perhaps no major country in the world in which the law has played a less significant role in the shaping of relations than in Great Britain and in which today the law and the legal profession have less to do with labour relations' (Kahn-Freund, 1954).

Most countries have quantities of individual and collective labour law. Individual labour laws specify terms to be found in individual contracts of employment and regulate the recruitment, employment and dismissal of individuals. Collective labour laws regulate trade unions and union–employer relationships. In the UK there has, traditionally, been a notable absence of both types of law. As Flanders (1965) put it, the British industrial relations system was 'voluntary' not only in the sense that it relied on collective bargaining rather than law to establish the individual terms and conditions of employment, but also (unlike, for instance, the USA) because the collective bargaining system was not supported or regulated by a framework of collective laws. Before we turn to the reasons for this torpor, and for its decline, we need to review the political activities of unions and employers.

THE POLITICAL ACTIVITIES OF UNIONS AND EMPLOYERS

Both employers and organised groups of employees are bound to be political, for they inevitably have an interest in political decisions that affect them. 'A completely non-political trade unionism hardly makes sense, and would today be about as unrealistic as a motor industry which claimed to have nothing to do with roads' (Hobsbawm, 1979). The demand that certain large pressure groups keep out of politics may be good propaganda by opposing interests, but if seriously meant, must rest on unrealistic 'liberal-individualistic' perspectives.

Social groups seek political influence in a number of ways. If group members have strong social contacts with people in political power, they will use the most direct method of influencing political decisions and will lobby the executive. Groups with less access to those in power will attempt to sway Parliament, or public opinion.

The first trade unions had no access to political decision-makers and initially relied on demonstrations and direct action to draw attention to their political demands. However these methods were soon supplemented by political pressure on Parliament. Unions joined the lobby for universal suffrage and began to encourage and support the election of labour-minded Members of Parliament. In the period from 1900 to 1906 trade unions formed a significant part of the alliance of socialist and working mens' groups that eventually established the Labour party. Since 1929 at least 30 per cent of Labour's parliamentary candidates have been put forward and sponsored by unions. Unions concentrate their support on the safest seats and Coates and Topham (1980) estimate that the proportion of union-sponsored Labour MPs in each Parliament has ranged from 95 per cent in 1910 to just over 30 per cent in the landslide Labour victory of 1945. In 1979 unions sponsored nearly half of the elected Labour MPs. Unions also help fund and govern the political Labour party. They provide about 80 per cent of Labour party funds. They control 85 per cent of the votes at Labour's governing annual conference, and because unions operate the block vote system, in which all the weight of the union's affiliated Labour party members are cast in favour of the union's majority decisions, regardless of the strength of minority opinion, the unions wield considerable voting power which outweighs constituency party votes in conference decisions. Unions can also dominate the choice of some of the nominees to the national executive, which is responsible for governing the Party between conferences.

Despite the close institutional ties between the unions and the Labour party, a traditional division of labour, separating the industrial and political wings of the Labour movement, was maintained for many years. Unions tended to use their political contacts for the narrow defence of their industrial activity, leaving most of the more general policy formation to the politicians (Richter, 1973). The sponsored MPs were usually used as spokesmen on any issue which directly affected a trade union's activities, but were not mandated on wider ranging policies, and from 1938 until 1969 unions concentrated their political lobbying on the executive and Whitehall, rather than rely on their MPs. This policy has changed with the development of proposals for trade union legislation from the late 1960s. Union-sponsored MPs threatened to vote against the Labour government's proposals for more restrictive legislation in 1979 and this marked the start of a period in which trade unions have sought to be far more actively involved in Labour party policy-making.

The political activity of employers is less visible. Only recently have companies been legally bound to disclose their 'political funds' and there is not the same open, institutional link between business and the Conservative party. Nevertheless, all employers' associations, most large and many medium-sized firms can make a case heard within Parliament by using MPs, usually from the Conservative party, as consultants or associates and as spokesmen. The CBI, large employers associations like the EEF, the NFBTE or the Retail Consortium and many large companies maintain contacts with the executive and Whitehall. Ford's direct contacts with Prime Minster Callaghan over the siting of their new motor plant at Bridgend, Wales, in the 1970s, is but one particularly important example of the regular involvement of businessmen with political decisions.

Both unions and employers seek political influence. The political power they can muster in their own cause is difficult to assess with accuracy. Both sides can use constitutional pressure through Parliament, they can lobby the executive, or mount publicity campaigns. The publicity campaigns of unions tend to feature demonstrations, mass meetings and marches. In 1980 the TUC organised a march of unemployed from Jarrow and South Wales to London to copy those of the 1930s although, in the context of considerable opposition in the media, the event had limited impact. Employers' publicity campaigns favour the use of the communications media by mass advertising or by funding events to attract media attention, like opinion surveys. Such methods have been used very effectively by insurance and building-industry employers against nationalisation. Both unions and employers have also adopted policies of non-co-operation against legislation they opposed. The TUC, as we see in Chapter 9, greatly increased its stature and influence in the 1970s by successfully co-ordinating a policy of non-co-operation to the 1971 Industrial Relations Act. Employer non-co-operation stymied the 1974–9 Labour government's proposals for planning agreements, and the CBI threatened massive non-co-operation, on the lines of the TUC's earlier campaign, if that government attempted to place trade unionists on company boards.

The relative political power of employers and trade unions is a subject of heated dispute which goes to the heart of the differences in theoretical perspective which we reviewed in Chapter 2. Objective studies of political power are difficult to conduct because power is difficult to measure and the exercise of power may be unseen. As a result, discussions of the political power of unions and employers readily degenerate to propaganda, with the 'other side' invariably 'too powerful' and rapidly increasing in power. Grant and Marsh (1977) studied the CBI as a political pressure group and concluded that the CBI could have a major impact on the technical, detailed drafting of legislation but would be less powerful if business interests were themselves divided. As we noted in Chapter 4, FBI and CBI attempts to protect the manufacturing industry have been weakened under Conservative monetarist governments because divisions among employer members arise when loyalty to a Conservative government is put at risk. Grant and Marsh did not take employer opposition to industrial democracy proposals as a case example, but this is an area where British employers have demonstrated remarkable unanimity which has given them a powerful political impact on British and European governments. Martin (1980) sensitively charts the growth of TUC influence to 1976, and the TUC's increase in power as it responded to governmental attacks on the trade union movement, but his study does not cover the TUC's decline with the mounting unemployment of the 1980s. Dorfman (1979) studied the TUC's impact on incomes policy and concluded that the TUC had enforced some changes in the policies government proposed. These studies are useful but they are not comparative, giving no guidance on the relative political power of employers and trade unions. In addition, their studies of employer or union impact on particular policies cannot deal with the important question of 'invisible power'. As Bachrach and Baratz (1962) emphasised, the ability to 'mobilise bias', i.e. to prevent certain policies even reaching the agenda of debate and to suffuse other proposals with legitimacy, is a powerful if subtle tool. Such ideological influence is extraordinarily difficult to assess, but in this context the link between business interests and the ownership of the press and media needs to be taken into account. Several studies of television and press news suggest a marked bias against trade unions which should be of considerable significance in assessing the political influence of employers and employees (Hartman, 1976; Glasgow University Media Group, 1976, 1980; Palmer, 1977).

Employers and trade unions have an interest in, and access to political decision-making. Nevertheless, for many years they deliberately sought to exclude the state from British industrial relations.

THE PERIOD OF VOLUNTARISM: COLLECTIVE BARGAINING AND THE WELFARE COMPROMISE

A lack of positive labour law does not imply the absence of any political activity by employees or employers, nor the abstention of the state from industrial relations. However, the period of voluntarism in Great Britain did mean that for many years neither employers nor unions relied on the state and its institutions to achieve their objectives. This remarkable restraint and unwillingness to use political means requires explanation, for the policy of voluntarism was, for a period, upheld by unions and employers, and by the courts.

1   Reasons for Union Commitment to Voluntarism

In the nineteenth and early twentieth centuries the general and industrial unions did press for legislation on individual issues like health and factory safety, and the removal of the worst injustices of truck, i.e. payment in goods or credit, rather than cash. However, as the new unions developed their collective bargaining strength they increasingly adopted the preference of the craft trade unions for industrial bargaining rather than political campaigns for legislation as their method of achieving results. The TUC constitution adopted in 1922 did contain a commitment to seek minimum wage legislation, but this was never achieved and the clause was finally deleted with little debate in 1978. Sporadic calls in 1946 and 1950 for legislation to enforce a forty-hour week and two weeks paid holiday never developed into a concerted political campaign. In 1979 when unions across Europe collaborated in a campaign to achieve a thirty-five hour week, the British unions sought to achieve this through industrial, not political, pressure. British unions have relied on collective bargaining as their method for improving employment conditions, and this contrasts sharply with the more politically-oriented union movements in Europe. In France, for example, unions have sought and obtained statute laws on hours of work, holidays with pay and minimum wage levels. In many countries on the continent the law is used to consolidate gains made by bargaining. British unions have not sought to legitimate or support their collective bargaining achievements by legislation. Instead the law has only been used where union organisation was weak or non-existent, for example among juveniles, women and selected 'sweated' industries (see Chapter 8). When laws on individual employee rights of the European type began to appear in the UK from the mid 1960s, the stimulus came from outside the British union movement.

Why have British unions not sought state support for minimum terms and conditions of employment when this is a common tactic for union movements elsewhere? K. W. Wedderburn (1980) suggests the reason lies in the historical development of the British working-class movement in the crucial formative period from 1867 to 1906. In this period when the relationship between the unions and the law was evolving, the UK had a relatively strong labour movement, but its strength was entirely industrial not political. Labour did not have a well-developed political organisation and the right to vote was only slowly extending to male workers. There was no universal suffrage. Unions gained industrial bargaining functions well before they felt able to exercise any political muscle. When unions first began to act on the political front, their demands were pragmatic, not ideological, and were processed through a labour/liberal alliance, not a strong or cohesive working-class party. The Labour party was not established with a political platform until 1906, and even then it was far less socialist or ideological than the Marxist-based, socialist parties on the continent. The Labour party was an uneasy alliance of radical socialists and trade unionists; many of the latter were notably 'moderate' – i.e. holding liberal-collectivist values and not strongly committed to radical ideologies or to the desirability of major social change. These tensions on political policy were exacerbated by the defeats suffered by the radical left. The collapse in 1921 of the Triple Alliance which was to have co-ordinated the miners, railwaymen and transport workers, and the crushing humiliation inflicted on the TUC in 1926 when the government clearly outmanoeuvred the unions' General Strike were important factors in the unions' retreat from attempts to achieve major political changes.

Union suspicion of legal reform was heightened by the particularly distant, if not hostile, relationship between trade unions and the British judiciary in the early development of British labour law. The dominance of judge-made law in Britain, particularly in the labour area, gave the judiciary a particularly significant role, and union folklore can quote many cases where judicial interpretation clearly stretched or redefined the law against union interests, the *Taff Vale* judgement (1901) and the *Osborne* judgement (1909) being the most famous historical cases. More recently unions have pointed to the *Rookes* v. *Barnard* judgement (1964) and to cases in the 1970s (see Chapter 9) to demonstrate that judicial interpretation still moulds the law against trade unionism.

The reasons for the unusually high degree of tension between unions and the judiciary in the UK are complex. In part they relate to the narrow social band from which British judges are recruited, which makes the judiciary unusually homogeneous in class origin, and ostentatiously unrepresentative of working classes. This has been recognised as a problem by many. In 1923 a leading judge, Lord Justice Scrutton, said:

> The habits . . . the people with whom you mix, lead you to having a certain class of ideas of such a nature that . . . you do not give as sound and accurate judgements as you would wish.

This is one of the great difficulties at present with labour. Labour says 'where are your impartial judges? They all move in the same circles as the employers, and they are all educated and nursed in the same ideas as the employers'... It is very difficult sometimes to be sure that you have put yourself into a thoroughly impartial position between two disputants, one of your own class and one not of your class. (Quoted in O'Higgins, 1976)

Winston Churchill, in 1911, argued:

It is not good for trade unions that they should be brought in contact with the courts, and it is not good for the courts. The courts hold justly a high and, I think, unequalled prominence in respect of the world in criminal cases, and in civil cases . . . but where class issues are involved, and where party issues are involved, it is impossible to pretend that the courts command the same degree of general confidence. On the contrary, they do not, and a very large number of our population have been led to the opinion that they are, unconsciously, no doubt, biased.

Another reason for trade union distrust of the judicial process derives from the common law's emphasis on notions of individual property and contractual rights which give little recognition to collective pressure group action. The training and traditions of British lawyers are oriented towards nineteenth-century liberalism. Neither the collective pressures of unions nor intervention by state agencies are legitimate in this tradition. However, it must be added that British judges have upheld the individualist, liberal traditions more consistently against trade unions than against business cartels in the UK. British courts have been more lenient to cartels and monopolies than their American counterparts, who operate with more rigidly specified statutory anti-trust laws. The traditions of British law and the historical experience of relationships between unions and the British judiciary have therefore helped deter British unions from using the law as a method for achieving their objectives.

2   *Employer Acceptance of Voluntarism until the 1960s*
Unions have been important supporters of voluntarism, but their non-legal preferences were supported for many years by employer acquiescence. British employers did not use the law to contain the industrial strength of trade unions, nor to structure the developing bargaining relationships. Collective laws have often developed in other countries as a result of employer pressure for state aid

against trade unions. In Britain, from the period from the late 1920s until the mid 1960s employers were reluctant to take trade unions to court. England and Weekes (1981) suggest that the absence of employer pressure in the late nineteenth and early twentieth centuries was because unions only affected a minority of employers and the employers who were affected felt able to cope with trade unionism by multi-employer bargaining through employers' associations. Certainly, the period of voluntarism coincides with very low levels of industrial conflict and strikes. Finally, England and Weekes suggest that with the increase in foreign competition, the employers' main preoccupation was with shopfloor productivity and the prospect of increasing control over the shopfloor by tighter management techniques. In this situation legal immunities posed less of a threat to managerial prerogatives on the shopfloor than a legal 'right to strike' or more positive political and judicial intervention. Employers, as a result, were not concerned to make use of the legal sanctions opened up for them by the *Taff Vale* judgement of 1901, and did not campaign either to prevent the passage of the 1906 Act, or to repeal it once passed.

Employer pressure for restrictive legislation on strikes, picketing, the closed shop and the enforceability of agreements emerged only in the 1960s, with the weakening of the Welfare Compromise, discussed below.

3   The Welfare Compromise

The voluntary, non-legalistic system of industrial relations was supported in the years from 1945 to the mid 1960s by social and economic government policies which established conditions under which voluntary collective bargaining was seen as broadly acceptable by unions and employers. It is the breakdown of these policies in recent years which has thrown industrial relations back into the type of political controversy that had not been seen since the beginning of the twentieth century.

Crouch (1977 and 1979) labels the policies the 'Welfare Compromise' and dates their inception from the postwar Labour victory in 1945. Labour won this crucial postwar election with a commitment to full employment and a Welfare State. These objectives were to be achieved by the use of Keynsian economic policies in which government acted to regulate demand and smooth trade cycles by controlling public expenditure. The policies involved increased employment, more state expenditure on such things as education, health and housing, and rising money wages. Government intervened to regulate macroeconomic variables but left the details of employment relationships to be resolved by employers and employees. The policy was a clear move away from the *laissez-faire* philosophy which argued for no state interference and the free play of market forces. Nevertheless, it did not seriously threaten either capital or labour interests, and received the support of both unions and business for several years.

Unions supported the policy because they believed it enabled them to maintain their autonomy in negotiations with employers while guaranteeing their members an improved and more secure life-style because of the support for employment and improvements in welfare. Trade union leaders could remain free of government pressure, and responsive to their members on the key issue of wage demands, and yet become more closely associated with government policy. Senior trade union leaders had experienced an involvement in the administration of government policy during the First and Second World Wars. The coalition government of the Second World War had placed Ernest Bevin, the general secretary of the TGWU, in the Cabinet as Minister of Labour and he had used this position to trade the unions' assistance in the wartime mobilisation of labour for state support in the extension of collective bargaining. With the policies of the postwar Welfare Compromise union leaders like Bevin and the TUC general secretary, Citrine, maintained their contacts in Whitehall and could encourage and participate in the extension of the welfare state without threat to their traditional collective bargaining activities.

Employers supported the Welfare Compromise policy because it offered to protect them from the sloughs of the trade cycle and from the social upheaval and class strife of the interwar years. When the Conservatives returned to government in 1951, they did not abandon the Keynesian economic policies; instead, they accepted the development of a mixed economy and union leaders still found their views were listened to in Whitehall. Indeed the most important and long-lasting institutional expression of the involvement of unions in government was established by the Macmillan government in 1962. The National Economic Development Council (NEDC) was set up to enable unions, employers and government to jointly discuss and study problems of economic policy.

In summary, there was a period after 1945 when there was 'possibly a unique consensus between politicians, civil servants and trade unions about the form of the post-war political settlement' (England and Weekes, 1981.) This consensus was aided by a sustained period of economic growth and relatively full employment. From 1945 to 1965 unemployment in each five-year period averaged less than two per cent, compared with the average of thirteen per cent from 1920 to 1940.

THE COLLAPSE OF THE VOLUNTARY CONSENSUS

The Welfare Compromise, while it lasted, kept trade unions away from political controversy. However, strains on the policy began to show as early as the late 1950s, and by the mid 1960s several groups were pressing for radical changes in public policy towards trade unions. Crouch charts the start of the breakdown from 1956 when the Conservative government produced a white paper on the *Economic Implications of Full Employment*, (cmnd. 9725), which questioned the commitment to full employment if price stability was to be maintained. It argued that full employment increased union bargaining power and was fuelling inflation. It urged employers to resist excessive wage claims and promised 'wage restraint' in the public sector. There followed the innumerable attempts by government to establish incomes policy shown in Table 8.3. Incomes policy cannot coexist with voluntarism and once state institutions are concerned to regulate wage levels a voluntary, non-political and completely free collective bargaining system is untenable.

As governments became increasingly concerned with the international competitiveness of the British economy, other aspects of the employment relationship came under government purview on the grounds that the voluntary system was failing to satisfy national economic needs. First there were laws designed to improve labour efficiency and labour mobility (the Industrial Training Act, 1964, and the Redundancy Payments Act, 1965). Next came laws influenced by the individual rights legislation of the continent and the USA, designed to provide a statutory floor of employee rights on contracts of employment, unfair dismissal, equal pay and opportunity regardless of race or sex, guaranteed pay levels and provisions for paid maternity leave. These incursions into the old voluntary system of regulation were broadly bipartisan, supported by Labour and Conservative governments, and were largely non-controversial in political terms. However, there were more fundamental pressures on the Welfare Compromise and the voluntary system of industrial relations with a source outside government circles.

The main attack on the Welfare Compromise came from employers concerned that the Keynesian social and economic policies were increasingly threatening the interests of capital. Businessmen argued that rising state expenditure burdened companies with heavy corporate taxation. Nearly full employment and the new statutory floor of individual rights after the mid 1960s increased employee power within companies and contributed to a squeeze on corporate profits in the 1960s. Initially, leading employers responded by attempting to increase the productivity of their labour force by renewed rationalisation, and by the productivity bargaining discussed in Chapter 8. However, some employers came to see the solution in terms of the need for political and legal changes that would alter the trades unions' role in British society.

Employer dissatisfaction with the old welfare consensus policies did not lead to employer agreement on alternatives. Strinati (1979) noted that in the late 1960s and early 1970s different sections of business developed different conceptions of desirable solutions. Most multinational enterprises did not see a need for legal changes. They were capital intensive and were confident that they could cope with their own labour relations by buying-out trouble or by sophisticated personnel policies. Small-scale businesses tended to feel far more vulnerable to rising labour costs and disruptive labour tactics. However, small-scale businesses were still attached to *laissez-faire* policies and did not want or trust state intervention. Small-scale businesses who were most vulnerable to competition therefore called for laws which would weaken union power, but not involve the centralised administration of economic policy. They sought curbs on the closed shop, and on employee power to strike and picket. In contrast, larger national firms with some monopoly control over their markets, together with UK subsidiaries of MNEs in the car industry, advocated the more centralised and bureaucratic administration of British industrial relations. They sought to reshape union government and negotiating structures (incidentally protecting the closed shop) so that employee pressures could be contained within rationally centralised, interventionist government policies on the economy. At least three types of policy were therefore being supported by different industrial groups.

State response to these pressures was evidenced first when judges began to interpret the law more restrictively in order to curb trade unions' power to strike. Judgements in 1964 (*Rookes* v. *Barnard* and *Stratford* v. *Lindley*) and 1969 (*Torquay Hotel Company Limited* v. *Cousins*) all narrowed the protection of the old immunities and made unions more liable to labour injunctions if they struck. The Labour government of the time set up a Royal Commission to investigate trade unions and employers' associations and it later established a new body to 'reform' industrial relations and made an abortive attempt to introduce restrictive legislation. Heath's Conservative government of 1970–4 attempted the most comprehensive and fundamental restructuring of British industrial relations in the massive 1971 Industrial Relations Act, which combined legislation to reduce trade union power with attempts to reshape trade unions to fit them into more bureaucratic administrative structures. From 1974 to 1979 Labour pursued policies designed to integrate unions into centralised government policy-making, while from 1979 a new Conservative government sharply reversed the direction of public policy by changing the law to narrow trade union immunities and reduce union power by monetarist economic policies.

All these contrasting, controversial policies are discussed in detail in Chapter 9. None have come near to achieving a new political consensus for public policy on industrial relations – instead policies are polarising as each new government seeks more radical solutions ever further away from the old consensus. There is every sign that the politics of industrial relations will remain a highly contentious and volatile subject in the years to come.

PERSPECTIVES ON THE ROLE OF THE STATE

The controversy about the direction of public policy on industrial relations has forced the reassessment and reconsideration of the role of the state in UK industrial relations. The analyses of the once-dominant liberal-collectivist school (see Chapter 2) which treated the role of the state as limited and passive, are not sufficient for understanding the present politics of industrial relations. However, the area is complex, and there are many issues that have yet to be given much attention.

1 *The state as a complex set of institutions*
The state itself is a complex set of institutions with different types of power, responsive to different pressures from outside. The separate institutions within the state apparatus do not necessarily act in concert, and may even favour conflicting policies. For example, even within the civil service the Department of Employment tends to espouse incomes policy, and policies which would involve the integration of union leadership into government policy-making and administration, whereas Treasury civil servants, with less contact with trade union negotiations and with different orientations and priorities, are more likely to oppose the integration of unions into government and favour legislation to curb union power. A more public conflict can at times be seen between Parliament and the Judiciary. The Judiciary is imbued with values and traditions opposed to the collectivism of trade unions. Parliament and the Executive are generally more responsive to labour interests and, faced with pressures from unions and the lobby of large-scale companies, are more likely to be interested in corporatist methods of resolving conflicts of interests. Judge-made law has in the past been more restrictive than statute law, and there have been occasions when judges have been very unwilling to give expression to the intention behind legislation designed to regularise or extend trade union powers. For example, in 1979 and 1980 leading Law

Lords expressed their disapproval of the social contract legislation of 1974–6, although the laws in question, as the more progressive Lord Justice Scarman pointed out, had only restored to trade unions the immunities originally granted in 1906. In the same period the Advisory, Conciliation and Arbitration Service (ACAS) found itself unable to administer legislation fostering the recognition of trade unions, in large part because of a number of court cases which restricted ACAS's powers to act, the most important being *Grunwick* (1978) where the Courts overruled an ACAS recommendation that the union be recognised, on the grounds that the employer's refusal to let ACAS ballot his staff had nullified their inquiry. There was a period, from 1974 to 1981 when ACAS found it lost every case heard before the Master of the Rolls, Lord Denning, a judge who made no secret of his support for liberal-individualism and his disapproval of policies which smacked of the corporatist integration of trade unions.

State institutions are complex, they do not act in total co-ordination and the detailed relationship between the various institutions is beyond the scope of this book. Nevertheless, state activities are co-ordinated by the Executive, and the public policy which emerges cannot be ignored in the analysis of behaviour at work.

2   A Passive or Interventionist State

States vary in the extent to which they actively regulate employment relations. The UK state has played an extraordinarily passive role in industrial relations. The nineteenth-century policy of *laissez-faire* was replaced by the Welfare Compromise, which involved some state intervention in the economy, but retained the voluntary regulation of the employment relationship. The system of legal immunities kept most trade union activities outside the scope of the courts. There was the abstention of statutory law, with little legal support for minimum standards or conditions at work, and no legal support for trade unions or voluntary collective bargaining. Direct state involvement was minimal, limited to arbitration, conciliation and inquiry services. Even the government's arbitration and conciliation services were 'voluntary', for they were and are normally used only if employer and employee both wish to make use of them, and an arbitrator's award is not legally binding. Inquiries could be set up by government in the form of *ad hoc* committees or courts of inquiry and these reported to government, but their use was exceptional and limited. The only other state intervention was the attempt to prevent the worst cases of low pay through wages councils and even this intervention, as we see in Chapter 8, was imbued with voluntarism.

Many British academic writers have been loud with praise for this passive state role, most notably those grouped together as the 'Oxford School'. Flanders, Clegg and Kahn-Freund have all argued that a reliance on voluntary collective bargaining rather than state regulation ensured that the rules that regulated the employment relationship were flexible, relevant to the particular conditions of each industry, and democratically determined by the parties who had to live with, and administer, the results. In the defence of a non-interventionist state it was not explicitly argued that the state was thereby neutral between the parties, that employers and employees necessarily had a balance of power, or that any power imbalance had been equalised by the state such that justice reigned in the employment field. Instead, these issues were not discussed in any detail, and the advocacy of the passive state tended to be put in the context of pressures for more restrictive, anti-union legislation. However, in the absence of a detailed analysis of the role that the state did play in the situation, or of the political context of voluntarism, the earlier writers have become an easy target for criticisms that their view of the state was based on unrealistic assumptions (see Hyman's debate with Clegg on Pluralism, Hyman, 1978; Clegg, 1979, Chapter 11; and Lewis (1979) on Kahn-Freund). Certainly the Oxford School's view of the state was too scantily developed to be used to analyse the pressures for state action that have arisen in the recent past.

The UK state is no longer passive. It now provides a statutory floor of individual rights in employment. These provisions are largely non-controversial, but they inevitably involve the growth of labour law and litigation and have been responsible for the first significant development of any legal expertise on employment issues in the UK, in the expanding industrial tribunals. More fundamental shifts in public policy are presaged by the ever-present consideration of incomes policy and of restrictive or more corporatist legislation. Even those who advocate non-intervention propose public policies which involve a significantly more active state. As we see in Chapter 9, the Oxford School had a considerable influence on the recommendations of the 1968 Donovan Report, which can be seen as advocating the continued abstention of the law, but a far more active state on incomes policy and the involvement of unions and employers in government and managerial policy. The Thatcher government, with its commitment to *laissez-faire* economics, nevertheless narrowed the ambit of statutory immunities in order to bring trade unions under the closer regulation of the judiciary. The British state is moving from its extraordinarily passive policies of the past but, with disagreements about the direction of change both between and within the major interest groups and political parties, it is far from clear what the more active state policy will look like.

Why is it unlikely that the UK will retain or return to the passive state role in industrial relations? State inactivity is unusual in industrial and economic relations. Only in certain socio-political conditions are the interested parties likely to sheath the considerable power of the state. The *laissez-faire* policy of nineteenth-century Britain arose in unusual economic and social conditions. In most countries the state has always been far more actively involved in developing and regulating its economy. Voluntarism in industrial relations is unique to the UK and survived only while it was supported by the factors outlined in the sections above. Employers and employees are invariably political in their activities. They use political pressure to achieve their ends and this, together with increasing government concern to influence problematic areas of the economy, will ensure a more active role for the state than has been traditional in the UK.

3   The state, capital and labour

The state is likely to be an active participant in industrial relations; we therefore need to consider the relationship between the state and the other main parties. As we noted in Chapter 2, and outlined in Figure 2.1, different theoretical perspectives make a variety of assumptions about this relationship.

From unitary and pure corporatist perspectives, the state is the neutral guardian of the superordinate national interest. The other perspectives hold a less sanguine, trusting view of state activity. Liberal-collectivists, with their preference for a passive state, tend not to give the relationship between the state and other parties too close attention, merely assuming that under systems of collective bargaining the state can 'hold the ring' or 'establish Queensberry Rules' (Kahn-Freund, 1956, 1969). Such notions do not help us understand the controversy surrounding recent shifts in public policy.

Marxists have given considerable thought to the state's relationship to other parties, although Marx himself did not develop a theory of the state, and there are disagreements and differences of emphasis within Marxism. For all Marxists, the state in a capitalist society is primarily the agent of the capitalist class. Far from being neutral, state institutions are usually used to support the interests of capital against labour. Two leading European Marxists – Miliband and Poulantzas – give slightly different explanations for this close tie between capital and the state. Miliband (1969) suggests that it occurs because people from capital-class origins dominate positions of power and use state institutions as instruments to their own ends. Poulantzas (1973, 1976) argues that it occurs regardless of the class origin of those in power, because those who govern are subject to so much pressure from the interests of capital that they have no choice but to appease capital if they are to maintain their position. Structuralist constraints therefore limit the policy options of socialist, avowedly working-class governments. All Marxists accept that the state has some element of autonomy from capital and may not always appear to be acting in capital's interests, but there are divisions within Marxism on whether social democratic reforms apparently designed to strengthen working class power *do* assist the working class, or merely serve to prevent more radical socialist change. Orthodox Marxists argue that though the state may adopt policies of tripartite administration and trade union participation that may appear to override short-term business interests, this is only done to protect long-term capitalist interests and ensure the survival of capitalism. Because labour is the most articulate and effectively organised interest opposed to the capitalist class, strategies may be adopted which incorporate the leaders of labour-representative bodies into the administrative apparatus of the state. Under such a system labour appears to have considerable formal power and political influence, but labour is, in effect, castrated. Labour leaders do not have the power or resources to oppose capital in such corporatist institutions. In return for their apparent responsibilities, they accept more restrictive legislation and act to discipline disruption from their own membership. Unions become, like the state itself, agents of capital with no genuine autonomy (see D. Coates, 1981, on the policies of Tony Benn). However other, non-orthodox Marxists see more value in social democratic policies. They follow the Marxism of the Italian, Gramsci (1971), to argue that such policies may represent a genuine advance in working-class interests and help to weaken the hegemony of the capitalist classes in the slow battle of attrition that will be necessary to create communism in the advanced societies of the West.

Non-revolutionary socialists assume that state institutions are sufficiently autonomous from the power of capital to be used in labour's interests. In the UK the Fabians have since the 1880s advocated state intervention on labour's behalf. Crouch (1977) suggests that a genuine, Bargained Corporatism is possible in situations when labour is strongly organised, when the state does not have the power to be coercive and when capital interests are themselves divided. The belief that the state can aid the working classes even in an essentially capitalist economic system, and that such intervention by the state is preferable to more radical social change, lies behind the support that many trade unionists and labour moderates have given to corporatist policies in the recent past (see Chapter 9).

The role of the state in industrial relations and the effect that policies of state involvement have on the respective powers of employers and employees is now a subject of considerable debate. Several recent attempts to introduce or tighten trade union laws are best understood as attempts to use the power of the state to shift the balance of power towards capital and away from labour. Several recent policies have had elements of corporatism, and whether corporatist policies incorporate and exploit trade unions or whether they can achieve a bargained consensus is a question of central concern to the UK Labour party, the Social Democratic/ Liberal Alliance and the Conservative moderates.

CONCLUSION

The state plays an important part in any nation's industrial relations system. Within the UK the role of the state has been undergoing radical, and as yet unpredictable, change. For many years the state was unusually passive and Britain had a 'voluntary' system of employment regulation. Unions used their political power to keep the state, and particularly the courts, out of industrial relations, and for some time they gained the support of business interests in this policy. Now there is business, trade union and state pressure for more interventionist government policy on employment relations, but no party is unanimous in its view of the future. Within trade unions there are tensions between those who believe that state intervention could be used to achieve political objectives, and those whose prime fear is of an incorporation which would separate union leadership from the membership and weaken both. Within business groups there are divisions on the type of state role preferred. Even the institutions of the state itself support different types of policy.

Theoretical questions concerning the passivity or interventionism of the state, and the extent to which the state is autonomous from dominant interests are likely to recur as politicians and interest groups struggle to re-establish a stable public policy for industrial relations. Meanwhile the turmoil in public policy has rekindled academic interest in the role of the state in industrial relations and we return to these issues in Chapters 9 and 10.

Chapter 8

The British System of Collective Bargaining

Collective bargaining is the main method used in British industry to handle conflicts at work. Collective agreements set basic terms and conditions of employment for most British employees. About 15.5 million people, or 70 per cent of all full-time workers, are covered by collective bargaining. In the public sector over 90 per cent of employees are so covered, while in manufacturing the figure is nearly 70 per cent (see Table 8.1). Only 5 million employees, concentrated in small workplaces and in white-collar employment, are not personally affected by either free, or the state-supported form of collective bargaining discussed on p. 160 below. Collective bargaining is therefore an institution of major importance affecting far more than the 50 per cent of employees who are members of trade unions in the UK.

Collective bargaining dominates the determination of pay and conditions of employment for British employees, but in recent years it has become the subject of much controversy. Governmental attempts to reconstruct the collective bargaining system are discussed in Chapter 9. In this chapter we chart the development of Britain's traditional, national-level system of collective bargaining. We trace the turbulence created in the system by the development of local bargaining in the 1960s and by the growth of state intervention in the form of individual labour law and tripartite administration. In assessing collective bargaining today we note the alternatives to the dominant tradition of free collective bargaining that may prove significant in the future.

THE DEVELOPMENT OF BRITAIN'S TRADITIONAL COLLECTIVE BARGAINING SYSTEM

Collective bargaining can be defined as an institutionalised system of negotiation in which certain decisions affecting employment are decided within specialised, joint employer–trade union negotiating committees. (In Chapter 10 we discuss the contrasts between collective bargaining and other types of institutionalised negotiation and control.) When collective bargaining developed in the UK

Table 8.1 *The Importance of Collective Bargaining in the UK*

| | Proportion of full-time employees reported to be affected by some form of collective agreement in 1978 | | | | | | TOTAL |
| | Men | | | Women | | | TOTAL |
	Manual	Non-Manual	TOTAL	Manual	Non-Manual	TOTAL	Men and Women
All industries and services	78.3	59.6	70.9	70.9	66.7	68.0	70.0
Manufacturing	79.2	45.4	70.3	72.4	48.0	63.5	68.7
Private sector service*	51.3	38.1	43.6	44.5	33.4	35.5	40.4
Total private sector†	73.7	41.2	62.7	66.0	37.5	49.0	59.0
Total public sector‡	93.0	88.1	90.5	88.0	96.7	95.4	92.3

Source: Elliott (1980).
* MLH Orders 705 and 709 and MOH Order XXIII to XXVI complete except for MLH 872.
† Manufacturing plus private service sector, construction and agriculture (this is a slight overestimate, since manufacturing includes publicly-owned iron and steel, shipbuilding, vehicles and aerospace manufacturing).
‡ All industries and services less total private sector.

the negotiating committees formed were both multi-employer and multi-union. Formal negotiations came to be conducted industry by industry at what was called the 'national' level with little government support or interference.

It is often assumed that collective bargaining introduced employee-group negotiations into the workplace, replacing individual arrangements between employer and employee (Webb and Webb, 1898; Flanders, 1968, pp. 1–26; Fox, 1975, pp. 151–74). However, recent studies in the development of work organisations show that many nineteenth-century industries were organised around employee-group negotiations in the form of sub-contractual relations between owners and clearly structured, semi-autonomous workgroups based on craft, family or gang-boss controls (Littler, 1982, Chapter 6, esp. Table 6.1). Collective bargaining first appeared in the industries which had been based on sub-contract forms of organisation. It started in the craft-based industries and spread at the end of the nineteenth century through the industries which had been organised around family- and gang-boss-based workgroups.

The initial development of collective bargaining in the old sub-contract-based industries can be explained as the compromise reached between employers and employees in the transition to more centralised forms of work organisation. As employers attempted to impose a more direct control over labour costs and worker performance, they met resistance from employees who organised both to oppose tightening managerial controls and to standardise and improve their pay and conditions of work. The compromise of collective bargaining was opposed by employers who sought total unilateral control over work and by employees who sought the more fundamental change of workers' control. The compromise emerged as some employers agreed to negotiate with union officials on basic rates of pay and hours of work. Employers acted together in these negotiations, signing agreements which initially covered local districts and eventually spanned entire industries. The contents of the collective agreements were limited to basic pay and conditions of work and procedures for handling disputes. Wider issues such as the criteria for recruitment or dismissal, detailed pay structures, methods of work, supervision and discipline, were rarely touched by the collective agreements. Such areas were left, depending on workgroup power, to the unilateral determination of management, to continued unilateral workgroup control, or to the realms of informal compromise and bargaining on the shop-floor.

By the end of the nineteenth century, craftsmen had local agreements on standard wage-rates and hours in the printing, shipbuilding, engineering, building and furniture industries. In the last quarter of the century, collective bargaining also took root in the industries built around family and gang-boss sub-contractors. Here employers were replacing the sub-contract system by more direct employment based on piecework methods of payment. Employees demanded a say in the piecework schedules and price lists, and collective agreements on such lists in the coal mining, iron and steel, cotton textiles, boot and shoe, and the hosiery and lace industries had developed by the end of the century. At the turn of the century the craft and piecework trade were still the main base of collective bargaining, but demands for collective agreements were being copied by other groups of manual workers. By 1910 a quarter of the industrial workforce was covered by collective bargaining.

THE GROWTH OF NATIONAL, INDUSTRY-LEVEL BARGAINING

The first collective agreements covered local firms, but once collective bargaining was established there were many pressures to lift negotiations to a national, industry-wide level.

Employer association strategy

Employers, as we saw in Chapter 4, acted through employers' associations to demand national procedure agreements. Under such agreements no strike or lockout was constitutional until a central meeting of employer and union officials had attempted to resolve the dispute. Some employers saw national agreements on substantive issues like pay and hours as a logical development from such procedures, replacing simple employer collusion in the regulation of labour markets. The first national substantive agreements were signed, primarily on the employers' initiative, in cotton weaving in 1892 and cotton spinning in 1906. Most trade union full-time officers also saw advantages in industry-wide negotiation because it rationalised negotiating efforts, emphasised the need for full-time officers and enabled unions in single agreements to demonstrate a widespread impact. However union demands for national substantive agreements met fierce employer resistance, organised by the employers' associations of some industries, and the period from 1910 to 1914 was marked by bitter confrontations on the issue.

Government pressure

A Royal Commission on Labour (1891) had recommended the development of national collective bargaining and with the First World War the government took the initiative to encourage national levels of negotiation. The government prohibited strikes and instituted compulsory arbitration on industrial disputes for industries vital to the war effort. Pay settlements by arbitration acted as a pressure towards the rationalisation of numerous local agreements into single industry-wide settlements. The government also took direct control of 715 munitions factories, the railways and the coal mines, favouring industry-wide pay settlements here. Wartime inflation and the associated need for constant adjustments in wage rates encouraged both employers and union officials to accept the more straightforward, less time-consuming system of industry-wide negotiation.

After the war, government policy was heavily influenced by the reports of the Whitley Committee (1917 and 1918). The Whitley Committee on the Relations between Employers and Employed was appointed in the context of considerable government anxiety about the management of postwar industrial relations because of the very high levels of prewar industrial unrest and the existence of a radical shopfloor movement for workers' control (see below). The Committee's reports on future government policy were welcomed by many employers and union officials, in part because they could be interpreted in either more, or less, radical ways. Whitley advocated the extension of industry-wide collective bargaining and proposed the establishment of formal, joint employer–employee institutions at industry, district and workplace levels. It was not clear from the reports how wide the decision-making powers of the various joint bodies would be, nor how equally power would be shared within them. The proposals therefore could either be seen as heralding a new world of democratic decision-making at work, or as a simple recommendation for the spread of industry-wide pay settlements across industry with some formal provision for management to consult with employees at their place of work.

When voluntary pay negotiations returned at the end of the war, the newly formed Ministry of Labour set about the promotion of the Whitley Committee proposals. It drew up a model constitution for joint industrial councils (JICs) under which equal numbers of trade union and employer representatives would meet at regular intervals to discuss, not just wages and conditions of employment, but wider areas of co-operation, labour efficiency and job satisfaction. Seventy-three JICs were established between 1918 and 1921, but few extended their scope beyond very basic issues of pay and hours. They were widely used to negotiate wage cuts in the 1920s deflation. The Whitley proposals made little difference to the major industries where collective bargaining had already been established, but were very significant for the public sector. In the civil service and the Post Office, Whitley Councils were established with relatively wide decision-making powers and this helped spread collective bargaining to white-collar staff.

The growth of industry-wide collective bargaining that occurred in the immediate postwar years ended as trade unions suffered major defeats in industrial conflicts in the 1920s and as unemployment rose with the onset of the Great Depression. By 1938 the number of JICs had fallen to forty-five as employers withdrew their support. In the coal industry, for example, negotiation reverted to the district level as employers, confident of their increased strength, refused to appoint representatives to the national machinery. The Great Depression of the 1930s therefore caused some slippage in the development of the national collective bargaining system. However, the worsening market for labour had a more crushing and long-term impact on the workplace activity which had, in the 1920s, presented a real threat to the establishment of industry-wide collective bargaining.

The decline of the first shop stewards' movement
Formalisation of collective bargaining at national levels implied, at least for many employers, that no significant negotiation should occur at lower levels. But the national agreements were skeletal, establishing certain very basic conditions and rates but leaving innumerable details to be decided elsewhere. Although employers might claim the exercise of managerial prerogative over all issues not determined at the national bargaining table, some other negotiation was always likely to exist. Indeed it can be argued that some form of domestic, company-based bargaining is inevitable because no managerial control system, no contract of employment and no national agreement can comprehensively establish rules to cover every contingency at the place of work. Even individual supervision is negotiated: 'it is possible to visualise the process of supervision as a method of bargaining between workers and supervisors. The details of the arrangements are left to be worked out through direct interaction between (them)' (Baldamus, 1961). Individual bargaining with one's superior is likely to be replaced by workgroup bargaining wherever groups form with the unity and strength to bargain their collective co-operation for some concession in their terms of employment and, as we saw in Chapter 5, the influence that workgroups exert varies with the tightness of control exercised by management or higher levels of negotiation and with the internal organisation and bargaining skills of shopfloor leaders. In the UK, there have been two main periods when shopfloor bargainers were able to exert sufficient power to make a noticeable impact on industrial affairs. On both occasions domestic bargaining has been seen as operating in conflict with national collective bargaining and as threatening its stability.

Shop steward activities first caught public attention in the First World War, but negotiating shop stewards have a longer history.

At the end of the nineteenth century, piecework and payments by results systems were introduced into British industry as employers centralised control over worker effort and productivity, and reduced the autonomy of foremen and workgroups. An important, though no doubt unintended, consequence of the change in managerial control techniques was the encouragement of bargaining between workers and rate fixers or foremen over the price or time for each job. G. D. H. Cole describes how it became a regular practice for workers to consult with each other before any questionable price was accepted, and for workers to negotiate on such prices as a group. In some works 'special workshop committees or piecework committees sprang up for the purpose, among others, of considering all prices before any man was allowed to accept them' (Cole, 1923). Some committees, like the Royal Arsenal shop stewards committee at Woolwich, or the Piece-work Committee at Crewe railway workshops were granted *de facto* recognition by local management, making their committee-men the first shop stewards in the modern sense of having powers of negotiation, in addition to the conventional workplace representative's role of collecting union subscriptions, maintaining membership and acting as a link with union branches.

The First World War speeded up the spread of shop steward bargaining throughout the munitions industries and to new groups of semi-skilled and unskilled workers. Military conscription and the associated manning problems at home, the wartime passivity of the trade union leadership who were supporting the war effort, and power derived from wartime full employment all stimulated the growth of shopfloor bargaining until 'workshop and works committees, with duly appointed convenors, in close touch with similar bodies in other establishments, became a regular feature of factory organisation' (Cole, 1923).

Actively negotiating shop stewards fit uneasily into a system of national-level bargaining and into trade union hierarchies designed to produce negotiating officials at national, district or at the lowest, branch levels of union organisation. The early trade union's branch structure was usually based on a worker's residence, rather than his or her workplace and so any workplace negotiators represented members in several branches of any one union. In addition multi-unionism made it even more difficult for higher trade union officials to co-ordinate the exercise of authority over workplace activities. In the period from 1890 to the late 1920s, the divorce between shopfloor representatives and the official union institutions was exacerbated by differences in ideology and policy. Workgroup activity became associated with the Shop Stewards' Movement which started on the Clyde in 1915. This movement opposed the official trade union's wartime truce, advocated an end to sectional divisions within the union movement, and argued for industrial unionism capable of class-based political action in the pursuit of workers' control. Although most stewards were not direct members, the movement influenced stewards in many big cities and served as an industrial link with the revolutionary ideas of the Socialist Labour party (a Marxist body), the Guild Socialists and the Syndicalists. All saw the official trade union support for industry-level collective bargaining as a betrayal of worker interests and a supporting bulwark for the capitalist system (Goodman and Whittingham, 1973).

The shop steward activity of the First World War stimulated several reactions. Several unions changed their rules to give stewards limited formal status and negotiating responsibilities, and in 1917 and 1919 the Engineering Employers Association and engineering unions formally gave some recognition to single-union shop stewards and to works committees, although *not* to senior stewards or convenors who represented members in more than one union. The government's reaction was to set up the Whitley Committee, and the Committee's proposals for works committees were intended to provide a constitutional outlet for demands for greater worker influence on the shopfloor. Within public mythology the Shop Stewards' Movement identified shop stewards with political revolutionaries, a stereotype which fitted only a small minority of workplace bargainers at the time and which was to be even more inappropriate when the stereotype was revived for the new generation of stewards which developed in the 1950s.

The Shop Stewards' Movement and the threat of steward bargaining evaporated in the interwar recession. With unemployment averaging 13 per cent between 1920 and 1940, many employers took the opportunity to terminate the recognition of shop stewards, and widespread victimisation and blacklisting turned the radical shopfloor representatives of the wartime period into the leaders of the 1930s unemployed. Domestic bargaining was reduced to insignificance and it was in the 1930s and 1940s that scientific management was introduced into British industry without the support of, but with remarkably little resistance from, a demoralised and weakened workforce. The collapse of the first shop stewards' movement smoothed the way for the firm establishment of national collective bargaining in the Second World War.

The strengthening of national bargaining since the Second World War
Prewar economic growth and wartime government intervention revived the national system of collective bargaining. During the Second World War government again intervened to control the

economy, unemployment dropped and unions bargained their co-operation with wartime measures for the extension of industry-wide collective bargaining. Fifty-six JICs were created or re-established from 1939 to 1945 and the wages council system of state-backed national negotiating machinery was extended in the belief that this would protect the industry-level bargaining system if there were a postwar recession similar to that following the First World War (see p. 160 below).

Wartime conditions again stimulated the growth of shop-floor bargaining but government, employers and unions took care to provide institutional channels for increased local activity. Productivity committees were established in all war-related industries to enable managers and stewards to argue out differences at the place of work. The extent and scope of domestic, shop steward bargaining expanded, especially in engineering, shipbuilding and construction, and some measure of the increase in this local activity can be seen in the large number of short, and at the time illegal, strikes. However in the Second World War domestic bargaining was *not* seen as a serious challenge to either official trade union policies or industry-wide collective bargaining. On this occasion shop stewards were not the bearers of a radical counter-ideology and the wartime bargaining did not stimulate very much public concern.

Britain's national, industry-wide system of collective bargaining was therefore well established by the end of the Second World War. All major industries and the bulk of manual workers were affected by it and by 1946 15.5 million out of a working population of 17.5 million in industry and services were covered by some type of voluntary or statutory national-level negotiations. By this time opinion in government, union and employer ranks supported the system as a mature, flexible and democratic method of employee involvement at work. Collective bargaining was pressed on the defeated wartime powers of Germany and Japan as a means of liberalising their political structures and creating a pluralistic bulwark against the return of totalitarian regimes. German unions followed TUC advice and adopted an industrial structure to suit industry-level negotiations. In Japan, however, the strength of company consciousness and the power of large companies led to the development of enterprise-level collective bargaining.

In the postwar years of the Welfare Compromise policies discussed in Chapter 7, with unemployment reduced to an average of 2 per cent in each five-year period between 1945 and 1965, the national system of collective bargaining appeared to thrive and was spread to new groups of employees.

The Nationalisation Acts put a statutory duty on the new controlling authorities and Boards to set up negotiating machinery for their employees, a requirement which spread collective bargaining to white-collar workers in the nationalised industries. The growth of education, health and the social services also encouraged the development of collective bargaining for white-collar professional employees. White-collar trade union membership rose by 33.6 per cent from 1948 to 1964, and although this increase barely kept pace with the 32.4 per cent growth in the white-collar workforce, it was to represent a significant change in the base of trade unionism. Collective bargaining for white-collar employees spread relatively smoothly through the public sector and national-level negotiation became widespread. In the private sector, recognition disputes over white-collar workers' collective bargaining rights were one of the main issues to disrupt a remarkably peaceful industrial relations scene. The national collective bargaining system therefore seemed well established and secure. By 1965 there were 500 separate institutions for reaching national level agreements ranging from the *ad hoc* meetings of unions and employers representing the vast engineering industry, to the permanent standing committee, complete with its own staff, of the Joint Industry Board for the small and specialised electrical contracting industry. The system was complex but comprehensive and had the unobtrusive support of the state.

THE STATE AND TRADITIONAL COLLECTIVE BARGAINING

British public policy during the development of the national collective bargaining system was relatively passive. Governments avoided direct intervention on terms and conditions of employment and did not use the law to encourage the growth of trade unions or the spread of collective bargaining. Nevertheless, as is evident from the history above, public policy did encourage the development of national machinery for collective bargaining. The state also acted to help stabilise the collective bargaining system by measures which provided some support for the bargainers and some protection for the most disadvantaged employees. These measures, though limited, became an integral part of traditional British collective bargaining.

Conciliation, arbitration and inquiry

Before the Industrial Revolution, government involvement in pay determination was conducted through the compulsory, binding arbitration of disputes between individual workers and employers by Justices of the Peace. When the state moved to divest itself of these responsibilities it initially retained vestiges of the old system, first by providing for nominated referees to arbitrate in disputes (Acts of 1800 and 1824) and then (in Acts of 1867 and 1872) for arbitration boards to be set up in conjunction with voluntary collective bargaining institutions, to make legally binding awards. These were little used, and the UK moved to reject legally binding arbitration in peacetime.

In 1896 all previous legislation on arbitration was repealed and the government gave itself three types of power to intervene. It could *inquire* into disputes and offer advice without the consent of the parties; it could appoint a *conciliator* or board of conciliators to try to help resolve a dispute, if asked by one of the parties; and it could appoint an *arbitrator* to make a positive recommendation, but only if asked to do so by both parties. In no case was an inquiry's advice or arbitrator's award to be legally binding and all the provisions for government intervention were only to be used after voluntary collective bargaining procedures had failed.

The provision of voluntary arbitration, conciliation and inquiry continues to the present day. The services were put on a permanent basis on the recommendations of Whitley, arbitration being entrusted to an industrial court, (now the Central Arbitration Committee) and conciliation became part of the function of the new Ministry of Labour in 1916 and since 1975 has been conducted by a tripartite Advisory, Conciliation and Arbitration Service – see p. 175 below).

Extending the terms of collective agreements

Compared with all other countries operating collective bargaining systems, British governments have given little support to either trade union recognition or to the extension of collective agreements once made. Only for a brief eleven years, between 1969 and 1980, did the state assist unions seeking recognition from reluctant employers. Public sector employers have, however, been expected to recognise trade unions and determine their employment terms by collective bargaining, and companies working on contract to the public sector are subject to 'fair wages' resolutions passed in 1891, 1909 and 1946, which require all government contractors to observe fair wages, hours and conditions of work for their employees. 'Fair' is defined as being those terms established by collective bargaining for the trade or industry in the district where the contractors operate.

A wider extension of collective agreements existed from 1940 to 1980. Wartime provisions to protect wages were replaced by section 8 of the Terms and Conditions of Employment Act (1959) which enabled individual workers to claim that the provisions of the relevant industry or district collective agreement should be applied to them, even if their employer was not party to the agreement. This clause existed for many years without being widely or actively used, although it may have encouraged the widespread practice of unfederated employers following their industry's agreement. In 1976, Schedule 11 of the Employment Protection Act widened this extension of collective agreements and was widely used by employers and unions in collusion against incomes policy and by white-collar unions for unrecognised members in private industry. Schedule 11's repeal in 1980 removed one of the slender supports given by the state to collectively agreed terms.

Demands for laws to protect individual rights in employment have traditionally been disregarded in the UK. Nevertheless, some legislation was enacted. The earliest legislation concerned the payment of wages and the hours of work of women and children. A series of Truck Acts, passed from 1831, ensured that employers paid their employees in cash and not in kind, and did not dictate how employees' wages should be spent. Factory legislation in 1802 and 1833 set limits to the hours worked by women and children in industries like coal-mining and textiles. There has been a more consistent government interest in health and safety and low pay.

Health and safety at work
From 1802 a succession of Factory Acts were passed laying down minimum standards on such things as ventilation and sanitation; on the guarding and proper maintenance of machinery and equipment; on the provision of drinking water; on the use of poisons and dangerous substances; and on the notification of accidents and industrial diseases. Fines and government-employed inspectorates were used to enforce these laws and by 1970 there were nearly thirty separate Acts in the area, enforced by seven separate inspectorates. These were rationalised in 1974 by the Health and Safety at Work Act (see p. 176).

Low pay and wages councils
The early general unions and the Anti-Sweating League (formed in 1906) demanded a national minimum wage to protect the lowest paid, a demand that was vigorously opposed by advocates of a free labour market. In 1909 the Liberal government produced a compromise in the Trade Boards Act. Trade boards, composed of representatives of employers, employees and independents, were set up for certain low paid industries with the function of deciding 'reasonable' rates of pay. Since then, new functions have been grafted on. The Whitley Committee in 1918 suggested that trade boards should be set up in any area not subject to collective bargaining and should regulate a wider range of subjects in order to mirror and stimulate the development of collective bargaining. This new role for the trade boards was bitterly criticised by employers and in the interwar recession the boards did, in practice

revert to their old, limited function of establishing minimum wages. In 1945 the system was revitalised and extended in the belief that the newly named wages councils would give some statutory protection to collective bargaining if there was a postwar depression similar to the one that followed the First World War.

Wages councils were therefore left with two complex functions: support for the low paid; and the encouragement of collective bargaining where it was weak. The two roles were contradictory. The function of encouraging collective bargaining hindered effective support for the low paid because council orders were too detailed and complex to be easily understood by employees and because wages council chairmen tended to define their role in terms of easing agreements, rather than acting on low pay. In turn, the low pay function probably hindered the spread of collective bargaining by removing some of the incentive to unionise or set up more genuine bargaining machinery (Palmer, 1974). Despite the complex wages council machinery (thirty-three councils or boards covering three million employees by 1980) and the efforts of the small inspectorate, few believe that wages councils provide an adequate solution to the problem of low pay.

By the end of the Second World War, the UK had a comprehensive system of industry-wide collective bargaining with government support which was widely believed to offer a responsible solution to the inevitable conflicts at work. The phases in the development of this traditional system, and the stresses that were to develop after 1955, can be traced in the statistics on industrial action.

THE HISTORY OF INDUSTRIAL ACTION IN THE UK

The development of the UK's collective bargaining system is reflected in the strike statistics. Two measures of industrial action are conventionally used, the number of strikes or lockouts reported to government in a year (strike incidence) and the man/woman days involved – i.e. the number of workers involved times the duration of the stoppage in days ('days lost' or striker days). The UK's Department of Employment records stoppages due to industrial disputes which involve 10 or more workers and which last for at least one day, or which involve over 100 days lost.

As can be seen from Figure 8.1, the years up to the Great Depression were characterised by periods of bitter confrontation involving massive numbers of 'days lost'. Disputes occurred in which entire industries were struck and/or locked out, generating figures for annual work days affected by disputes far higher than anything seen in the UK since.

From 1919 to 1925 nearly 150 million out of 194 million striker

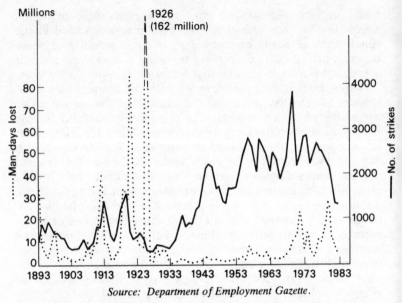

Source: *Department of Employment Gazette.*

Figure 8.1 Strike Activity in Great Britain and Northern Ireland, 1893–1981

days were lost in 17 official disputes occurring in a total of over 6,000 disputes. Seventy-two million days went in the coal lockout of 1921. Of the 30 million days lost from 1927 to 1933 over 18 million came from 5 national textile strikes. These major national disputes came to an end as labour power fell with the 1930s recession. They did not return when the economy revived during and after the war.

After the Second World War the figures for annual days lost showed a remarkably peaceful picture compared with the industrial conflicts of the 1920s. The establishment and widespread extension of the traditional, national collective bargaining system was accredited with the successful institutionalisation of industrial conflict. However the apparent success of the national institutions was greatly assisted, if not primarily caused, by the UK's most sustained period of real economic growth since the 1880s, and by the policies of the Welfare Compromise discussed in Chapter 7. There were no official national disputes from 1933 to 1953. Lockouts were rare and strikes became very much shorter and smaller in scale, giving a dramatic reduction in the figures for striker days, despite a larger labour force.

Although the number of days lost dropped over the period in which collective bargaining became the dominant institution of employment relations, the number of disputes notified to the government increased. At the beginning of the century, strikes were limited to a very few industries where union membership was well established. Coal was responsible for over half of the disputes each year until the late 1960s. The gradual increase in the incidence of industrial action shown in the chart reflects the spread of trade unionism and collective bargaining to new groups of employees. Before 1941 there were only 5 years when the number of stoppages reached 1,000 a year. Since then there have always been over 1,000 and the annual average is now over 2,000 stoppages a year.

The fall in striker days, despite the rise in the number of stoppages, is explained by a reduction in the length and average size of strikes from the earlier massive confrontations over the establishment of the national bargaining system. The size and length of strikes also fluctuates with the state of the labour market and economic demand. On the whole, in periods of recession there are fewer strikes but they are longer, because major issues are at stake and there is little pressure on the employer for an early settlement. In periods of prosperity collective bargaining has generated more but shorter disputes.

Countries with political systems which permit free collective bargaining usually publish statistics on industrial action. International comparisons are now published by the DE showing the days lost per 1,000 employees in the normally strike-prone industries of mining, manufacturing, construction and transport. As can be seen from Table 8.2, in the statistics available for recent decades, the UK figures for industrial action are not peculiarly severe. On most recent averages the UK ranks lower than the USA, Canada, Australia, Finland, India, Ireland, Italy or Spain in days lost per 1,000 employees. The UK figures are not exceptional for a country which relies on collective bargaining as its main mechanism for handling conflicts in the employment relationship (in contrast, for example to West Germany's worker participation schemes) and which has problems associated with an ageing industrial base and contracting heavy industries.

Although international comparisons suggest that the aggregate level of industrial action in the UK is not unusual, Britain's strike record has, since the mid 1960s, been seen as demonstrating a serious national problem. The argument that Britain is 'strike prone' has fuelled mounting criticisms of British trade unions and of the traditional collective bargaining system. One of the factors behind this dramatic change of mood towards British industrial relations was a rising strike incidence (see Figure 8.1) arising from stronger shopfloor bargaining and the spread of industrial action to new areas. The second factor was the advent of incomes policy

Table 8.2 Comparative Strike Proneness

| | Days lost by industrial stoppage per thousand employees | | | | | |
| | 1 In all industries and services | | | 2 In mining, manufacturing, construction and transport[4] | | |
	1971–80	1971–75	1976–80[1]	1971–80[2]	1971–75	1976–80[1,3]
United Kingdom	575	585	566	1,132	1,146	1,118
Australia[5]	662	728	596	1,327	1,464	1,155
Belgium	228	236	219	454	422	495
Canada	892	919	864	1,774	1,848	1,700
Denmark[6]	264	436	92	627	990	173
Finland	684	753	615	1,248	1,426	1,025
France	209	232	186	327	342	308
Germany (FR)	54	57	52	92	92	92
Irish Republic	739	415	1,064	1,229	746	1,833
Italy[7]	1,271	1,367	1,174	1,780	1,746	1,823
Japan	115	188	43	200	326	74
Netherlands	37	43	30	88	90	85
New Zealand	264	150	378	596	386	858
Norway	47	52	42	87	104	70
Spain	856[2]	141	1,749[3]	1,352	240	2,743

Spain	856[2]	141	1,749[3]	1,352	240	2,743
Sweden[8]	163	85	241	50	76	18
United States[9]	452	484	420	1,073	1,136	1,010
India	—	—	—	1,537	1,532	1,543
Switzerland[9]	—	—	—	3	2	5

Source: Department of Employment Gazette, February 1982.

[1] Provisional.
[2] Average for 1971–79 where the 1980 figure is not available.
[3] Average for 1976–79 where the 1980 figure is not available.
[4] The figures are restricted mainly to those four relatively strike-prone industry groups by the ILO to reduce the effects of different industrial structures and improve the basis of comparison of strike rates between the countries.
[5] Including electricity and gas; excluding communication in columns 4, 5 and 6.
[6] In columns 4, 5 and 6 figures up to 1974 relate to manufacturing only and are therefore not fully comparable with later figures. Columns 4, 5 and 6 include gas, electricity and water.
[7] Including political strikes from 1975 onwards.
[8] In columns 4, 5 and 6 figures for 1971 relate only to manufacturing, and are therefore not fully comparable with those for later years.
[9] Including gas, electricity and water in columns 4, 5 and 6.

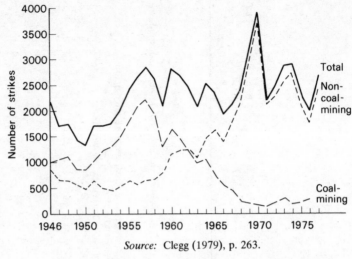

Source: Clegg (1979), p. 263.

Figure 8.2   Strike Trends in Coal-mining and Other Industries, 1946–77

and the return of major confrontations on the principle of free collective bargaining.

Although the increase in strike incidence in the postwar years was not dramatic, and although annual days lost were still remarkably low compared with the turbulent period from 1914 to 1926, the overall figures masked changes in strike activity which worried the critics. The use of the strike 'weapon' was spreading through industry. Whereas coal-mining had dominated the strike statistics of earlier years, after 1955 there was a rapid decline in mining strikes as the industry declined, pits closed and local pit-based bargaining strength and activity faded. However coal-mining's reduced industrial activity was more than matched by the spread of industrial action to previously strike-free industries and this can be seen from Figure 8.2. Another cause for concern from 1955 was that increasing numbers of strikes were not related to national-level negotiations and by-passed the national disputes procedures. Shop stewards were apparently acting autonomously in workgroup bargaining and using the strike sanction without reference to higher authorities. Ninety-five per cent of strikes were estimated to be unofficial, i.e. not sanctioned by union executives in 1968 (Donovan Report). The growth of small, usually short, shop-steward-led strikes, not associated with negotiations on national agreements, fuelled the charge that British industrial relations was out of control and by the 1960s there was a widespread public belief that Britain was the most strike-prone nation on earth. Public confusion and concern was increased by the return of major confrontations as unions reacted to government attempts to intervene in the determination of pay. The challenges presented to the traditional collective bargaining system by the growth of domestic negotiations and by changes in the role of government are the subject of the next two sections.

THE CHALLENGE OF DOMESTIC BARGAINING

The renewed growth of domestic bargaining that attracted attention from 1955 provided the first indication that the traditional collective bargaining system could not resolve all conflicts in modern employment relations. Improved labour market conditions increased the ability of workgroups to act on their own. Even though shop stewards were not, on this occasion, associated with radical politics or with the rejection of national collective bargaining, the increase in shop steward activity from the 1950s to 1970s undermined the regulatory force of the national collective agreements and was viewed with alarm.

The rising number of small-scale, shop-steward-led strikes was the most public indicator of the growth of domestic bargaining. Wage drift was another indicator, seized upon by economists who argued that domestic bargaining was a prime source of inflation, because unregulated local accretions to wages were pushing up costs. In 1968 the Donovan Report expressed considerable concern about wage drift – i.e. the drift of take-home earnings away from nationally negotiated wage-rates. Donovan (1968) noted that the gap between national wage-rates and take-home pay had increased between the 1930s and the mid 1960s because piecework earnings, overtime payments and domestic additions to national rates had all grown until they together contributed a high proportion of actual earnings. All three sources of wage drift were seen as a cause for concern:

Rising piecework earnings were seen as evidence that the piecework schemes, originally introduced as a means of motivating workers and giving employers tighter control over worker effort, were being used by well-organised workgroups to increase their earnings by presenting claims based on comparability and precedent at every job change. Constant domestic negotiations over piecework prices and times had served, in the context of tight labour and soft product markets, to weaken managerial control over labour costs.

Overtime was seen as a problem on the grounds that systematic and high levels of overtime were worked by workgroups wishing to increase their earnings, rather than because there was any managerial need for extra hours of work. The length of the working week specified in national agreements dropped from 47.2 hours in 1938 to 40.3 hours in 1966, and yet the actual hours worked between 1946 and 1966 fell only by one hour. Case studies suggested that the control of overtime, and the distribution of overtime opportunities across the workforce, formed a significant part of the shop steward's bargaining role.

Factory additions to nationally agreed rates had mushroomed and most employers' associations turned a blind eye to the evidence that their negotiated agreements were being treated as minima. These domestic agreements were seen as a problem, not because they existed – for they had clearly developed because they were seen to be in the interests of workers and local management – but because of the non-institutionalised form they took. Flanders (1965) argued that the new domestic bargaining was 'largely informal, largely fragmented and largely autonomous' resulting in 'chaotic' relationships outside the control of senior managers or the full-time union officials. This argument had a profound effect on the Donovan Commission and was resonated by all who were concerned to introduce more centralised and formalised pay determination into the British economy.

To What Extent Was Domestic Bargaining a Problem?

By the 1960s shop steward activities were therefore again defined as a major national problem. There were various demands for government action, from calls for changes in collective labour law to outlaw unconstitutional strikes and so curb workgroup power, to calls for the restructuring of collective bargaining to integrate domestic negotiations into a new framework of institutions. Government response to these proposals are discussed in Chapter 9. Here we need to note that, although domestic bargaining was widely presented at the time as posing problems for managers, government and trade unions alike (Donovan, 1968) not all groups shared this perception.

Most domestic bargaining developed between local workgroups and local managers, with the connivance or explicit acceptance of officials higher in their respective hierarchies. Domestic bargaining was not widespread in areas where management had for many years adopted bureaucratic, central controls over personnel policy, for example in the public sector or for the white-collar workers of many private companies. Spontaneous domestic bargaining was essentially a feature of the less bureaucratic construction, engineering and shipbuilding industries and even in these industries it was often not seen as a problem by the unions or managers directly involved. Batstone *et al.*'s (1977, 1978) study of domestic bargaining in the vehicle industry, conducted at the height of shopfloor power, found that stewards worked closely and cooperatively with their union full time officers. The government agency established to restructure domestic bargaining found many employers and senior managers who were not prepared to view their existing domestic arrangements as in need of change (see p. 192). Only those employers faced with increased international competition, tightening product markets and a concern to cut labour costs viewed their domestic arrangements with concern and many of these took the initiative in instituting or reshaping their own domestic negotiations as we see below. It can be argued that domestic negotiations were primarily seen as a problem by the advocates of incomes policy who sought to control inflation by more centralised wage determination. Whether domestic bargaining *did* fuel inflation was, and still is, hotly contested. Ranged against the 'wage-push' theories that it was a cause were the arguments of 'demand-pull' theorists and of monetarists (Blackaby *et al.*, 1980; D. Jackson *et al.*, 1972).

Employer Initiatives and Productivity Bargaining
As early as 1960 some large, multi-plant companies were moving to create new institutions for domestic bargaining which would enable them to develop more detailed agreements with their workforce than were possible in national levels of bargaining.

The Fawley Agreement. Flanders (1964) wrote a detailed analysis of the agreement at Esso's Oil Refinery at Fawley which pioneered this development in the UK. Fawley's management conducted a long and complex series of negotiations to centralise domestic bargaining into a single, plant-level agreement. In the negotiations the employer gained a reduction in the size of the workforce and changes in working practices (the relaxation of job demarcation, the withdrawal of the craftsman's mate and their redeployment to other work and greater freedom in management's use of supervisors). In return, employees received pay increases of 40 per cent, job guarantees, the extension of fringe benefits and a reduction of the working week from forty-two to forty hours. Finally, a high and systematic level of overtime (18 per cent of hours worked) was to be reduced over time with the guarantee of no consequent loss in earnings. This 'productivity bargain' was acclaimed by Flanders as a rational approach to the problems arising from the gradual *ad hoc* accretion of shopfloor bargaining power. He argued the agreement was 'without precedent', not only because of the unusually wide scope of the bargained subjects, but also because the negotiation process was elaborately designed to involve shop stewards as well as full-time union officers and was conducted within a new, formalised joint negotiating institution for the plant.

The Esso initiative created a wave of interest in the pharmaceutical industry, and some large employers in chemicals and also in engineering began to establish plant or company-level joint negotiating committees or councils and to adopt policies of strategic independence (see p. 60). The Chemical Industries Association came to welcome and encourage domestic negotiations but the Engineering Employers' Federation was initially less willing to accept the reduced importance of its own negotiations and several large engineering employers left the Federation in order to take charge of their own relations with trade unions at domestic level.

The Spread of Formal Domestic Bargaining

Government in the late 1960s encouraged employers to follow the lead of those who had instituted more formalised domestic bargaining. The Donovan Commission and the Commission on Industrial Relations endorsed and encouraged the formalisation of domestic bargaining (see pp. 187–92). The National Board for Prices and Incomes (1965–70) expounded the advantages of formal domestic productivity bargaining in most of its reports.

Survey evidence suggests that domestic bargaining at establishment, plant or factory level did become more formally conducted in the late 1960s and 1970s. Brown *et al.* (1981) surveyed the manufacturing industries in 1977 and 1978 and concluded that the previous ten years had seen radical changes at the workplace with formal joint negotiating committees for domestic bargaining spreading throughout the industries surveyed. Sixty-eight per cent of manual employees, in fifty-three per cent of establishments, had their pay principally affected by single-employer bargaining conducted at plant level or above. Shop steward organisation had also developed, matching the greater institutionalisation of domestic bargaining. Brown found regular shop steward meetings and the development of shop steward hierarchies with senior stewards and multi-union convenors. Shop stewards existed in 73 per cent of establishments for manual workers, 34 per cent for white-collar workers, giving an estimated 119,000 manual stewards and 37,000 non-manual stewards in manufacturing. An estimated 3,500 of the manual stewards and about 300 white-collar stewards were full-time, making more stewards paid by their companies to spend all their time on union business than there were union officers paid by trade unions. Management not only paid to support the shop steward hierarchies, but aided trade union organisation through agreements on check off and the closed shop. Check-off schemes (in which employers help collect union subscriptions by deduction from wages) had spread to cover nearly 60 per cent of establishments and over 70 per cent of employees in manufacturing. The closed shop had spread to cover 50 per cent of trade unionists in the manufacturing sample – 55 per cent of the manual and 20 per cent of the non-manual union members.

There has been considerable debate about the causes of the spread of formal domestic bargaining. Brown presents in the change as largely initiated by management. Employers, faced with steady inflation, a volatile foreign trade position, more overseas ownership of industry, growing industrial concentration and a marked increase in government intervention in employment relations, reacted by seeking a firmer grip on labour costs and a more effective control over the labour process. They saw more centralised domestic bargaining as the means to achieve the workplace changes they desired. Employers replaced the old piecework incentive schemes with measured daywork, which ended the constant steward bargaining at each job change, but required more centralised negotiations. Check-off and closed shops were supported by managers in the interests of simplifying union administration and helping create domestic union structures with sufficient cohesion to implement agreements. Brown's interpretation, that management was the instigator of formal domestic bargaining, is endorsed by the Chemco research (see page 89, see also Cliff, 1966). Employer initiative was important in the development of formal domestic bargaining. The impact of government policy we discuss in Chapter 9. Here we can add that shop stewards themselves provided some of the pressures towards formalisation. Redundancy, an escalating problem from 1960, caused the centralisation of shop steward organisations as workgroups sought to protect their jobs. Hyman (1979) has noted that stewards have sought more bureaucratic arrangements as a means to greater effectiveness. The traditional fragmentation of workplace struggles had disadvantages for employees and the move to more structured steward organisation was essential if stewards were to retain or increase their influence in the face of more sophisticated managerial policies or were to affect decisions made higher in company management. The formalisation of shopfloor bargaining did not, in general, face shop steward or worker resistance.

What were the effects of more formal domestic bargaining? For some the development suggests a significant increase in workgroup power (Donovan, 1968), for others it implies the emasculated incorporation of unions and shop stewards into vastly more sophisticated managerial controls (Nichols and Beynon, 1977, and Herding, 1974, in the US context). We return to this discussion in Chapter 10. However it is relevant that even at the height of stewards bargaining power in the 1970s, formal domestic bargaining usually took place at the level of the individual plant or establishment rather than for an entire multi-plant company. In Brown's survey, in only 11 per cent of the establishments covered by formal domestic agreements did the agreement cover more than one plant and these multi-plant agreements were normally found in industries *without* a tradition of strong shopfloor bargaining. Formal multi-plant bargaining occurred where the employer had taken the initiative to move straight from the old multi-employer to multi-plant, single-employer bargaining, or in foreign-owned companies with a preference for centralised, bureaucratic personnel policies. Where shop steward organisations were already strong, employers were likely to keep the determination of pay and conditions decentralised to the establishment level even when formalising domestic bargaining arrangements. Gowan (1976) found only 14 of the 150 largest British companies gave any official recognition to combine committees representing stewards from different plants.

Without employer assistance shop stewards have found considerable difficulty in building the necessary communication and organisational links between the workgroups of separate plants of a company within one country. The difficulties in the face of trade union co-ordination of the workforces of multinational enterprises are immense. Writing in 1978, Brown and Terry argued that the survival of effective collective bargaining could be in doubt if unions were unable to breach this gap in the structure of union and workplace representation and effectively operate at the new levels determined by large-scale, complex company structures. This fear was repeated in several TUC reports in the late 1970s. Formal bargaining may strengthen trade unionism within the plant, but the development of formal domestic bargaining in the 1970s did not give unions access to corporate levels of decision-taking.

The recession of the 1980s weakened the shop steward organisations that had grown to such prominence in the 1970s. As unemployment rose, some employers chose to mount an offensive against shop steward power. In 1981 the ACAS chairman, an ex-British Leyland director of personnel, was warning employers not to take too much advantage of their new-found power over the shopfloor, because the bonfire of old agreements was building up resentments to bedevil the future. In British Leyland itself the changed climate was symbolised when the chairman, Sir Michael Edwardes, successfully dismissed the company's senior convenor, Derek Robinson, in 1979 and went on to adopt an aggressive labour policy, threatening to dismiss all unconstitutional strikers and countering the stewards call for a strike over the 1981 pay claim by directly communicating to all employees that he would dismiss all the workers of the most affected plants. Across the motor industry, once the strong heart of domestic bargaining, shop steward strength crumbled as employers pushed forward their frontier of control on such issues as payment of lay-off pay for workers affected by others' disputes, the speed of the line in assembly plants, or the length of rest periods. The short, shop-steward-led strikes which had caused such concern in the 1960s were not a feature of the 1980s.

How far the roll-back of shop steward power caused the decay of the formal institutions for domestic bargaining has yet to be studied. Many, especially those initiated by managers, remain. However a new count of the shop stewards able to spend all their time on steward business would almost certainly show a significant reduction from the days of Brown's survey.

Britain's traditional collective bargaining system, based on multi-employer, industry-wide agreements has therefore been altered by the growth and formalisation of single-employer, domestic bargaining. Both national and formal domestic agreements now co-exist to give an increasingly complex collective bargaining structure. The relative importance of the two levels of bargaining is the subject of dispute. Brown (1981) argues that national agreements now have little significance except to act as a safety net for the occasional support of the lowest paid; the brunt of pay determination occurs at domestic levels. Elliot (1980, 1981), and Elliot and Steele (1976) dispute this analysis and use New Earnings Survey data to argue that national agreements continue to be the only or most important form of collective bargaining for substantial areas of manufacturing as well as for much of the public sector, and that for several of the manufacturing industries the proportion of standard weekly earnings accounted for by national negotiations actually rose in the ten years to 1978.

GROWING LEGISLATION ON INDIVIDUAL RIGHTS AND TRIPARTITE ADMINISTRATION

As domestic bargaining re-emerged and became formalised, another major change was affecting the traditional collective bargaining system. Governments continued to maintain their services of conciliation and inquiry, voluntary arbitration and wage council support for the low paid, but began to discard the traditional passivity for more active and interventionist measures. Government response to the growth of domestic bargaining and changes in collective labour laws are the subject of Chapter 9. In this chapter we review some of the less highly publicised and politically contentious, but nonetheless significant, moves towards state intervention.

Legislation to Provide a Statutory Floor of Individual Rights
From the 1960s the UK began, for the first time, to develop a substantial body of labour laws concerning individual rights. Many of these laws were modelled on earlier and more comprehensive

continental legislation and the laws on equal opportunities followed the more advanced legislation on equal rights of the USA. The development of state intervention in these areas was therefore seen as following practice abroad and was largely non-controversial in the UK, but it marked the first steps in the shift away from the traditionally passive state role in industrial relations.

i   *The Contracts of Employment Act (1963)* gave employees, for the first time in Britain, the legal right to written particulars of their terms and conditions of employment, and it specified periods of notice that an employer must give before terminating employment.

ii *The Industrial Training Act (1964)* gave government support to the training of employees by requiring employers to pay a training levy which was used to fund government-approved training schemes approved or administered by new Industrial Training Boards.

iii *The Redundancy Payments Act (1965)* gave employees the right to claim compensation for the loss of their jobs, if dismissal was caused by technological or economic change. This acceptance by the state that workers had 'property rights' to their employment was a recognition of deep seated feelings among employees, and was supported by managerial arguments that this would help overcome resistance to the restructuring of British industry.

iv Legislation against discrimination in employment on the grounds of race or sex was passed in the *Race Relations Act* (1968), the *Equal Pay Act* (1970), and the *Sex Discrimination Act* (1975). These attempted to outlaw discrimination in access to jobs, treatment within jobs, and payment. Discrimination has proved to be extraordinarily difficult to prove in court and the practical effects of this legislation disappointed many of its advocates.

v   Legislation against *unfair dismissal* has had more impact. This was recommended by the Donovan Commission (1968) and employees were first given the right to claim compensation or reinstatement in the Industrial Relations Act (1971). The provisions on unfair dismissal were retained when that act was repealed.

vi *The Employment Protection Act (1975)* added rights to a modest guaranteed payment when laid off, the right to payment during medical suspension, to itemised pay statements, written reasons for dismissal, paid time off to look for work or arrange training in the event of redundancy, paid time off for shop steward training, the right not to be dismissed for pregnancy, and the right to reinstatement after a period of maternity leave.

In 1978 many of these individual rights were drawn together in the Employment Protection (Consolidation) Act. In fifteen years a body of individual labour law had been created, putting the UK more in line with other industrialised states. Politicians now argue about the detailed terms of individual protection, but the existence of these statutory floors now seems established. When the Thatcher government took office in 1979 it acted to restrict the scope and limit the application of the employment protection given by its predecessor. It extended qualifying periods and exempted small firms, but the framework of individual protection survived; indeed, pregnant women were granted time off to attend ante-natal clinics in 1980.

The Growth of Tripartite Agencies

With the development of legislation on individual rights went a growth of state agencies to implement and enforce such rights.

Industrial tribunals were established in 1964 and have since developed to have jurisdiction over claims arising from all the laws listed in (ii)–(vi) above. The tribunals now employ about 600 staff in 25 regional offices and consider over 50,000 cases a year. Industrial tribunals are the nearest the UK has come to a well established system of specialised labour courts. However the tribunals have been designed to make them as 'voluntary' as possible and to separate and protect them from the politically turbulent waters of collective labour relations. The tribunals themselves consist of a chairperson with legal experience, and two assessors, drawn from two panels nominated by the CBI and TUC. Applicants and respondents may present their own case without solicitors or barristers. Appeals on points of law are heard by the *Employment Appeal Tribunal* (established in 1975) and the House of Lords.

The *Equal Opportunity Commission* and the *Commission for Racial Equality* review and help promote the laws on sexual and racial discrimination. The Commissions are part of the state's administrative machine, responsible for administering public policy and law, and yet they are tripartite, with governing bodies composed of representatives of the CBI, TUC and independents.

In 1973 and 74 some of the traditional functions of the Department of Employment (D.E.) were 'hived off' to be administered by similar tripartite institutions.

The *Advisory, Conciliation and Arbitration Service* (ACAS) continues the traditional conciliation and arbitration services once carried out by civil servants. Its governing council consists of a full-time chairman, 3 CBI, 3 TUC and 3 independent members, chosen after consultation, by the Secretary of State for Employment. ACAS has about 730 staff in London and 9 regional offices and handled 50,000 requests for conciliation and arbitration, and resolved 19,000 conciliation cases in 1981. Some requests for arbitration are passed to the *Central Arbitration Committee* (CAC), a tripartite panel which heard 8 requests for voluntary arbitration in 1981. CAC also provides unilateral arbitration on disclosure of information (see p. 203) and on the Fair Wages Resolutions (p. 59).

The *Manpower Services Commission* was established in 1974 to take over traditional DE functions in manpower forecasting, the encouragement of training and the administration of labour exchanges. It contains an Employment Services Division which runs over 1,000 local employment offices and jobcentres, providing a placement service and employment advice. It also provides a training service which supports the Industrial Training Boards, and finances some training. Since 1975 it has run special programmes to provide some relief to unemployed schoolleavers, which by 1981 spent £277.5 millions of the MSC's total budget of £869.3 million. The Commission has about 25,000 staff.

The *Health and Safety Commission* was established to take over the administration of health and safety legislation, rationalised into a comprehensive Health and Safety at Work Act in 1974. The various inspectorates (see page 160) were grouped into a *Health and Safety Executive*, with about 4,000 staff, which is responsible for the enforcement of the health and safety regulations, aided by union-appointed safety representatives at the place of work.

Wages councils, the tripartite institutions with the longest history have remained broadly unchanged except for rationalisation to reduce their numbers. They continue to be serviced by the DE.

The extension of laws on individual rights and the growth of tripartite administration represent a small but significant movement from the traditionally passive to a more active and interventionist state. The tripartite agencies are usually concerned to work with and support the traditional institutions of free collective bargaining but they changed the role of the state and represent a hint of 'corporate government' to anyone vehemently opposed to any deviation from liberal principles.

ALTERNATIVES TO THE FREE COLLECTIVE BARGAINING
TRADITION IN THE UK

The traditional system of collective bargaining still pervades employment relations within the UK but is now under considerable strain from the challenge of domestic bargaining, from state intervention on individual rights, and from the torrent of legislation on collective labour relations which we discuss in the next chapter. In the context of a system in the process of change, it is relevant to note the traditions which suggest possible alternatives to free collective bargaining in the UK. The ancient policies of direct state intervention to regulate pay and employment conditions have always had some adherents, and this tradition continues among advocates of incomes policy and national planning. More radical demands for workers' control and industrial democracy also continue to present a challenge and an alternative to collective bargaining. Meanwhile an anti-union advocacy of unilateral managerial control, long heard in the USA, is beginning to be voiced in the UK.

Workers' Control and Industrial Democracy
In several periods demands for workers' self-government have made an impact on British industrial relations. The first was in the early decades of the twentieth century. Radical political change seemed highly probable, the Labour party was being formed and working-class power and discontent were very evident in the 'great unrest' so visible in the strike statistics. Demands for workers control were made by Syndicalists, Guild Socialists and many advocates of industrial unionism who argued that trade unions should be involved, not in accommodative collective bargaining, but in the management and government of industry. *The Miners Next Step* (published in 1919), which called for the nationalisation of the mines and their management by a board on which half the seats were held by trade unions, was an example of the specific proposals being made. However the optimism for new methods of workers control dissipated with the Great Depression.

Demands for workers' control re-emerged in 1945 when the Labour government gained office on a programme of radical social and economic change. However, the government adopted the policy of extending and supporting collective bargaining. Even the nationalisation policy, which brought one-fifth of British industry under government ownership, endorsed collective bargaining as the method of employee participation and left management to operate in the conventional way, through separate channels. For those who had hoped for more direct industrial democracy, nationalisation was a disappointment.

Industrial democracy was again widely discussed in the general review of industrial relations in the 1960s and 1970s and proposals were made for the involvement of unions in management. An interesting example of such proposals originating from shop stewards was the Lucas Aerospace Joint Shop Stewards Committee Alternative Corporate Plan, which in the late 1970s argued the need for the development of alternative products in order to protect Lucas' UK workforce in the face of declining defence sales and to turn Lucas resources to socially useful production (see Coates and Topham, 1980). The 1970s saw a spate of new workers' co-operatives and of sit-ins or work-ins challenging managerial decisions to close plants. Although the motive behind many of these was largely job protection and resistance to redundancy, they represented new opportunities for the advocates of workers control (K. Coates, 1980).

Britain's membership of the EEC brought European practices of worker participation by works councils and workers on company boards into discussions in the UK. Despite many union suspicions of the dangers of European forms of industrial participation, the TUC was drawn into the debate on worker directors and in 1974 proposed that 50 per cent of company board seats should be taken by workers elected through the trade union machinery. The Labour government's response to the rising interest in industrial democracy is discussed in Chapter 9 (pp. 204–6).

Government Intervention – Variants of Corporatism
There have always been critics of the traditionally passive government role in British industrial relations. For a period from 1918 to the 1930s there were many calls for policies for reconstructing British industry in which government would actively help to co-ordinate both capital and labour. Guild Socialists argued that industry should remain privately owned but that the state should co-ordinate economic activity and ensure that the control and management of each industry was in the hands of Guilds of employees. Beatrice and Sydney Webb argued for two Parliaments, one Social and one Political. The Social Parliament would supervise economic activity, with Standing Committees of the Social Parliament responsible for each socialised industry. An industry's Standing Committee would appoint a board of representatives of management, trade unions and some customers to be responsible for day to day administration (Webb and Webb, 1920). Some Conservative MPs joined this debate, the most famous being Harold Macmillan. In 1932 he advocated representative national councils for each industry to be recognised by the government as 'the authority with which it would deal on all matters affecting the interests which they represented', with labour associated with

these councils 'in all matters affecting the welfare of the workers with a view to avoiding Strikes and Lockouts'.

The Mond – Turner Talks

In 1927 attempts were made to give concrete expression to the ideas about reconstruction outlined above. A group of twenty large employers, led by Sir Alfred Mond (founder of ICI) began a series of talks with the general council of the TUC under Ben Turner. The talks were intended to develop closer collaboration between unions, employers and government following the crisis of the 1926 General Strike. Proposals were drawn up for a central body, representing the TUC and the two central employer organisations of the time – the BEC and FBI – to act as a forum for central discussions on industrial disputes and on wider issues of industrial reorganisation and the government's economic policy. These proposals were welcomed by the weakened TUC but were opposed by many employers. In particular the engineering employers, a powerful group within the BEC, saw no need to grant trade unions this central recognition and distrusted the centralisation of power that would occur within the employers own organisations. The employers therefore rejected this historically unique, peacetime attempt to establish the more centralised, and corporate regulation of industrial affairs in the UK (Gospel, 1979).

The National Economic Development Council

Proposals for the peacetime involvement of government in economic and labour affairs revived with the Macmillan government of 1957–62. Macmillan sought the involvement of employers and employees in economic planning, and the planning of incomes. Macmillan's contribution to the trials with incomes policy that have been a feature of post war public policy, can be seen from Table 8.3. A more permanent contribution to the development of tripartite planning was the establishment in 1962 of the National Economic Development Council, which still exists. Senior government ministers, the TUC and the CBI have seats on the NEDC and have used their meetings to discuss the shape of many government policies. NEDC ('Neddy') is supported by a staff of 211 in its National Economic Development Office and there are 'little Neddies' established for individual industries.

Incomes Policy

The retreat from passivity and the growth of government intervention has been most obvious in incomes policy. Table 8.3 illustrates the complex history of government attempts to intervene in the regulation of incomes since the Second World War. Policies have been introduced by governments concerned to become involved in

Table 8.3 Post-war Incomes Policies

Date	Instrument: Agreement, White Paper or Act	Policy norms on pay, etc.	Implementing institutions	TUC/CBI position
1948–50 *Attlee Govt* Wage restraint	'Personal Incomes, Costs and Prices'	No general increase in money incomes except for labour shortages	None	Grudging support of TUC at 1949 congress. Employer support
1961 *Macmillan Govt*	i) Pay pause in public sector	Private sector asked to follow pay pause	None	No TUC support
1962	ii) Incomes policy: the next step	2–2½% pay increase	National Incomes Commission	
1963	iii) Norm revised	2–3½% pay increase		
1964 *Wilson Govt* Voluntary policy	Tripartite declaration of intent on prices, productivity and incomes	Pay increases to keep in line with national output		TUC, CBI agreement
1965	'Prices and Incomes Policy' 'Prices and Incomes Policy: an early warning system'	Norm of 3–3½% with exceptions for low pay, increased productivity, manpower needs or anomalies. Restraint on price increases	National Board for Prices and Incomes to vet and approve claims	TUC set up own early warning system to vet claims

Date					
July 1966–1970	Statutory policy freeze	Prices and Incomes Act 1966	General standstill. Exceptions as above emphasising productivity	NBPI given power to delay increases. Early warning compulsory	TUC continued own vetting system
	Period of severe restraint	'Prices and Incomes Policy after June 1967' 'Productivity, Prices and Incomes in 1968 and 1969'	2½% to 4½% increases		
1971	*Heath Govt* Public sector policy	Public sector restraint	n–1 policy to decelerate pay increases		No TUC support. CBI initiated 5% limit on price increases in private sector
1972	Statutory policy	Counter Inflation Act 1972 Stage I	5 month freeze on pay, prices, rents and dividends	Pay Board 1973–4	No TUC support
1973		Stage II	£1 + 4% up to a maximum of £250 p.a. except for moves to equal pay or for frozen agreements. 12 months between pay increases	Prices Commission 1973–. Powers to vet agreements. Rigid codes to determine when increases allowed	

Table 8.3 Post-war Incomes Policies (Continued)

Date	Instrument: Agreement, White Paper or Act	Policy norms on pay, etc.	Implementing institutions	TUC/CBI position
1973–4	Stage III November 1973–July 1974	7% of total wage bill with minimum of £2.25 per worker per week and maximum of £350 p.a. Threshold payments of 40p per person for each 1% the retail price index rises above 7%. Exceptional increases for equal pay, efficiency schemes, unsocial hours, major anomalies		
1974	Wilson/Callaghan Govt Social Contract	TUC Congress approved guidelines	Guidelines to maintain but not increase real incomes except for low paid where aim at £30 per week. Increases only every 12 months		TUC active support

1975/6	'The Attack on Inflation' endorsed policy proposed by TUC in July 1975	Flat rate £6 per week. Nothing for those over £8,500 p.a.	Prices Commission to reject applications for price increases where pay limits not observed	TUC active support
1976/7	'The Attack on Inflation – the Second Year'	5% general limit with a maximum of £4 per week and a minimum of £2.50. 12-month gap between settlements		TUC active support
1977/8 July	'Winning the Battle Against Inflation'	October 1977, 10% limit with extra for productivity. October 1978, 5% limit		Not supported by TUC
1978/9		5% limit with exceptions for lowest paid, productivity schemes and anomalies	Standing Commission on Pay Comparability established to resolve public sector disputes	Not supported by TUC
Thatcher Govt		Exhortation to reduce expectations		
Winter 1981		Cash limits of 6% in public sector		
1982		Cash limits of 4% in public sector		
1983		Cash limits of 3.5% in public sector		

social and economic planning – like Macmillan's, or the Wilson governments from 1964 and 1974. They have also been introduced by governments which initially adopted non-interventionist principles. Policies have sometimes been voluntary, sometimes compulsory; some specified simple pay norms or guidelines, some complex formulae. All restricted free collective bargaining by setting government objectives to override the possible outcome of negotiated settlements on pay. The pressures which have tempted so many postwar governments to attempt to affect the results of free collective bargaining have been discussed in Chapter 7 and the problems of these centralised regulations over pay are discussed in Chapter 10.

So far, incomes policies have had mixed success. Even those which succeeded in reducing pay and inflationary pressures have often degenerated in time into a backlash of frustrated claims based on upset differentials. Incomes policies have been responsible for the return of major official strikes. Macmillan's early pay pause provoked the unprecedented protest of nurses in 1962, Heath's n-l policy for the public sector was defeated by a seven-week coal-mining strike in 1972 which extracted increased concessions from the coal board, an enhanced award from a court of enquiry and final concessions from the Prime Minister negotiating at Downing Street. Heath's statutory policy was challenged again, by the miners in 1974, and on that occasion the government introduced a three-day week throughout the economy to save fuel, and called a 'Who Governs Britain?' election. The period from 1970 to 1974 was marked by postwar records in the days lost by industrial action. In four of the five years, annual totals were higher than in any year since 1926 because of a series of major public sector strikes in coal-mining, the Post Office, local authorities, gas supply and the National Health Service over the application of the government's successive incomes policies. The following government's 'Social Contract' policies were initially based on firm trade union support, and industrial action fell to very low levels. However, further attempts to limit pay rises collapsed in a 'winter of discontent' in 1978–9. There were 29.4 million days lost in 1979, 10.3 million in national stoppages in the engineering industry, and many disputes occurred in parts of the public sector which had previously been largely strike-free.

There have been innumerable attempts to construct a viable incomes policy in the UK in recent years; none, so far, have achieved lasting success. Nevertheless, state intervention in the regulation of pay and other forms of income remain (often in protective disguise) on the agenda of debate in the Labour, Social Democrat, Liberal and moderate wing of the Conservative parties. Incomes policy has developed into a new tradition of state inter-

vention in open conflict with the tradition of free collective bargaining.

CONCLUSION

Relations between employers and the emerging British trade
unions were slowly regularised in the UK as industry-wide employers' associations reached agreements with trade unions to
establish industry-level disputes committees and set standard pay
rates and conditions of employment. The national substantive
agreements set a framework of basic conditions, leaving detailed
interpretation to be resolved at the workplace. In the period after
the Second World War this system of national, industry-wide collective bargaining, and the associated absence of government
involvement in employment relations, was widely regarded as a
firmly established, mature and democratic method for handling
conflicts at work.

Since 1960 the traditional system of collective bargaining has
been subject to strain arising from the growth of workplace, shop-
steward-led bargaining, of formal single-employer negotiations
and of increased government intervention.

Collective bargaining still dominates the determination of employment conditions for the majority of British employees. The
collective bargaining structure is complex, with the network of still
active national negotiating bodies, especially in the public sector,
now supplemented by many institutions for plant-level and multi-
plant bargaining. However, the spread of formal domestic bargaining rarely involves negotiation for all plants of large multi-plant
companies and does not cross the international boundaries of the
MNEs.

With the strains imposed on traditional collective bargaining,
old demands for workers' control, alternative forms of worker
participation and for greater control by the state have re-emerged.
Government reactions to this controversy are the subject of
Chapter 9.

Government Attempts to Reconstruct British Industrial Relations

The last fifteen years have seen a series of government-initiated attempts to alter British industrial relations. The postwar consensus which supported collective bargaining and a passive, background role for the state, has crumbled. All recent governments have produced major and radically different proposals for change.

An analysis of these government policies highlights the increasing significance of the role of the state, discussed in Chapter 7, and illustrates the conflicting theoretical perspectives outlined at the start of this book. Government attempts to promote the 'reform' of industrial relations have been premised on different theories. Old-fashioned liberalism is revived in recurrent attacks on the closed shop. Liberal-collectivist justifications for collective bargaining have been used to support state intervention both to increase and to decrease trade union power. There have been elements of corporatism in many of the new institutions and laws proposed, although corporatist arguments have rarely been used openly. Finally, neo-Marxist analyses have provided a critique of the proposals for legislative change. The different interpretations and judgements of the policies tried so far have generated fierce academic debates on pluralism and corporatism, mirrored at the political level by increasingly virulent arguments between social democrats (within and outside the Social Democratic party), democratic or parliamentary socialists, and socialists who reject the parliamentary means to radical social change. The end of the old consensus is all too evident in the conflicting legislation and the turmoil of political debate!

In this chapter we review the major prescriptions for changing collective labour relations in the UK and analyse the theoretical perspectives underlying different government policies. Some recent policies are now seen as catastrophic failures responsible for threatening constitutional crises, others have introduced permanent change. Together they demonstrate the central position now taken by industrial relations in British domestic policy. In the absence of the emollient of economic growth and with no new consensus on the handling of employment relations, the controversy surrounding public policy in the area is likely to continue.

THE DONOVAN REPORT: THE EXTENSION AND RESTRUCTURING OF COLLECTIVE BARGAINING

The recent series of changes started with a Royal Commission on Trade Unions and Employers' Associations chaired by Lord Donovan. The Donovan Commission was set up by the Labour government in 1965 in the context of mounting pressure from business interests for legal changes to curb unofficial strikes, of trade union concern at judge-made changes in labour law, and of a government concerned to regulate the economy. The Commission's Report (1968) accepted that unofficial strikes were a cause for concern but argued that they were only a symptom of underlying ills and not in themselves the most significant problem. Neither the strikes nor the underlying problems would be solved by changes in labour law; instead, British industrial relations were in need of 'procedural reform'.

The Donovan Report is worth analysing because it was welcomed by many trade union and management specialists, it represented the views of the Oxford School of academics, important in industrial relations at that time, and it had some impact on later government policy. Donovan advocated government action but not the use of law, to encourage employers to shift the collective bargaining system into a more widespread, centralised and bureaucratic form that would match new levels of managerial decision-making and would be consistent with a state-administered incomes policy. We look first at Donovan's prescription for the reform of British industrial relations and then at the extent that Donovan envisaged a change in the role of the state.

Donovan's Procedural Reform

Donovan advocated the reform of industrial relations procedures, rather than industrial relations laws. 'Procedure' was used in two rather different ways by the authors of the report. One meaning, derived from the old National Disputes Procedure agreements, defined procedures as negotiated provisions specifying the rights and processes to be used by the parties to collective bargaining. The other meaning was much wider, and derived from Dunlop's sociological discussion of substantive and procedural norms (pp. 15–17). Under this second meaning, procedural rules were all non-substantive rules at work, including 'methods used in determining differential levels of rewards, rights and privileges, or in recruiting employees and allocating them to jobs, or in promoting, supervising, disciplining and dismissing them' (Flanders, 1965). Procedural reform with the first meaning meant the restructuring of existing collective bargaining arrangements along more bureaucratic lines. Procedural reform under the second meaning meant the extension of collective bargaining to new groups of employees and new subject areas.

1   *Procedural reform as the restructuring of collective bargaining institutions*   This was presented as the solution to unofficial strikes and to the underlying problem of increased workgroup bargaining power in a tight labour market. Restructuring was necessary because the old industry-level negotiating institutions were ill-equipped to handle the pressures arising from shopfloor bargaining and the UK had developed two systems of collective bargaining: (1) the old national system with formal, industry-wide institutions playing an increasingly irrelevant role; and (2) informal unco-ordinated and 'chaotic' bargaining on the shopfloor. The shopfloor relations satisfied those directly involved as they were flexible and customary, but they caused inefficiencies which acted against the long-term interest of both unions and management. Negotiation at domestic levels could not, and should not be stopped, but should be conducted through new institutions which enabled senior managers and union officials to control its results.

Donovan advocated the bureaucratisation of domestic collective bargaining (see also Goldthorpe 1974). In place of constant, often covert bargaining it recommended formal periodic negotiations conducted through properly authorised Joint Negotiating Committees for factories and plants. The division of labour surrounding such negotiations would be clarified and in particular the authority and responsibilities of shop stewards would be defined and main board directors would be held responsible for their managers' negotiations. The existing confusion of locally agreed terms – some written into agreements, some in minutes of meetings and some in remembered precedent – would all be replaced by single comprehensive agreements clearly specifying in written form the jointly determined rules applied to work.

2   *Procedural reform as the extension of collective bargaining*   This aspect of procedural reform was dealt with more superficially, but did, potentially, have a much wider relevance than restructuring, which applied primarily to the engineering, construction and shipbuilding industries. Donovan argued that employment terms should be regulated by collective bargaining, and supported this with the traditional liberal-collectivist arguments that collective bargaining was democratic, flexible and provided a channel for institutionalising conflict at work (pp. 13 and 14).

Proposals for more direct industrial democracy were dismissed almost contemptuously in the Report. Donovan supported collective bargaining, but its proposals for the extension of collective bargaining were sketchy. It suggested that unions be given the right to a government-sponsored inquiry into recognition disputes (i.e. where employers refused trade union demands for collective bargaining) and that wages councils be reviewed to see if independent collective bargaining could replace them. However, the question of extending the depth and coverage of existing collective bargaining was only touched on, with the hope that bargaining be extended to cover disciplinary procedures at work, the facilities granted to shop stewards and redundancy arrangements and terms.

Donovan and the role of the state
Although Donovan's recommendations were presented as in the tradition of the unique British 'voluntarism' they did, in reality, represent a significant shift from the traditional, passive state.

In one respect, Donovan took a traditional view of the role of the state. It opposed the use of law as an agent of state intervention and its rejection of the mounting demands for legal change was strong and clear. The law was irrelevant to the structural problems underlying unofficial strikes and to use law would hamper the necessary restructuring, as it would be seen as unjust and irrelevant, merely bringing the law itself into disrepute. Only when domestic bargaining was reformed and formalised should the possibility of using legal sanctions against any remaining unofficial strikers be reviewed.

Donovan rejected the use of law as a change agent, but it did call for government action to promote the procedural reforms it wished to see. Given its dislike for direct legal action it suggested that a state register of domestic agreements and a new state agency, combining research and consultancy functions, should be used as the agents of change.

All boards of companies over a certain size (e.g. 5,000 employees) would be required to register all their local collective agreements with the government. These agreements would be vetted by the Department of Employment and any company having difficulties restructuring its local arrangements along the lines advocated by Donovan would be referred by the government to a new industrial relations commission (the CIR). This would have powers to conduct an inquiry and make recommendations, and although these recommendations would not have legal force the CIR was envisaged as an interventionist agency. Its brief was to promote the changes outlined in the Donovan blueprint for reform (in contrast, for example to the US Federal Mediation Service's strictly servicing role to industry) and it was hoped that by research, consultancy and advice the CIR could guide even reluctant parties along the specified path. Some legal pressure would be put on employers who refused to implement a recommendation to recognise a trade union, but even this would take the indirect form of compulsory arbitration on terms and conditions of employment.

In what way should the Donovan proposals be interpreted? Goldthorpe suggested that Donovan sought the bureaucratisation of domestic bargaining in order to assist management and increase labour productivity. However in the light of the considerable managerial resistance to some of the proposals and the experience of the CIR discussed below, a better interpretation is that Donovan sought to extend, restructure and formalise collective bargaining in order to create institutions consistent with increased state involvement in the regulation of employment. Although the Report did not discuss the details of incomes policy, arguing that this was not in its remit, it did say that incomes policies were a desirable and necessary part of public policy. It argued that its proposals would make effective incomes policy easier to sustain and it envisaged the new agency working in parallel with the existing incomes policy agency – the National Board for Prices and Incomes, which had already argued the need to rationalise domestic bargaining and increase labour productivity. As Donovan avoided too direct a reference to incomes policy, the philosophical and practical problems associated with such policies were not discussed. It was apparently assumed that national, tripartite negotiations between government, unions and employers could create a new level of collective bargaining that would, in a voluntary way, provide a rational form of incomes policy. More bureaucratically structured domestic negotiations would aid the administration of centrally determined employment policies. How the state would use its considerable powers against the opponents to central policy, and how it would bargain with the representatives of capital and labour were not discussed.

The Donovan Report can therefore be interpreted as supporting collective bargaining but wishing to reshape the collective bargaining system so that it could be integrated into political decision-making, with tripartite negotiations on employment policy taking place at the centre of the structure of negotiations. This corporatist element of Donovan's prescription was not explicitly spelt out but did, nevertheless, lie behind the main proposals. The usual liberal-collectivist argument that collective bargaining removed employment relations from politics is conspicuously missing from Donovan's defence of collective bargaining. More explicitly corporatist arguments were later developed in an article by Flanders and Fox, 'The Reform of Collective Bargaining: From Donovan to

Durkheim' (1969), which argued that Donovan's more centralised, formalised agreements would cure the anomic loss of agreed regulation within British industry. This analysis may not have been endorsed by other academics in the Oxford School, but it did highlight the corporatist elements of Donovan's prescription.

Donovan's corporatist tendencies were mild and not coercive. It was assumed that more centralised regulations would derive from genuine bargaining, and the report contained no proposals for tighter government control over trade unions' internal affairs. In this area the Report merely stated that union rules should be clear and unambiguous, should contain safeguards for individual members in dispute with their union and that there should be an independent trade union review body, chaired by a lawyer, to hear union members' appeals against disciplinary action taken against them by their unions and to judge disputes between unions and the government registrar over the adequacy of union rules.

The Response to Donovan's Proposals
Donovan claimed to reflect the consensus of expert and reasoned opinion in its Report, and it relied on the existence of such a consensus for the implementation of its proposals. This consensus proved not to exist. The Labour government did not accept the arguments for gradual, non-legal reform and chose instead to seek the legal sanctions of *In Place of Strife* (see below). Many of Donovan's arguments were accepted by unions and by some employers. The proposed CIR was welcomed and the TUC ran a series of 'Post Donovan' conferences. However, the proposals that might have been most relevant to incomes policy were quickly rejected. Four months after Donovan was published, the TUC and CBI drew up a joint statement welcoming many of its recommendations but rejecting the proposal that *all* local agreements be registered with the government and calling instead for the voluntary notification not of all agreements, but only those concerned with procedures for negotiation, handling grievances, etc. The government accepted this modification and the Registry of Agreements became a nominal and largely ignored exercise within the Department of Employment.

The Commission on Industrial Relations 1968–1974
One recommendation which did receive widespread support was for a third party research and consultancy agency to stimulate voluntary procedural reform. The CIR was established in March 1969, headed by George Woodcock, the retiring general secretary of the TUC. The CIR became the main agent for the promulgation of Donovan's policies and although the CIR's final report regretted the lack of government support for this work, the twenty-three

reports produced before the CIR became entangled with the following government's legislation, and some of the 62 reports produced thereafter, provide a practical test for Donovan's procedural reform.

The restructuring of collective bargaining did not go entirely according to Donovan's plan. The CIR attempted to apply the Donovan blueprint wherever it found domestic bargaining, but found some parts of the plan for bureaucratic domestic institutions were more readily accepted than were others. Single, comprehensive agreements specifying all mutual obligations in a written, easy-to-register form where quickly dropped, as no one in the companies concerned could see their advantage. In contrast, proposals to increase the status and facilities of domestic negotiators received active support by those groups which benefited. The CIR left strengthened personnel departments and improved shop steward facilities in many of the companies it studied. The creation of new, formal bargaining committees at local level proved problematic. Although the need for such formal arrangements was usually accepted, the level at which these JNCs should operate often caused fierce controversy as managers sought to divide the workforce in ways that cut across local union unity, and strong groups of employees resisted negotiating as minorities in larger groups. There was no consensus on this aspect of bureaucratisation. Nevertheless the CIR helped reinforce the moves to extend and centralise domestic bargaining in the 1970s, later recorded in the surveys of Brown (1981) and Marsh (1981).

On the expansion of collective bargaining, the CIR produced 45 reports on recognition disputes. The CIR's general advocacy of collective bargaining probably helped spread union recognition in areas, like the finance industry, where employer resistance was still prevalent and acted as a block against the strategy of using internal, employer-sponsored staff associations to provide an inferior version of collective bargaining. Eight reports were written on wages councils, and the CIR recommended mergers, the abolition of some councils and the introduction of 'statutory JICs' which would bargain normally but have their agreements supported by the inspectorate. The CIR simplified the wage council system, but whether this helped the low paid or radically extended collective bargaining must be open to some doubt. The extension of existing agreements to cover new areas proved highly problematic. The CIR met resistance from employers when it recommended that bargaining cover areas previously determined by management, and resistance from workgroups when it called for bargaining over employee-determined work practices. There proved to be no consensus on extending the subjects covered by collective bargaining.

'IN PLACE OF STRIFE' AND THE 1969 INDUSTRIAL RELATIONS BILL

Although the Labour government of 1964–70 welcomed the Donovan Report and established the CIR, it did not accept Donovan's advice. Instead, no doubt encouraged by the media's attack on Donovan's 'toothless proposals', it proposed legislation to give the government power (1) to impose a twenty-eight-day conciliation pause on unofficial strikes thought to harm national interests, and (2) to impose a compulsory ballot of union members before official strikes similarly thought to harm the public interest. It also agreed to implement some of Donovan's proposals, but this was given secondary importance and in April 1969 the government announced that it intended to legislate on the so-called 'penal clauses', leaving the other matters until after the election. The Prime Minister, Harold Wilson, and his Secretary of State for Employment, Barbara Castle, clearly believed that anti-strike legislation would be an asset in the polls. The move threw the Labour Movement into turmoil. Pressure from the unions and the TUC was supported by a significant number of backbench MPs, and the government was forced to climb down with the assurance of a 'solemn and binding undertaking' from the TUC to tackle the strike problems by changing its own rules to permit TUC intervention in unofficial and inter-union disputes. The 1969 Bill which emerged from this compromise excluded the penal clauses and concentrated on those Donovan measures which had the TUC's approval.

The Labour government therefore started the recent moves to legislate against strikers. It had already made history, in 1966, by introducing a statutory incomes policy backed by criminal sanctions against those who struck against government orders to delay pay awards. These sanctions had not been used, but the government was presumably encouraged to believe that other curbs against strikers would be similarly, if reluctantly, accepted. The TUC's successful campaign against the penal clauses was immediately followed by a battle against far more radical legislation.

THE 1970–4 CONSERVATIVE GOVERNMENT AND THE INDUSTRIAL RELATIONS ACT

In 1970 Edward Heath's Conservative government came to power with the reform of Britain's industrial relations a major part of its manifesto. Rejecting Donovan, industrial relations problems were seen as derived from excessive trade union power and it was confidently assumed that the creation of a new framework of collective labour laws would provide the solution. The 1971 Act therefore repealed much of the previous law on collective labour relations and in place of the old immunities and 'legal abstention' put an interventionist system centred on a new labour court, the National Industrial Relations Court (NIRC). A new list of civil wrongs, named Unfair Industrial Practices (UIPs) were introduced as the means of reshaping trade unions' relationships with their members and regulating employee power in bargaining.

The Act's short and stormy life provides one of the most dramatic stories of recent public policy. Although the Act no longer survives on the statute book, its history is worth studying because of the remarkable constitutional crisis it provoked, and because legislation with similar intent is likely to occur again. The history clearly illustrates the pitfalls surrounding collective labour laws.

The Provisions of the 1971 Industrial Relations Act
Before the Donovan Commission reported, the Conservative party had produced a policy paper which identified the unions as the main cause of industrial relations problems and proposed legally binding agreements, the outlawing of the closed shop and penalties on unofficial strikes as a general cure-all. These proposals were put in the 1971 Act, but in addition some of Donovan's arguments about the need to restructure bargaining and strengthen official unionism were taken on board, together with institutions and laws transplanted from the USA, the whole making an Act of extraordinary complexity and length. The most important provisions were:

1   *Labour Courts:* a new system of labour courts was created, incorporating the existing industrial tribunals (see p. 175) and headed by the NIRC, with High Court powers.

2   *Trade union registration:* Before 1971 trade unions could register with the Registrar of Friendly Societies in order to gain tax exemption on provident benefits. The registrar's significance was, however, slight. The 1971 Act created a Trade Union Registrar with power to vet and regulate trade union rules, specifying over twenty requirements on, for example, who had the power to authorise official strikes. Non-registered unions lost not only the old tax advantage (worth £800,000 per annum for a union like the TGWU), but lost immunity against claims for damages for breach of employment contracts, put their officials at risk of similar claims, could be subject to unlimited damages in court actions, and could not benefit from new provisions to assist trade union recognition.

3   *Outlawing the closed shop:* Pre-entry closed shops (see p. 108)

were declared void and post-entry closed shops were nullified by giving all employees the right *not* to belong to a registered or unregistered trade union. Closed shops were, at the time, widely used among manual workers in certain industries to support union organisation and encourage membership unity, and the authors of the act realised that the liberal individual freedom *not* to join could undermine collective bargaining. Equity, the actors' union, lobbied the government, emphasising their need for a closed shop during the passage of the Act. Provision was therefore made for complex procedures to grant 'approved closed shops' for unions like Equity or the National Union of Seamen, and 'agency shops' to provide a limited union security for anyone else.

4 *Legally binding agreements:* Written collective agreements were presumed to be intended to be legally binding unless they specified otherwise. Shop stewards calling strikes in breach of disputes procedures could be sued if agreements were binding, and the CIR could draft procedure agreements to be imposed where none existed.

5 *Emergency ballots and cooling-off periods:* The Secretary of State for Employment could apply to the NIRC to prohibit any industrial action thought to be gravely injurious to the economy for up to sixty days, and to order a compulsory ballot to gauge membership support of strike action.

6 *Union recognition and the determination of bargaining agents:* Provisions here reflected a desire to rationalise and spread collective bargaining, as Donovan recommended, but by using legalistic methods. Registered unions could request CIR investigation of their recognition disputes. However, complex new procedures for determining bargaining agents and units were added and the NIRC was given the power to enforce recommendations which benefited registered unions.

The Act deferred to liberal-collectivist traditions by emphasising the value of voluntary conciliation and requiring the NIRC and the CIR to try conciliation before resorting to law. It acknowledged Donovan's influence by retaining the CIR's powers to promote procedural reform and by instituting a 'Code of Practice' based on Donovan's prescriptions, to be issued by the Department of Employment as guidance to good practice.

The Theoretical Confusions of the 1971 Act
The provisions of the 1971 Act were not only ambitious and far-reaching: they were riven with theoretical contradictions. Moran

(1977) and Weekes *et al.* (1975), in their separate studies of the Act, note the problems caused by its contradictory objectives. Some of the provisions, like the registrar to vet trade union government, the granting of privileged status to registered unions and government support for recognition, had some affinity with the reformist values and analysis of Donovan with its collectivist, mildly corporatist prescriptions for the strengthening and rationalisation of collective bargaining. Many other provisions harked back to a unitary dislike of unions and a distrust of all their activities in the labour market. The outlawing of the closed shop, the rights for individuals to join or not join unions, provisions for individual union members to take complaints against their union to the registrar or the NIRC, and for small groups of individuals to challenge established bargaining arrangements, were all desirable from a unitary or liberal-individualist perspective which put individual liberties above collective rights. However from a liberal-collectivist or corporatist perspective such individual rights were disruptive of necessary social regulations, they were likely to encourage the splintering of bargaining arrangements, and they weakened a union's ability to discipline disruptive members or maintain the unity needed for effective bargaining. The 1971 Act sought to strengthen both unions as agents of control over their members, and the individual in dispute with his union and its regulatory arrangements.

The contradictory provisions of the 1971 Act have been blamed on the contrasting influences of conservative lawyers – with their strong liberal-individualist traditions – as opposed to conservative businessmen, more attuned to a pluralist perspective and more attracted to corporatist arrangements (see K. Wedderburn, 1980). However, although the influence of conservative lawyers, notably Sir Geoffrey Howe, was very important in the drafting of the Act, as Moran points out, businessmen were also calling for the abolition of the closed shop and for general curbs on union influence and power. The unitary, individualistic perspective underlay much employer rhetoric and this encouraged the drafters of the law to assume that employers would not only support but also use the new provisions, an assumption which proved incorrect. Moran notes similar contradictions within the electorate. Opinion polls showed over 80 per cent of the adult population initially in favour of anti-union legislation. Nevertheless once the laws were operated this liberal support evaporated: not only was there widespread collusion between employers and workpeople to negate the legislation, but there was also massive sympathy for the unionists who defied the new laws. Moran concludes that there is a widespread acceptance of liberal, individualist ideologies in the UK but no corresponding willingness to abandon pluralist practice.

An analysis which recognises the importance of class relations would add that the 1971 Act was primarily an attack on union bargaining power but that it was attempted at a time when labour markets were still sufficiently tight to prevent employers risking outright confrontations with their workforces for the sake of an over-complex law of confused objectives.

The Discrediting of the 1971 Act

In 1971 the Act was presented as one of the most ambitious attempts to reconstruct a major social institution and it was the main plank of the government's domestic social and economic policy. By 1974 the Act was discredited. Conservative politicians were admitting that major amendments were needed, and the director general of the CBI was reported as saying that it had had a detrimental effect on industrial relations – a remark which many Conservatives believed helped lose them the election of that year. Labour returned to office in 1974 with the repeal of the Act as one of its most popular election pledges.

The extraordinarily rapid destruction of one of the most significant Acts of Parliament in the century highlights the complexity of relations between the state, trade unions and employers. As legislation with similar intent has reappeared under new guises, the actions and events which brought down the 1971 Act merit analysis.

1   *The TUC Policy of Opposition*   The TUC declared the legislation a fundamental attack on unions legitimate rights to operate. The government refused to discuss the TUC objections and the TUC mounted a policy of opposition to the Act as a whole. It boycotted all the agencies of the Act, withdrawing union nominees from the industrial tribunals and the CIR. More importantly, it adopted a policy of deregistration.

Many of the Act's controls were exercised through the registrar. The rewriting of union rules to control steward activity and union discipline, and the provisions for bargaining units and agents depended on union registration. It had been assumed that unions would register and when it became apparent they might not, extra penalties against unregistered unions were added to the draft bill. However, the TUC saw non-registration as the best demonstration of their rejection of the Act and one which had the advantage of being entirely constitutional. It was not illegal to deregister, just very disadvantageous. Even so there was no evidence, in 1971, that the policy would gain union support. For a few unions with large provident funds – like the National Graphical Association (NGA) – the extra tax burden was financially devastating. More widespread concerns arose from deregistration's threat to membership. The National Union of Bank Employees (NUBE) feared the membership gains that would be made by its registered rivals, the Bank Staff Associations, and would not risk deregistration. Both NUBE and the NGA registered and it was clear that, if any major union broke ranks, others would follow to protect their membership from poaching by registered rivals. TUC conferences in March and September 1971 wavered over whether to advise affiliates not to register, or to make it an obligatory policy backed by the threat of expulsion from the TUC. It was recognised that the second policy would not be tenable if one of the larger unions registered. Although there was a small majority for a mandatory policy in March, by September it seemed that unity on deregistration was crumbling.

The TUC's policy of opposition by deregistration was saved by a number of events which boosted union morale at precisely the time when the policy needed to be established. The first event was the NUM's success in breaching government incomes policy by strike action in 1972. This provoked a U-turn in government policy, and the earlier refusal to consult with the TUC was replaced by the establishment of tripartite talks on wage restraint, economic expansion, welfare measures and price controls. The 1971 Act had been premised on the need to remove government from active intervention in the economy, relying instead on the new legal framework to help employers control their own affairs. Therefore the U-turn towards more active government interference both undermined the philosophic basis of the legislation and made the unions feel they could bargain their co-operation for the repeal of the Act. Meanwhile, the experience of the Act in operation, detailed below, was swinging public opinion against the Act. By the next TUC congress in 1972 the mandatory policy of deregistration was assured and only thirty-four unions with a small total membership were expelled.

2   *The Experience of Emergency Ballots*   The first experience of the emergency ballot provisions shook the credibility of the government's claims that a legal framework would guarantee harmony at work. The government chose to use the cooling-off and emergency ballot provisions against the railwaymen in 1972. The unions had started a work to rule after rejecting a government-appointed arbitration award, and it was known that the union executives were not unanimous on a call for further action. The government was therefore confident that a cooling-off period and ballot would prove the members to be unwilling to follow their 'militant' leadership into a strike. The government applied for a cooling-off period and a ballot. To the government's great surprise the ballot showed the railwaymen to be 6 to 1 in favour of their

leader's call for further action. Many years of American experience, which shows that union members treat emergency ballots as a vote of confidence in their union, were confirmed. Faced with the weight of employee opinion, the Railway Board conceded the claim in full without strike action. The government never used its emergency provisions again; when they once more faced industrial action which they felt was gravely injurious to the nation, they tried a ballot of the electorate instead.

3 *Disputes over Containerisation in the Docks, and the Jailing of Stewards* The employment opportunities of dockers were threatened by the development of containers to handle goods sent by sea, especially when the loading and unloading of containers was carried out in inland depots. The demand that this work be done only by dockers brought the dockers into conflict with the owners and employees of the inland depots. Several of these disputes reached the NIRC.

First the NIRC granted an order to a Lancashire firm, Heaton's, ordering the TGWU to stop its dockers blacking the firms' containers at the Liverpool docks. The TGWU refused to appear in court, in line with the TUC policy of opposition to the court, and it was fined £5,000 for contempt. A second firm followed and obtained a similar order. As the blacking had spread, the NIRC fined the TGWU £50,000 and warned that it would freeze all the union's assets. This broke the union boycott of the court and the TGWU obtained TUC permission to defend itself in court. It paid the fine and argued that the union could not be held responsible for the stewards actions. The NIRC's president, Sir John Donaldson, rejected this plea, judging that the intention of the legislators had been to make unions responsible for shop stewards actions because the penalties against the new UIPs were to be applied against organisations and not individuals who might become martyrs. However, this strategy was destroyed, most unexpectedly, by the Court of Appeal. Lord Denning and his colleagues quashed the fine against the union and argued that it was the stewards, not the union, who must be held responsible for the blacking.

An appeal on the Heaton's case was set in motion, but meanwhile the NIRC acted on the new ruling. Stewards leading the blacking of a London depot at Chobham Farm were called to appear before the NIRC. They refused to appear and their imprisonment seemed inevitable when Lord Denning, 'having played his part in torpedoing the Court, now helped launch a lifeboat in the form of the official solicitor' (Moran, 1977, p. 141). The Official Solicitor argued in court on the shop stewards' behalf that there was not sufficient evidence that the stewards were blacking the depot. Several of the stewards were, at the time, gleefully telling news reporters that they *were* picketing the depot and hoped their imminent imprisonment would sway opinion against the Act. The NIRC accepted the Official Solicitor's plea, the stewards were relieved of martyrdom, and the crisis subsided with the authority of the court diminished.

In spite of this dramatic intervention, it was still stewards who were to be held responsible for their actions. With the dispute unresolved and still spreading, a month later the NIRC ordered five shop stewards to Pentonville for refusing to cease their picket of a blacked depot in London operated by Midland Cold Storage, a subsidiary of the giant Vesteys firm of butchers. The result was predictable. By the evening of the same day, docks in London, Liverpool and Hull were at a standstill. Lorry drivers, who had been counter-picketing the docks in support of TGWU members in the blacked depots, withdrew their counter-picket in sympathy with the jailed dockers. The USDAW cold-storage workers who had brought the original action to court expressed their support for the dockers their action had jailed. Strikes broke out in other industries, especially engineering and the publication of newspapers ceased for five days. The general council of the TUC voted for a one-day national strike in protest – although they deferred the date to allow time for a solution to be found – and they withdrew from the tripartite talks with government. The government was saved from this crisis by an unusually speedy decision in the House of Lords reversing the Appeal Court ruling. In less than a week the Lords restored Donaldson's original judgement on the Heaton's case and ruled that the union, not the stewards, must be held responsible for the blacking and picketing. The 'Pentonville Five' were released.

The jailing of the Pentonville Five had an immediate impact on the TUC's deregistration policy. Major unions which had been anxious to remain registered bowed to the opposition to the Act and announced that they would follow TUC policy. With its new legal framework increasingly discredited, the government made more open moves for a bargaining relationship with the unions, but its conciliatory posture was to be constantly disturbed by the fireworks still surrounding the NIRC and the AUEW.

4   *The AUEW in Conflict with the NIRC*   When the TUC relaxed its boycott of the NIRC to allow unions to appear and defend themselves, one union – the AUEW – continued in absolute refusal to recognise the court. This gave rise to some fierce legal battles. The first occurred in 1972 when a Mr Goad obtained an order from the NIRC instructing the AUEW to accept him into membership, despite the local branch's opposition. The union refused to comply and was fined £5,000 for contempt. The fine

was not paid and so was obtained from the union's bank. Mr Goad was still not admitted and the AUEW was fined a further £50,000 and union assets were sequestered to pay. As engineering employees struck in protest at this action, Mr Goad shattered the pomp and sanctity surrounding the court action by publicly offering to withdraw his case in return for a cash settlement.

The next confrontation concerned a closed shop which proved to have the support of the employer. An employee of Chrysler resigned from the AUEW, which had a closed shop at the plant where he worked, went to court and obtained judicial confirmation of his right not to join a union. Mr Langston was proceeding with his case in the higher courts and attempting to sue the AUEW, when Chrysler sacked him, conceded unfair dismissal and paid him compensation. The NIRC was faced with clear evidence that the workforce would not work with him, and that Chrysler was not prepared to risk its output for the sake of the individual freedom of the odd non-unionist. The NIRC judged that it would be impractical to order Mr Langston's reinstatement and the closed shop was seen to have survived the change in law.

The final fiasco concerned a strike for trade union recognition in a small engineering firm, Con Mech. In 1973, Con Mech obtained an order from the NIRC that the AUEW should call off its strike for recognition, and that the case should be investigated by the CIR. The AUEW did not obey the order to stop the strike. The NIRC sequestrated £100,000 of union assets, eventually confiscating £75,000. The AUEW claim for recognition was then supported by the CIR's inquiry, but the CIR recommendation in favour of the union was rejected and ignored by the employer. The NIRC could not give legal force to the CIR recommendation because the AUEW was not registered. There was a series of one-day strikes in support of the AUEW and the strike at Con Mech continued. In April 1974, with the Labour government in power and the bill to repeal the 1971 Act published the day before, the NIRC exacerbated the situation by awarding £47,000 damages to Con Mech. The AUEW refused to pay and its assets were seized. The union executive called for a national strike of indefinite length, large sections of industry were affected and most newspapers closed down. At this point rescue arrived in the shape of an anonymous group of businessmen who offered to pay £65,000 for the union's fine. The offer – possibly coming from members of the Newspaper Publishers' Association – was accepted by the court on behalf of the still contemptuous union. The incident ensured that the NIRC ended its life in a blaze of controversy and a widespread concern that the law was being brought into disrepute by legislation that did not have popular support and could not be enforced.

5   *Employer Avoidance of the Act*   By 1974 employers were openly disillusioned with the Act, but even from the start their desire to use the new provisions had been minimal. Most employers were prepared to go to considerable lengths to give illicit support to their banned closed shops (Weekes *et al.*, 1975). No large employers used their new rights to apply for court orders against UIPs. During the docks disputes, Ford shifted business away from a blacked depot in order to avoid legal entanglement. Only individuals and small employers used the Act, and the employers who used it did so to sue other firms' workers, not their own (Thompson and Engleman, 1975). Even with the mass picketing and secondary boycotts of the miners' strike in 1972, with battles with police around the Saltley coal stock-pile in Birmingham, the legislation was not used and there was a universal and apparently willing employer acceptance of the TUC opposition to legally binding agreements. All major negotiations, even in the public sector, inserted clauses in their agreements that they were not legally binding.

The 1971 Act reflected the breakdown of the consensus between class interests on the postwar Welfare Compromise, and demonstrated that the unions were too powerful at the time to be neatly shackled into a new legal framework of controls. The dramatic failure of the Act influenced the contrasting policies of the governments which followed. The Labour government responded to the greatly increased stature of the TUC by involving it in policy-making. When the next Conservative government introduced its changes in labour law, it was careful to do so gradually and without conspicuous new institutions and agencies. For trade unions, the experience of the 1971 Act persuaded some leaders that increased legislation was likely but could be used to the union's advantage. The TUC abandoned the abhorrence of legalism it had argued so forcefully before the Donovan Commission, and pressed for positive, pro-union legislation.

THE 1974–9 LABOUR GOVERNMENT AND THE
SOCIAL CONTRACT

The TUC and Labour party were drawn closer together through their opposition to the 1971 Act. In 1972 a TUC–Labour party liaison committee had been formed by the TUC general council, the Parliamentary Labour Party and Labour's national executive committee. This drafted joint proposals for the next Labour government. The 1971 Act and the statutory incomes policy would be repealed. There would then be legislation to increase employment protection for individual employees, to strengthen collective bargaining and consultation rights in the workplace, and to extend industrial democracy by giving trade unionists seats on company boards. After Labour's election victory in 1974 the TUC published *Collective Bargaining and the Social Contract*, which outlined what was, in effect, an agreement to exchange legislation favourable to trade unions for union support in voluntary pay restraint.

Pro-Union Legislation

The Trade Union and Labour Relations Acts (TULRA, 1974 and 1976) repealed the 1971 Act, abolished the NIRC and CIR and reinstated the statutory legal immunities to protect the right to strike. The 1971 Act's provisions on unfair dismissal were retained and a Parliamentary battle developed centring on the position of employees in closed shops, now that it was possible to claim compensation for unfair dismissal and closed shops were no longer outlawed. It was not until labour had a majority of one in the Commons in 1976 that various amendments from the Lords were removed and the government enacted the provision that dismissals arising from a refusal to join a closed shop should be judged fair unless the individual had strong religious objections to trade unionism.

The Employment Protection Act (EPA, 1975) provided a range of new individual rights (see pp. 173–5). On collective labour relations the EPA re-established several of the previous state institutions, although with different names and powers. A *Certification Officer* replaced the Registrar without the 1971 Act's power to vet union rules, but retaining the responsibility of judging a union's independence from employers and therefore suitability for collective bargaining. The *Employment Appeals Tribunal* replaced the NIRC in hearing appeals from industrial tribunals and the certification officer but did not have the NIRC's wide areas of original jurisdiction; the *Central Arbitration Committee* replaced the Industrial Arbitration Board and under Schedule 11 could extend collective bargaining to give workers the 'recognised or general level' of pay and conditions in their area, and the *Advisory, Conciliation and Arbitration Service* was established as an independent, tripartite body (see p. 175).

The EPA strengthened trade union rights within the workplace by giving shop stewards the right to paid time off work for union activities and for training approved by the TUC, by the reintroduction of a procedure to help unions gain recognition, and by a legal duty on employers to disclose information to unions relevant for their collective bargaining. Perhaps most important, in view of mounting unemployment, was the granting of a period for compulsory consultation with recognised trade unions before major redundancies could be announced.

The collective labour law changes in the EPA marked an extension of state support for collective bargaining and although the procedures for trade union recognition and the extension of collective agreements were repealed by the next Conservative government, most of the provisions remain although sometimes in more restricted form. The Labour government enacted further consultation rights for trade unions in the *Social Security Pensions Act* of 1975, covering occupational pensions, and the *Health and Safety at Work Act* (H & S AW, 1974) which enabled recognised unions to appoint safety representatives with statutory powers to receive information and inspect work premises. Two or more safety representatives can call management to attend a safety committee, and in many smaller establishments this right has stimulated closer co-operation among different unions, providing the first formal committee to involve management with all its unions.

The TUC also hoped for legislation on planning agreements to give government and unions a voice in the investment and employment plans of the largest manufacturing companies; for tighter supervision of multinational enterprises and for the extension of public ownership through the National Enterprise Board. Although the Industry Act (1975) contained some of these provisions, controls over private capital proved difficult to enact and to enforce and the government was pushed back from these commitments and away from the initially close relationship with trade unions by mounting employer resistance and by growing economic difficulties. The proposed planning agreements were modified to exclude trade union involvement but even this was strenuously opposed by employers and Chrysler Motors was the only company to sign a planning agreement, as a condition of a massive government loan to rescue the British plants (see D. Coates, 1980, pp. 100–106). This employer resistance to the TUC's wishes on industrial democracy goes to the heart of our subject and deserves fuller consideration.

The Bullock Proposals on Industrial Democracy

The TUC sought legislation to give trade unionists seats on company Boards. Various proposals for worker directors had been under discussion in the UK since its accession to the EEC, and the TUC moved to support the idea of worker directors, provided that: (a) they represented trade unionists and did not introduce a new, second channel of employee representation; and (b) that they exercised real power, having parity with shareholders in the allocation of seats. In 1975 the government set up the Committee of Inquiry on Industrial Democracy, chaired by Lord Bullock, with a brief to consider how best to put trade union representatives on company boards. Bullock's majority Report (1977) aroused a storm of protest from employers. The CBI mounted a campaign of opposition and threatened to match the TUC resistance to the 1971 Industrial Relations Act: it would use all its powers to defeat and if necessary defy the policy.

Bullock proposed a statutory right for trade unions to claim seats on the boards of about 740 companies employing over 2,000 employees in the UK. Any recognised trade union which represented 20 per cent or more of a company's employees should be able to request a secret ballot of all the company's employees to see if they supported the introduction of employee directors. If a majority, totaling at least one-third of the electorate, agreed then employee directors would be chosen through the trade unions and the board would be reconstituted on a 2X + Y formula – employees and shareholders would have equal representation (2X) and, to prevent the possibility of deadlocked voting, there would be a small, uneven number of independents (Y) chosen with the support of the two sides. If employees chose to adopt worker directors, then all the unions in the company would establish a joint representation committee (JRC) to decide how to allocate employee directorships and to co-ordinate the employee side. A new tripartite agency, an Industrial Democracy Commission, would assist and guide the implementation of the necessary changes.

The Bullock Report advocated these fundamental changes in the government of private companies on two main grounds. First, it argued that the proposals would ensure more efficient and effective work relations by providing a better framework to resolve conflicts at work. Employees would be more adequately represented and employers would find that the greater involvement of employees in company decisions would aid the implementation of difficult decisions and unleash energies and resources currently unused. The second ground was the moral need to extend democracy. Just as universal suffrage was a necessary and desirable reflection of the growth of middle- and working-class power in the nineteenth century, so the proposals for industrial democracy should be seen as a similar response to the growth of organised employee power in the twentieth. Just as the controversy surrounding the granting of the right to vote to ordinary people is now forgotten, so industrial democracy would eventually be seen as unexceptionable.

The employers' vehement antagonism to Bullock was stronger than the Labour government could resist. By 1977 the Social Contract between the TUC and government was already weakening as workers resisted further pay restraint in the face of rising prices.

Government motivation to fight for the TUC-supported Bullock proposals was lessened as splits appeared within the union movement. Although Bullock was strongly supported by many unionists, especially Jack Jones of the TGWU, it was opposed by Hugh Scanlon of the AUEW, and by Frank Chapple of the EEPTU, plus many left-wingers. With the CBI and the British Communist party equally virulent in their attack on the proposals, the Labour government produced a highly tentative White Paper in 1978 suggesting the voluntary adoption of some form of minority employee representation, not necessarily selected through trade unions and not on the main board, but on a supervisory board created, with limited functions, above it. The White Paper did, however, support the creation of joint representation committees with statutory rights to discuss investment plans and organisational changes like mergers, takeovers, expansions or contractions that would affect employees. The Bullock and White Paper proposals for industrial democracy can be seen as the most corporatist of the several mildly corporatist policies of the 1974–9 government. As such, they became the focus of many of the arguments for and against the development of corporatism which we discuss below (pp. 207–9).

The Social Contract Incomes Policy

The TUC's exchange of voluntary wage restraint for the pro-union legislation achieved some success for two to three years. The TUC initially produced guidelines on the time period between wage claims and the type of claims to be submitted which were generally applied. However, the guidelines did little to ease the rapidly rising average earnings which had been stimulated by the threshold clauses of the Heath government's incomes policy (which granted increases when inflation touched certain levels), and by rapid worldwide inflation following the four-fold increase in oil prices over the Arab–Israeli War. As early as 1975, the government found itself with inflation moving towards 20 per cent, average earnings rising faster than this (some settlements for Civil Servants, power workers and miners were over 30 per cent), a massive balance of payments deficit, sterling under pressure and Civil Servants proposing a statutory incomes policy. Faced with government pressure for greater commitments to wage restraint, Jack Jones of the TGWU produced a paper for the TUC suggesting that the unions support a flat-rate increase on basic rates and a freeze on higher incomes, as long as the government tightened price controls and reduced unemployment. The government supported these proposals although with a lower (£6 a week) flat-rate increase and without increased price controls. The TUC congress gave its overwhelming approval.

The 1975 policy was succeeded by another agreed policy in

1976. In 1977 income tax was reduced in exchange for a commitment to a 10 per cent limit on wage increases and the TUC
acquiesced, although it was finding it harder to gain membership
support for wage restraint in the context of rising unemployment,
public expenditure cuts dictated by the IMF and a reduction in real
wages of 5.5 per cent in 1974–5, 1.6 per cent in 1975–6 and nearly
1 per cent in 1976–7. Nevertheless the policy broadly held, backed
by a government blacklist on firms in breach of the policy. From
August 1975 until August 1978 the TUC therefore actively supported a government incomes policy designed to reduce the real
level of earnings in the hope of reducing unemployment, avoiding
accelerating inflation and keeping the Labour government in power.

The government then announced a 5 per cent pay guideline to
operate from August 1978, despite warnings from the TUC that
they could not support such a guideline and did not believe it
would hold. The policy was challenged by several unions and was
broken in a 'Winter of Discontent' in 1978–9 which started with a
successful strike at Ford and continued in the public sector. A
Standing Commission on Pay Comparability was set up to ease the
tension over public sector claims in March 1979. However, this
period of incomes policy failed. Settlements were considerably in
excess of the 5 per cent norm and the government, which arrived
in office in the wake of the miners' successful strike against the
Heath incomes policy, lost power in the context of another pay
revolt of wider scale.

Bargained Corporatism from 1974 to 1979

The 1974–9 government represents the best example so far of
British government attempting to govern in open alliance with
trade unions. The experience inevitably sparked a debate about
corporatism, and fears about the impact of corporatist policies
were widely aired, not only by the Thatcher-led opposition, but by
liberal and Marxist critics.

From 1974 to 1979, collective bargaining was replaced, as the
most important method of negotiation on employment, by
state–party negotiations between Labour ministers and the TUC.
This level of negotiation was most dramatically illustrated by the
government's offer to involve unions in forming budget policy by
exchanging tax cuts for wage restraint. At the level of individual
companies, the Bullock proposals presaged a change in the role of
collective bargaining at domestic levels. By providing for shop
stewards to be given seats as employee directors on company
boards, the proposals contained the potential for shifting domestic
union–management negotiations from collective bargaining
institutions to the boardroom. The traditional separation of collective bargaining from government and management structures of

decision-making was being replaced by the closer integration of trade unions onto the central decision-making bodies of British industry. Government policy had strong elements of corporatism, but the corporatism proposed attempted to avoid direct coercion of the individual; the industrial democracy proposals, for example, were ringed with requirements for choice.

Criticisms of this experiment in bargained corporatism were voiced from unitary, liberal individual, liberal-collectivist and Marxist perspectives (see Chapter 2). Those on the right of the political spectrum castigated the policies on two grounds. The liberal–individualist argument was put that state–party negotiations undermined the sovereignty of Parliament by giving governmental status to groups who were not responsible to the electorate. Unitary arguments were also used, especially that Bullock's attack on the authority and power of shareholders would make the efficient and profitable running of business impossible to achieve.

From traditional liberal-collectivists came fears that once unions became involved in the shaping and implementation of government or management policies they would inevitably lose their freedom to represent their membership. It was asserted that the offer of tax concessions for wage restraint marked 'the beginning of the end of collective bargaining, and with it the representative influence of trade unions' and that 'the usefulness of trade unions as instruments of social control could be entirely destroyed' (Anthony, 1977, pp. 290, 292). Once trade unions became the agents of government policy, then rank and file opposition would be crushed and unions would lose their ability to represent and channel grievances. Similar fears were echoed by many of the trade unionists who voiced their opposition to Bullock's proposals for industrial democracy.

From a more Marxist perspective came arguments similar to those of the liberal-collectivists, but without the same faith in collective bargaining. Panitch (1981) argued that trade union gains under corporatist bargaining are severely limited by the dominant, class-based structures of power in society which limit the advantages any government can offer its workers. In return for the illusion of some influence over government policy, union leaders accept greater restrictions over their use of industrial action and impose more elaborate disciplinary controls over their own membership. So, from 1974 to 1979 the TUC allowed real wages to fall and issued restrictive guidelines on the conduct of strikes, picketing, negotiating procedures and the operation of closed shops, but found its policies for economic expansion and import controls rejected in face of IMF influence, planning agreements nullified by employer opposition and its demands for a return to free collective bargaining rejected for a rigid pay restraint.

Defendants of the bargained corporatism from 1974 to 1979 argue that government intervention was inevitable, that intervention which attempted to act with union support was better than the alternative and that many of the Social Contract policies brought real benefits to employees which increased rather than reduced union ability to represent member interests at the place of work. For example, Jack Jones of the TGWU argued that the Bullock proposals would enable workers to extend their influence at work, that statutory JRC's would provide the joint union co-ordination at company level that unions had found difficult to establish, and that this would help bridge the widening gap between collective bargaining and managerial centres of power.

The debate on corporatism receded as the succeeding government adopted radically different policies, involving the minimum recognition of, or consultation with, trade unions.

THE CONSERVATIVE GOVERNMENT 1979 – MONETARY ECONOMICS AND RESTRICTIVE LEGISLATION

The economic and industrial relations policies of the incoming Thatcher government were far removed from corporatism, and from the TUC's desires for interventionist economic policies.

The economic policy of the new government marked a radical change from the welfare compromise. Britain was to be used, in Galbraith's phrase, as the first major experiment in monetarism. In line with a determination to reduce the role of the state, direct taxes were cut and VAT increased to pay for income tax deductions. The public sector was reduced by widespread cuts in expenditure and by the sale of public assets to the private sector. The government encouraged freer capital markets by lifting restrictions on the export of capital and it aimed at tight monetary policies in order to reduce inflation. At the time of writing, these policies have not produced the hoped-for regeneration of British industry. Instead, combined with the worst international recession since the 1930s, the UK has seen a cataclysmic fall in national output, greater than that experienced by her competitors with unemployment rising from 1,267,500 in October 1979 to 3,097,000 by December 1982.

Industrial relations policy was also based on dogmatically held theories based on a faith in freer markets. Trade unions were seen to have harmful effects on national profitability by exercising monopoly control over labour markets and by encouraging unrealistic expectations among employees. The solution was the adoption of realistic economic and monetary policies, backed by legal changes to reduce trade union bargaining strength and so free the labour market. With the experience of the 1971 Act still in mind, the government made no attempt to repeat the massive legal changes of 1971. Instead amendments were made to existing labour laws to reduce the scope of the employment protection legislation and to restrict and control trade unions' strike powers and internal discipline. The theory behind the legal changes was straightforwardly restrictive. There was none of the partial commitment to the corporatist integration of trade unions which confused the 1971 Act.

In 1979 changes were made to reduce the scope of some of the EPA's individual rights, and to reduce the compulsory warning period for certain redundancies. The 1980 *Employment Act* reduced individual rights to unfair dismissal compensation and maternity leave, and repealed the procedures for aiding trade union recognition and for extending collective agreements. These changes served to roll back some of the employee benefits gained under previous administrations. More fundamental changes in collective labour legislation were brought in gradually in 1980 and 1982.

The Employment Acts 1980 and 1982, and the Closed Shop

The government did not repeat the 1971 attempt to outlaw the closed shop; instead it made them more difficult to maintain. The 1980 Act amended the law on unfair dismissal so that a wider range of people, not just those with religious objections, could claim unfair dismissal if sacked for non-membership of a union membership agreement (UMA). People could not be fairly dismissed if they had conscientious objections or deep personal convictions against membership, if their employment predated the agreement or if the UMA was recent and had not been approved by a ballot. The 1982 Act extended the obstacles to fair dismissal, most importantly requiring regular ballots, at least every five years, and the endorsement of the UMA by 80 per cent of the electorate or 85 per cent of those entitled to vote. A special award of between £12,000 to £22,000 was to be added to the basic award for unfair dismissal if reinstatement was claimed, with a minimum of an extra £17,000 if an order for reinstatement was disobeyed. These damages are not necessarily paid by the employer. The 1980 Act gave the employer, and the 1982 Act the dismissed non-unionist, the right to join the union or union official as liable for the payment.

The Restriction of Statutory Immunities Protecting the Right to Strike

The 1980 Act restricted the trade union immunity to picket and take sympathetic strike action. Only picketing outside one's place of work remained protected. Trade union officials were only permitted to picket if accompanied by one of their own members and yet were expected to limit the numbers picketing each entrance. Sympathetic or secondary industrial action lost protection unless it met certain complex conditions. The 1982 Act restricted the scope of the statutory immunities by changing the definition of a trade dispute to exclude inter-union, political and foreign-based disputes. The general effect of these changes excludes from legality vast areas of industrial action which had been seen as lawful for over six decades, and increased the scope for legal action over a wide range of industrial disputes (Lewis and Simpson, 1981; K. Wedderburn, 1982).

Internal Union Government   Changes in union government were strongly advocated by the government but initial legal changes were slight. The 1980 Act made public funds available for unions using secret ballots for the election of officers, or for policy decisions. The TUC boycotted the fund.

Union-Labour-Only Contracts   The 1982 Act made unlawful all commercial practices like contracts, tenders, lists of suppliers or refusal to contract, which required work to be done by trade unionists.

The Taff Vale *Doctrine of Trade Union Liability*   The *Taff Vale* judgement of 1901 ruled that trade unions funds were liable to be seized in legal proceedings for tort. Before that judgement it had been assumed that the 1871 Act protected union funds, and the 1906 Trade Disputes Act gave unions statutory protection for most liability in tort. The 1982 Act removes that protection and exposes unions to injunctions and their funds to claims for damages. An upper limit is set on such damages ranging from £10,000 to £250,000, according to union size. Complex clauses in the Act attempt to resolve the dilemma, apparent under the 1971 legislation, of deciding when a union is or is not legally responsible for the actions of its members and officials.

The industrial relations policy of the Thatcher government is clear. The law is being changed gradually to reduce trade union power to take industrial action and to weaken membership unity in such action. The objectives are not cluttered by the reformist desires of the previous Conservative administration, indeed even the traditional obeisance to collective bargaining is faint, and the liberal-collectivist perspective is not evident behind 'the most comprehensive and the most effective statutory protection for non-union employees that we have ever had in this country' (N. Tebbit in the House of Commons, 1982).

Where the government is itself a partner to collective bargaining, it has sought to heighten the impact of market forces. Rigid cash limits have been instituted for the public sector and where possible the tradition of paying public servants on the basis of comparability studies has been abandoned.

The consequences of the Thatcher government's legal changes are unpredictable. More industrial disputes will become involved in British courts, but how far litigation extends will depend on employer attitudes to their new rights and on the number of people who seek compensation for leaving or not joining unions with UMAs. The unions are, not surprisingly, opposed to the Act and do not share its theoretical assumption that they exercise a monopoly control of labour markets. Whether the unions can defy the new laws as they did the 1971 Act must rest on the extent to which the 1980s recession has weakened union membership moral and bargaining power. K. Wedderburn (1982) suggests the fear of bankruptcy from the Taff Vale doctrine will ensure union executive committees and union officers spend more time policing rather than supporting industrial action, so driving a wedge between union officers and rank and file members. Certainly British courts and industrial tribunals will play a new role in collective labour relations but how unions, employers and the Judiciary itself adapts to the increased significance of judicial regulation of employment relations has yet to be seen.

CONCLUSION: CONFLICTING PERSPECTIVES, CONFLICTING PRESCRIPTIONS

The violent swings in government policy towards industrial relations in recent years highlights the existence of different theoretical perspectives on industrial relations and the end of the post war policy consensus.

In retrospect, the broad postwar consensus supporting the traditional collective bargaining system up to the mid 1960s can be seen as having been bolstered by the most successful period of economic growth that the UK has enjoyed, even if that success was diminished by the faster growth rate of industrial competitors. Most social institutions work more smoothly in periods of growing prosperity and in the period 1945 to 1965 the spread of collective bargaining, together with the growth of government-funded welfare, served to satisfy the expectations of most powerful groups of employees at a time when employers were not too severely squeezed. The background to employment relations is no longer so accommodating. Dissatisfaction has provoked a series of criticisms that collective bargaining itself is to blame. Employers complain that it permits too much open conflict, generates unwarranted pressure to raise wages and restricts the efficient and mobile allocation of labour to jobs. Employees complain that it is too narrowly based to accommodate their legitimate demands. In the climate of increasing criticism of the old institutions, there have been a wide range of proposals for reform, all of which involve the state in a more active role in the regulation of employment relations.

Different proposals stem from radically different theoretical perspectives, and relating back to the distinctions made in Chapter 2 we can identify the following influences:

Liberal, market-based prescriptions: A liberal aversion to the closed shop has influenced the legal changes of both the recent Conservative administrations. In contrast to the Heath government, the Thatcher government has been more resolutely committed to the liberal objective of reducing the role of government in the economy. However the restrictions on trade union immunities are designed to increase the role of the state law-enforcement agencies in industrial relations. How far the attempt to return trade unions to the uncertain legal status they held before 1906 succeeds, remains to be seen. In favour of success can be placed the effect of mass unemployment on union resources and on workgroup morale and resistance. Against success might be placed the long history of independent trade union development in the UK and the wide coverage of trade unionism across the working, and the middle classes.

Liberal-collectivist support for collective bargaining: Collective bargaining still has many supporters, but even those who distrust radical change usually suggest that British collective bargaining needs to be altered, either to extend the depth of its regulation of employment issues, or to rationalise and centralise negotiations so that national counter-inflation policies can influence negotiations. In 1979 the CBI proposed the synchronisation of bargains, so that agreements across the workforce were reached together, and similar suggestions for the public sector have been made by the general secretary of the GMBU. However it would seem that voluntary rationalisation of collective bargaining machinery is unlikely in the context of wide support for a variety of more radical legislative changes.

Variants of corporatism: All governments in the last fifteen years have sought to increase the role of the state in the regulation of employment relations. All except the Thatcher government have sought to achieve this increased state involvement through various tripartite institutions and through attempts to restructure employee representation and negotiation in a way that would increase the integration of trade union, employer and government decision-making. Although the term corporatism is rarely used, these policies contain corporatist elements. However there are many variants of corporatism and the policies tried so far have ranged from the Social Contract policies, partly designed to increase employee influence and involvement in decisions at work, through the Donovan proposals for the rationalisation of voluntary collective bargaining, to the 1971 Acts' vision of socially responsible bargaining constrained within a framework of law. The Social Contract and Donovan proposals were clearly linked to the need for incomes policy, the Heath policy was not initially premised on incomes policy although it rapidly became entangled with it. Corporatist policies have met with considerable resistance within the UK, but corporatist proposals still form an important part of the official Labour, Liberal and Social Democratic Party programmes and find support among left-wing Conservative groups.

The Thatcher government is anti-corporatist and ideologically opposed to state intervention. Nevertheless its revision of collective labour law is designed to increase the control of the courts over employee relations. Its policies increase the role of the State in labour relations, though by different mechanisms.

No recent government policy for industrial relations has gained widespread support, or been claimed as an unqualified success. The wide range of conflicting proposals still on the political agenda demonstrates the absence of any new consensus on public policy. The role of the state is increasing but without agreement on how this should be done.

Chapter 10

Negotiation and Control

This book has been concerned with the processes of control over employment relations in Britain. We have looked at employer objectives, employer strategies towards the labour process, different methods of organisational control and the historical importance of employers' associations. We have studied employee objectives, employee action within workgroups and within more formal representative institutions, and we have traced the slow development of the British system of collective bargaining. We have reviewed the politics of industrial relations and the increasingly active role of the state and noted that British industrial relations is now the centre of political debate, with radically different policies advocated by the main political parties.

The political controversy over British industrial relations has renewed an academic interest in fundamental and theoretical questions. The days when industrial relations could be taught as if it was concerned only with the technical details of well-established and accepted collective bargaining institutions have passed, and the social and political theories underlying current debates, as we noted in Chapter 2, are under review. This chapter concludes the book by looking at the relationships between negotiation and management- or state-run structures of control. A clarification of sociological theory in this area illuminates the discussion on the merits of collective bargaining, industrial democracy and corporatism which have recurred throughout the book. At the end we attempt a brief look into the future.

NEGOTIATION AS A SOCIO-POLITICAL PROCESS

Negotiation is a pervasive social process. Studies of industrial relations have traditionally focused on collective bargaining, and collective bargaining is certainly the most visible form of negotiation to occur at work: it is conducted through formal and specialised machinery, it may involve visible sanctions like strikes, and the negotiators themselves often use the news media to inform or persuade employees. However, the high visibility of collective bargaining obscures the existence of the many other negotiations at work that may well be more important than the precise percentage of some workgroup's pay-rise. Collective bargaining needs to be analysed in the context of other types of negotiation at work.

Within sociology there has long been a divide between *structuralists*, who focus on the co-operation and co-ordination in social life, and the *conflict* or *interaction* school, a rival tradition focusing instead on competition and social conflict. The interactionist tradition has recently come to the fore in industrial sociology to argue that business organisations are not totally structured and rationally administered by central management, but contain numerous internal conflicts over budgets, plans and priorities which are resolved by many different bargains. Indeed, organisations can be seen as held together by a 'negotiated order' (Strauss *et al.*, 1971) and comprised of overlapping and hierarchical sets of bargaining zones (Abell *et al.*, 1975). Bargaining might occur between different factions on the company board, between different management departments or divisions, between management specialisms, between unions and management, union members and their representatives, between unions or different levels of union official. An organisation can also be influenced by bargaining in external zones, for example between the organisation and its customers, and within Parliament, national tripartite institutions or international bodies like the EEC.

Negotiation has been defined as 'the deliberate interaction of two or more complex social units which are attempting to define or redefine the terms of their interdependence' (Walton and McKersie, 1965), and this interaction may take place between individuals or nation states, covertly or in formal institutions. In the next section we analyse different types of negotiation and review the development of negotiation within British organisations, in order to place collective bargaining in a social and historical context. In the sections following we discuss the power that can be exercised through different types of negotiation, and the relationship between negotiation and bureaucracy.

The Degree of which Negotiation is Institutionalised

If people negotiate on similar issues time and again they invariably develop structured procedures to regulate their bargaining relationship. The development of norms in any regular social interaction is a basic sociological and psychological process, the details of which need not concern us. However, we can distinguish different types of negotiation in terms of the degree and form of normative regulation, or institutionalisation, that emerges.

A very low degree of institutionalisation exists when bargaining occurs in situations where the dominant norms state that one party should have the authority to take decisions, or that decisions should be taken on non-political or rational criteria. Examples are the furtive deals that Dalton described between managerial cliques (see p. 83) or the earliest negotiations between the TUC and government when TUC delegates reached the Prime Minister by a secret passage from the Treasury. In both cases, bargaining was furtive because the dominant norms did not legitimise negotiation and these norms were supported by one of the parties, or by external powers no one cared to challenge. If bargaining continues in this form, then one norm likely to develop to protect the bargaining relationship is that knowledge of all deals should be kept secret.

At very low levels of institutionalisation, negotiation may be difficult to detect and there is the problem of deciding where to draw the boundary between bargaining and the unilateral imposition of control by one party. A supervisor may tell a skilled man to sweep the floor, be met by a stare of disbelief and move on to ask an unskilled labourer. Such an exchange can be classed as bargaining, even though no special meetings, no specialist negotiators and no elaborate procedures are involved. It is enough that there was the attempt to 'define or redefine terms of interdependence'. In this example the negotiation, though brief, is governed by norms known to both parties about appropriate work for apprenticed craftsmen and the scope of supervisory authority.

A high level of institutionalisation exists when an elaborate set of norms regulates the negotiating process. Norms then specify the parties entitled to negotiate, negotiable issues, the timing, membership and format of meetings, acceptable arguments, threats and sanctions, the format of agreements, and procedures for the implementation and administration of agreed terms. When norms governing negotiation are this specific and elaborate they are likely to give rise to visible and concrete forms. Some of the norms will have a formal status as 'rules' written into agreements, constitutions or government laws. There are also likely to be specialised roles to cope with the work involved, hierarchical structures of meetings, and mountains of paperwork. It has been estimated that the institution of collective bargaining employs about 150,000 people in the UK (Clegg, 1979) and similar startling estimates might be made for other forms of negotiating institution. The works council institutions in West Germany would make an interesting comparison. In 1975 the Deutsche Bank employed only 25,000 but their statutory works council machinery involved the employment of 30 full-time works councillors, plus their administrative support staff. Works council business was a tightly regulated, formalized affair.

Bargaining over employment relationships therefore takes institutional and non-institutional forms. The degree of institutionalisation for other types of organisational bargaining also varies: for example, capital budgeting can be seen as a process of bargaining between departments competing for investment funds. This process may be openly institutionalised in a negotiating round of meetings, like Alcan Aluminium's regular series of divisional budget meetings culminating in a central meeting each spring to establish departmental budgets (Tugendhat, 1973) or the bargaining process may be covert and disguised. As Pondy (1967) notes of the US, 'whereas the visible procedures of bargaining are an accepted part of the labor–management relations, there are strong pressures in budgeting (particularly business budgeting) to conceal the bargaining that goes on in the guise of rationality'. There is a similar unwillingness openly to institutionalise budgetary bargaining in many British companies. In contrast, Japan institutionalises much of its managerial bargaining, in the *ringiseido* system of extensive formal consultation across the management structure before major decisions are taken whilst open collective bargaining is a foreign import (Hanami, 1980). The degree to which bargaining is institutionalised both reflects and affects the power of the negotiating parties, but in all industrialised societies some type of institutionalised negotiation has developed around the employment relationship.

Types of Negotiating Institution
What negotiating institutions exist for employment relationships? There is a tendency in UK and USA literature to equate the institutionalisation of negotiation on employment matters with collective bargaining (Jackson, 1977, Clegg, 1979). This is, perhaps, understandable in the Anglo-US context where collective bargaining has been the dominant form of institutionalised negotiation, but by ignoring other types of institutional negotiation this tendency reduces our ability to analyse negotiation at work. We look first at the negotiating institutions that can surround managerial organisation, and secondly at the formalised negotiations that relate to state administration.

1 *Institutionalised negotiation and management's structures of control.* Negotiation on employment relations may be integrated within management's organisation or kept separate in various ways. Many pre-modern organisations institutionalised negotiations between capital and labour through sub-contractual relationships that were an integral part of the management process. A vivid description of this process in the Welsh slate quarries shows that work in the three main quarries, each employing 2,000–3,000 men, was organised around subcontracted work teams of 4 or 5 men. The teams, led by their 'bargain taker', negotiated each month with the 'setting steward' the price they would get for the

slate they quarried in the following month. The teams had a customary right to their own area of rock face and controlled their own work hours, methods of work and the recruitment, discipline and rewards of their own members. There 'was a startling absence of management' and the quarries 'were not much more than a collection of bargains' (Jones, 1977). Sub-contract systems of organisation were widespread throughout large sectors of British industry and the system was able to reflect various power relationships within the sub-contracted workgroups. Some sub-contract groups were dominated by petty dictators. Others contained their own internal system of participation and negotiation. The docks provide examples of both, for the corruption and exploitation by many of the old gangers in the London docks was notorious, and yet in 1898 Schloss described one gang of Scottish dockers run as a co-partnership, with the 51 members holding annual elections for their foreman and 5 ganger leaders (Littler, 1982).

The history of organisational development in the UK has seen the virtual elimination of this type of institutional negotiation. In most industries entrepreneurs have built more centralised, bureaucratic organisations around a directly employed workforce. Although the early industrialists may have hoped to eliminate negotiation from the new, centralised organisational structures (aided, if they were aware of them, by the organisational models of Weber, Fayol, F. W. Taylor and others in the structural school of organisation theory), their control was not sufficient to eliminate all bargaining. Negotiations persisted and in bureaucratic organisations negotiations over employment have been formalised into institutions that are integrated with, parallel to, or completely separate from the normal structures of management.

In the UK, distinct collective bargaining institutions, clearly separated from the institutions for managerial decision-making, developed because employers wished to preserve or create the managerial prerogative to determine the details of workplace administration and because both employers and employees believed they were divided by fundamental conflicts of economic interest and felt threatened by closer collaboration.

The separation of collective negotiations from the normal process of organisational control was unambiguous as long as collective bargaining was conducted at industry levels. It is more difficult to maintain the separation of collective bargaining when it is conducted at the workplace and when negotiators also relate through their roles in management's organisation. For example, the Chemco studies (see p. 89) describe how shop stewards may be used by local managers to gain worker acceptance of difficult managerial decisions, and in the reverse direction, Batstone *et al.* (1977, 1978) show powerful stewards cultivating managers in order to increase their mutual control of local events. Nevertheless collective bargaining at the place of work can be kept as a separate part of organisational structure by specialist meetings and careful attention to agendas.

Britain traditionally negotiates on employment issues through collective bargaining, but examples of more integrated institutional structures can be found. Some British companies, led usually by employers with a strong religious or philosophical commitment to employee participation, are managed through structures which incorporate employee representative onto company boards and managerial meeting. Scott Baader, Glacier Metal (Gray, 1976) and the John Lewis Partnership (Flanders *et al*., 1968) are the best known UK examples. The co-operative organisations in the Mondragon group of Spain (Oakeshott, 1978) and the decentralised producers' co-operatives within Yogoslavia (Vanek, 1975) provide more significant examples of organisations which conduct negotiations on conditions of employment through the main organisational structures.

Between the separated institutions of collective bargaining and the full institutional integration of producer co-operatives lie various institutions which aim to run employee negotiation in parallel with the structures of managerial decision-making. West German co-determination provides the best example of parallel institutions. Under West German law, companies must establish works councils, one for each establishment with over 300 employees, and in multi-establishment companies there are central works councils and economic committees. These institutions represent employee interests and have rights to information, joint consultation and co-determination. Co-determination covers social welfare; personnel policies including criteria for recruitment, job evaluation, training and work methods or production procedures; individual recruitment, classification, redeployment, transfer or dismissal; and general economic issues like mergers, or the subdivision of the company. Managers must achieve works council approval of their policies in all these areas, and the works councils' power to 'co-determine' these issues is backed by the right to take the company to arbitration. West German unions have been active in developing this system and generally regard it as an effective way of institutionalising workplace negotiations.

In the UK the most widespread institutions running parallel to management structures have been joint consultation committees or councils. Recommended by Whitley in 1917 (p. 153) as a means of involving employees in domestic decision-making, they had only consultative rights and none of the state-backed powers of the German works councils. Joint consultation did not become widespread in the UK until the Second World War, when consultation and productivity committees were used to secure greater employee involvement in the war effort. Although the institutions persisted after the war, they became increasingly discredited as powerless 'talk-shops' or 'kiss and cuddle' institutions and fell into disuse wherever domestic collective bargaining was firmly established. However, there was a resurgence of the old joint consultation committees in the early 1980s, as employers made some slight concessions to the demands for worker participation heard in the 1970s, and as increasing unemployment lessened employee hopes for more radical institutional reform (*Employment Gazette*, 1981).

The increased interest in worker participation schemes in Britain in the 1970s produced some interesting, if temporary, examples to show how variable the institutions of employee negotiations can be. At Chrysler, just before its collapse in the UK, shop stewards were invited to sit on the divisional management boards, to discuss general policy. The Ryder scheme for the rescue of British Leyland in 1975 increased worker participation by establishing a *third* set of institutions within the company. Besides the traditional structure of management control, and the conventional, separate, institutions of company collective bargaining, would be a third set of institutions which would parallel the most significant management meetings at regional, factory and department levels. These 'joint management' committees gave shop stewards equal seats with managers in meetings concerned with the development and implementation of the company's plan for survival (see *Financial Times*, 29.10.75).

2 *Institutionalised negotiations and state structures of control* If governments openly intervene in the regulation of employment relations in collaboration with employers and trade unions, then they create new levels of institutionalised negotiation. There are, as we saw in Chapters 8 and 9, many variants of corporatism and employee representation may be integrated into state administration, as under Fascism, or separate institutions may be created for limited purposes. In the UK the tripartite institutions (see pp. 175–6) provide for bargained corporatism on a limited range of special areas of public policy, while the most ambitious attempts to involve the state in the regulation of employment relations have been incomes policies.

Many incomes policies have been presented as government designed and administered, that is, as *not* negotiated. However Clegg, who involved himself in the adminstration of several policies, argues that both the design and the administration of incomes policy are usually negotiated, although with various degrees of success, and 'the negotiators have normally been curiously shy of acknowledging it' (Clegg, 1979). Most government policies are subjected to the lobby of interested pressure groups and civil servants regularly consult with the relevant pressure groups on draft legislation. British governments have sought the support of employers and trade unions for their incomes policies, although so far only the 1964–8 policy has been openly agreed in formal, tripartite negotiations. In 1972 the Heath government used a tripartite institution to agree its statutory incomes policy but the negotiations failed when unions demanded the repeal of the 1971 Industrial Relations Act as their price for collaboration. The 1974–9 policy was negotiated in a formal *bi*partite institution, the TUC-Labour Party liaison committee.

Even those policies designed entirely by government have been enforced through a mixture of bureaucratic administration and bargaining. Clegg argues that the main weakness of British incomes policies to date has been the failure to find a workable balance between the necessary bargained flexibility and the administration of effective controls. In 1965–6 the reference of pay claims to the NBPI became the subject of such heavy bargaining that the policy became discredited on the grounds that powerful groups were avoiding control. In contrast, the policy from 1972 to 1974 allowed neither the government nor the administering pay board sufficient room to manoeuvre in 1974 to make a special case to increase miners' pay in the context of the oil crisis. In the next policy (the Social Contract) no attempt was made to administer rigid regulations through the Civil Service or through a tripartite agency. Instead, the government and the general council of the TUC policed their agreement together. They agreed to minor adjustments to meet particular difficulties, just as parties to a disputes procedure might, and maintained the general policy against attack on the grounds that both had something to gain from its success. It was when the policy was no longer agreed, and when the government dictated a 5 per cent norm against the TUC's strong advice, that the policy broke down (for more details of these policies, see Table 8.3).

The various British incomes policies can therefore be seen as attempts to construct new, more centralised institutions for the negotiation of pay. Despite various experiments with different types of institution for policy design or policy administration, so far all recent incomes policies have been broken as groups of employees, sometimes with employer support, protested at wage restraint in the context of rising prices. The anti-corporatist elements opposed to incomes policy in the UK are strong, and Britain has yet to establish institutions to integrate government, employer and employee influence on the main conditions of employment.

In summary, negotiation at work takes many forms. Negotiations over employment relationships vary in the degree to which they are institutionalised. Institutions for negotiation can be separated from, integrated with, or structured to parallel the institutions of management or government control. Any judgement on the value or effectiveness of these different types of negotiation needs to consider the complex question of power.

NEGOTIATION AND POWER

Who exercises power in the various negotiating institutions and to what extent do different types of institution affect the distribution of power? Such questions lie at the centre of the theoretical perspectives on industrial relations discussed in Chapter 2 and go to the heart of recent political debate. Opinions range from the left wingers who assert that no negotiation within capitalism can do other than confirm the dominant power of capital, through the liberal-collectivist's insistence that employees can only improve their position with the power of the strike sanction, to liberal-individualists' counter-claim that strikes provide no benefit to employees but merely increase unemployment and inflation, and onto the corporatist belief that the integration of employee representatives onto management or governmental bodies can create a balanced distribution of power.

Power is a notoriously difficult question to study. Weber defined power as 'the probability that one actor within a social relationship will be in a position to carry out his will despite resistance'. However as Bachrach and Baratz (1962) and Lukes (1974) point out, if there is a considerable disparity of power between parties, then the dominant party may be in a position, not only to carry out his own will, but also to suppress all signs of resistance. This may be because the weaker party is aware that he has suffered a massive defeat in this area in the past and is not prepared to mount another challenge whilst he believes he will be defeated. Alternatively, the dominant party may be able to mobilise bias in a way that ensures that his claim to control certain areas goes unchallenged because the weaker party accepts his claim to have a moral, legitimate right to control. The subordinate may accept, as morally right, his or her disadvantaged position. If power is exercised invisibly, then it becomes extraordinarily difficult to study. In this section we look at the bases of power before discussing the power relationships within different types of negotiating institution.

The Structural Bases of Power
Power derives from relationships of dependency. A can exercise power over B, if B is dependent on A for the achievement of his objectives. In employment relations dependency works many ways. Employees are likely to be dependent on their employer for

objectives like income, job satisfaction and desired social contacts. Employers are dependent on their employees' effort and co-operation to achieve output or profit. Both employers and employees are dependent on the state for the maintenance of the infrastructure which supports economic activity. And the state is dependent on employers and employees for capital accumulation and co-operation in the implementation of government policy. However, different groups exert different degrees of power, and degrees of dependency need to be explored.

The state of the labour market, the form of the labour process and the organisation of work all help to structure power relationships between employers and employees. The structural bases of power which derive from these factors are often discussed in terms of non-substitutability and strategic importance. In Chapters 5 and 6 we analysed workgroup and trade union power in terms of non-substitutability (i.e. A exercises power over B because B depends on A's contribution and would find it hard to find a substitute if A withdrew it) and strategic importance (i.e. that A's contribution has a particular and strategic importance for B in the achievement of his objectives) (see pp. 85–9 and 99–103). Strategic and non-substitutable positions can be held by employees and employers. The earlier chapters noted that a high degree of skill or a crucial position in the work-flow increase employee power, provided that the employer is dependent on the goods or services that the employees produce. Conversely, an employer exercises power over employees to the extent that he offers employment opportunities that are in scarce supply and that the income from employment is crucial for the achievement of individual objectives. The power of the state increases as its activities become more important for the achievement of individual goals. Relationships of dependency are engrained into all social organisation and help structure the distribution of power at work.

Employee power rests, in the last resort, on the threat or possibility of the withdrawal of labour needed by the employer. How significant is this power? Strikes are the most measured and studied aspect of employment relationships and the impact of the strike weapon has been extensively discussed (see Crouch, 1982, Chapter 3; Hyman, 1972; and, for a review of the economic analysis, Sapsford, 1981). The right to strike is a fundamental safeguard against the authoritarian and totalitarian mobilisation of labour and yet strikes are not necessarily powerful. A strike is only likely to exert pressure on an employer to change his mind if the employer is dependent on the labour provided by the strikers, and if the employers' ability to wait until work is resumed is lower than the employees' ability to withstand their loss of income. The first national steel strike for many years, in 1980, failed because the

British Steel Corporation actually benefited from not having to pay wages at a time of excess supply, when steel products could not be sold. As Crouch notes, the longer a strike lasts, the weaker the employee position becomes because strikers bear considerable personal costs and their resources are quickly used. Employees may attempt to increase the impact of a strike by timing it to cause maximum embarrassment for employers or by attempting to borrow the bargaining power of other workers by widening the action through picketing or sympathetic action. However the law sets new limits to both sympathetic action and to picketing (see p. 210). Employers may react to counteract the power of strikes by dismissing the strikers, by substituting their labour power by employing other workers, or by buying in the product they produced. Employees face personal costs when they take strike action; striker unity is therefore never guaranteed. Employers can seek to weaken union unity and strike capacity by mounting a publicity campaign to persuade the strikers that their action is irrational and immoral and mobilising public opinion against disruptive action. Employers therefore have powers to offset the strike sanction although for most it will still be a sanction to be avoided.

In the interwar period, when virtually every industrialised country was experiencing major, often violent, confrontations between capital and labour, the potential power of the strike sanction seemed considerable. Syndicalists believed that a general strike would eventually spearhead a workers' revolution. The strike weapon in the UK has not evinced this potential. As Crouch notes, even the revolutionary Clydeside Shop Stewards Movement of the First World War (see p. 155) was unable to mobilise workers for any radical campaign; indeed, the major strike in which the movement was involved was a *defensive* protest over the dilution of craft skills by the introduction of unskilled women. Striking is a costly and risky process and workers are rarely prepared to shoulder the risks except on clear-cut defensive issues, or for small, incremental improvements that seem to be easy to achieve. The strike weapon has not proved to be a flexible power resource.

Although relationships of dependency and power sometimes seem impervious to change they are, of course, formed by human action and current social structures can be influenced, at least to some degree, by present activity. Chapter 5 noted both shop stewards and managers acting to affect the non-substitutability and strategic significance of the employees' contribution at work. Many of the managerial strategies described in Chapter 3 are designed to reduce the strategic importance and increase the substitutability of employee work. Government policies can have a similar impact, for example attempts to reduce unemployment or let unemployment 'reach natural levels' crucially affect employee power and the restrictions on the right to strike, the weakening of the closed shop and the reduction of supplementary benefit to strikers' families introduced by the Conservative government since 1979 are designed to weaken employee ability to present a united, 'non-substitutable' front towards employers. As groups manoeuvre to increase the power resources that they hold and weaken those of rivals, the influence of ideas and of subjective beliefs comes into play. This area has been mentioned briefly in Chapters, 2, 3 and 5 and is therefore dealt with in more detail below.

Power and Authority: The Mobilisation of Ideas

Ideas can reinforce or undermine objective power bases, and all bargainers will use arguments as a means of boosting morale on their own side, gaining the sympathy of external groups and attempting to convince their bargaining opponent of the legitimacy of their case. This aspect of bargaining power is best understood by looking at Max Weber's work on legitimated power or authority. Weber argued that power arising from the possession of objective resources is not the only source of control in social relations because the beliefs that people hold also influence behaviour. Beliefs affect people's willingness to be influenced by power. If power-holders can convince others that they have the moral, legitimate right to control certain decisions, then they exercise not only power, but authority. Authority provides invisible power (see p. 223), for ideas and beliefs are not simply used instrumentally by negotiators but may become internalised, becoming part of the individual personality and sense of self-respect. Negotiators are themselves likely to be influenced by dominant ideologies and this sets limits on the issues they raise and pursue with confidence and conviction (Armstrong *et al.*, 1981). Authority, therefore, is legitimated power and whereas power can expect to be challenged by other power-holders, authority proclaims the moral superiority of being above political battles. Authority claims to be non-negotiable, it assumes the right to decide issues irrespective of the immediate distribution of power. In practice this means that any group challenging an established authority will find it more difficult to mobilise sympathetic support from other power-holders, and will find it difficult to convince the waiverers on its own side that they have a justifiable case and are not making immoral demands.

Because authority is a valuable additional resource enabling its holder to economise on the use of power, most groups attempt to give their claims ideological support. What arguments are used in the propaganda battle for minds within British industrial relations?

Employer ideologies: employers claim the authority to manage industry and argue that this authority derives from simple property rights or, more subtly, from the long-term interest of everyone concerned (Hyman and Brough, 1975; Bendix, 1956). The case that managerial authority is in everyone's long-term interest can be supported by bureaucratic arguments, that society needs to be hierarchically structured and rationally organised and that managers have the necessary status and expertise to enable them to run the economy in a rational and efficient way, or by the more liberal argument that society needs the economic growth which can only be assured by allowing employers free rein to manage their concerns on commercial principles. Such arguments have been used to claim total control of employment relations or, once control has been ceded, to maintain control of areas like job design, the use of labour, or the investment or commerical decisions affecting employment.

Employee ideologies are less coherent or confident than those of employers and dominant, radical and subordinate value systems all make conflicting claims for employee support (see Chapter 5). Most institutionalised employee bargaining is backed by arguments based on subordinate values. These give a broad acceptance to managerial authority but attempt to limit and contain its scope by demanding the authority be exercised in 'rational–legal' and ethical ways.

Employees exploit the argument that managerial authority rests on the need for rational administration, and bureaucratic rationality is used to back employee claims based on precedent, comparability, seniority or tenure. Precedent has been widely used by British workgroups demanding that local management act rationally in the light of its own past decisions (Brown 1972). Well-organised shop stewards keep detailed records of managerial precedent in order to use this argument to good effect. *Comparability* arguments state that if a pay structure or personnel policy is to be seen as rational and just, applying to everyone equally, then certain groups of workers need to receive the same pay or conditions as similar groups treated more favourably elsewhere (Brown and Sisson, 1975). British workers have often fought for *tenure*, or the right to be retained once employed by an organisation. The claim to job 'property rights' has sometimes been interpreted as an expression of radical values; however, it is often heard from those who broadly accept managerial authority but dispute management's right to deprive others of work for other than disciplinary reasons. As the right to tenure was recognised by Weber as part of the rational, bureaucratic employment relationship (see p. 38), this pressure from employees is best seen as a demand that management operates within certain rational constraints, rather than as a total rejection of management authority.

Employees may argue that a rational criterion for the distribution of pay or promotion is *seniority* or length of service, on the grounds that assessment of merit is too subjective. Seniority arguments are widely used in American negotiations and in the USA, and employee pressure for tenure and the recognition of seniority has resulted in widespread agreements for 'bumping'. If a redundancy is announced, then the person in the redundant post can 'bump' or take the job from anyone in a lower position in the job hierarchy that the redundant person once occupied. Redundancies are therefore 'bumped' down an organisation until the most junior members of staff are dismissed, a formal practice that is not found in the UK where employees have been less bureaucratic in their orientations (see Littler, 1983).

What impact does the propaganda war have on the distribution of power between employers and employees? Some interpret Marx as claiming that the distribution of power in our society is shaped by the structure of property relations and that ideological arguments have no impact on this material base. However, this is over-deterministic. As Weber noted, although material resources like capital or control over administrative, research and communications resources do give considerable advantages in the struggle to mobilise bias and influence people's views, nevertheless the ideological arguments of less-powerfully resourced groups can influence society. In the UK, employees' claim to have a voice in the determination of pay and conditions is, on the whole, accepted as legitimate at least if this is through some form of collective bargaining. When employee claims are couched in bureaucratic terms they are often difficult for employers to ignore and employees, as we see below, have therefore played a part in shaping modern bureaucratic organisations.

Power Within Different Types of Negotiating Institution
To what extent is the exercise of power affected by the form of negotiating institution? Does collective bargaining with its institutionalised right to strike provide the only countervailing power against capital? Does the constitutional right to be represented on company boards provide an effective base for employee representation, or are all institutional arrangements equally vacuous under capitalism?

Institutions reflect and affect the power relationships within them. In negotiating institutions the superior power of one party may be reflected in the provisions for chairmanship or minute-taking, the allocation of seats, the control over agendas and the type of arguments and sanctions that are endorsed. Institutional arrangements are often hotly contested in the belief that they will influence decision-making thereafter. Most argument takes place over the sanctions backing negotiation and the relative merits of the strike sanction versus constitutional rights to speak, vote or take one's case to arbitration.

Liberal-collectivists insist that employees exercise little power unless their bargaining is backed directly by the strike threat, but given the 'harmony bias' that is widespread in society (see p. 51) there have been many advocates of more peaceful 'distributive', 'integrative' or 'problem-solving' bargaining (Walton and McKersie, 1965). Many joint employer-employee institutions are premised on the assumption that genuine negotiations can occur without a confrontational setting or the strike sanction. Crouch labels the non-conflictual bargaining 'concertation', and we can ask what is the difference in power exercised by institutions designed for concertation or for conflictual bargaining?

In some joint institutions based on concertation, institutional arrangements definitely work against the exercise of power by the employee representatives. Institutions established by management as part of a policy for improved communication rarely enable employees to oppose management effectively on issues where interests conflict. Employees in briefing groups or joining consultation committees may be able to make some impact on managerial decision-making by the force of their argument, but they will not be given information with which to challenge the rationality of management's decisions, and if they do not have their own independent organisational links with their constituents they will not be able to back their arguments with the sanction of non-co-operation. Many arrangements for putting worker directors on company boards are similarly emasculated. A small minority of employee directors are likely to find themselves powerless to penetrate the labrynthine intrigues of boardroom politics, and at a loss to analyse what is happening, because of insufficient information or because they have been deluged with incomprehensible statistics and out-manoeuvred as managers and shareholder directors settle major decisions outside the boardroom. Employee directors have all too often found themselves patronised by other board members and resented by their electors as puppets of management whose privileged position provides no tangible benefits for employees (see CIR Study 4, 1974; Brannen *et al.*, 1976; Batstone, 1979).

However there is evidence to suggest that institutions based on concertation are not necessarily powerless and that even within collective bargaining, sanctions other than the strike do have an impact. Herding (1974) studied American plant bargaining and contrasted it with the achievements of West German works councils. The American unionists were adamant that conflictual bargaining must be more effective than works council concertation, but Herding found that the issues being dealt with by the Americans were very similar to works council business and that there were some issues where works councils would probably have achieved more success. Crouch notes that 'the differences between different types of system are nothing like as great as immediately appears' and that it is important not to assume that institutional form implies employee strategy – people are likely to put to use whatever bargaining institutions are available.

Herding noted that his American collective bargainers often operated as if in a concertation set of institutions. Collective bargainers may also seek to avoid strikes and concentrate on the accommodative resolution of disputes and in some circumstances such tactics succeed (see Anthony 1977, p. 227). Christine Edwards (1975; 1978) studied the power relationship between the colliery manager and the union secretary at two National Coal Board collieries from February 1972 to August 1974 and attempted to measure both the visible and invisible power exercised by the two sides. Power to overcome open resistance was measured by listing all the disputes known to have occurred at each pit and asking union and management representatives whether they had 'won' or 'lost' in terms of their objectives at the time. Invisible power was measured by asking the negotiating partners to list the significant issues in their relationship with the other side and to assess who exerted most control over those issues. Under both measures Edwards found that the colliery managers exercised considerably more power than the union secretaries, and that management's dominance was more pronounced under the measure of invisible power. Issues of significance to the negotiating parties were determined more often by the less visible techniques of control than by open bargaining. However there were differences between the two pits and the differences demonstrated that non-confrontational power was not the sole preserve of management. There were more open disputes at the Midland colliery than at the northern one; indeed, very few issues were openly contested by the northern union secretary. Nevertheless Edwards calculated that the northern union exercised more control over issues of significance in the employment relationship than did their Midland colleagues. They did this through a negotiating strategy of conciliation and pleas for mutual accommodation, rather than open dispute. From Edwards' study it is clear that non-confrontational methods and tactics can be effective in collective bargaining.

The impact of institutional arrangements on the underlying distribution of power is difficult to assess. Some Marxists believe there can be no institutional redistribution of power within present political and economic structures and, in this vein, David Coates attacks the New Reformism of Labour party policies for naivety in believing that compulsory planning agreements, the expansion of industrial democracy and increased public control of the finance industry or of major industrial firms would increase employee influence in the British economy. He argues that no government, constrained by Parliament and the economic power of international finance and the MNEs, could implement policies to increase employee power: 'In a world crisis of present proportions states compete with one another to attract in capital by shackling their own working classes' (Coates, 1981, p. 129). Such arguments are often premised on the assumption that radical improvements could be made if only the tempting lure of institutional reform was rejected by employees. However, British workers have not shown themselves convinced by the possibility or desirability of revolutionary change, they *have* sought institutional negotiation within the existing society. Consistent employee pressure for institutional negotiations and vehement employer resistance to schemes like the Bullock proposals for industrial democracy in the UK, parity representation for worker directors in West Germany or the Meider plan for trade union control of company assets in Sweden, all point to the fact that employers also believe that institutionalised negotiations can reallocate power.

NEGOTIATION AND BUREAUCRACY

An analysis of employee negotiations and the effect of different institutions on the distribution of power needs to consider the relationship between negotiation and bureaucracy. It has often been assumed that bureaucratic structures of control exclude negotiation (Weber, 1947; Crozier, 1964), and there has been a conventional division of academic labour between industrial relations specialists, studying negotiation, and organisation theorists, studying bureaucratic structures of control. The growing interest in management strategies within industrial relations (see Chapter 3) and the emergence of the interactionist school of organisation theory (p. 216) point to the artificiality of this division (see Thompson and Warner, 1981; Gospel 1973; Gottschalk in Warner 1973.) This section underlines that bureaucracy can be negotiated, and notes the bureaucratic organisational features that are likely to be supported by employees.

Most writings in the structural school of organisation theory assume that the bureaucratic structures of modern business are designed by management. However, employee pressure can play a more active role in organisational design than this implies. Child noted that one of the contingencies affecting management's choice of organisational strategies may be employee power (Child *et al.*, 1973) while Gouldner and Crozier, in their different analyses of bureaucracy, touch on the significance of employee negotiation in the shaping of bureaucratic structures.

Gouldner (1954) produced a detailed case study of the bureaucratisation of a small gypsum plant in the USA. He charts the reaction to management's attempts to tighten control over labour and production processes by the imposition of more bureaucratic rules and notes that employee reaction to bureaucratic rules varied according to the rules' source and purpose. Some rules, for example the safety regulations, had the support of both managers and employees on site: their purpose was approved and they were jointly enforced, they could be seen as 'representative bureaucracy'. In contrast, there were rules imposed by management on, for example, lateness, absenteeism or pilfering which were regarded as punishment-centred and were resented and initially opposed by employees. The no-smoking rules, prominently displayed throughout the works, were ignored by both management and men. Their source was external – the plant's insurers – and Gouldner classifies these unenforced regulations as 'mock bureaucratic' rules. Punishment-centred rules therefore are designed and seen as instruments to control recalcitrant employees, but the regulations of representative bureaucracy can be supported and endorsed by different interests at work.

Crozier (1964) emphasises the control function of bureaucratic rules, but notes that employees as well as managers can use bureaucratic rules as instruments of control. He studied a French government-owned tobacco monopoly, concentrating on three plants near Paris, and shows how, in one plant, workers restricted their plant manager's inspections of the shopfloor by insisting on the letter of the rulebook. (The trade union tactic of work-to-rule provides another example of turning management-originated bureaucratic rules against management). Crozier also describes how employees as well as managers act to structure their environment through the elaboration of regulations to make their situation more predictable. In an illuminating footnote he writes: 'There is an important distinction to be made between rules prescribing the way in which the task must be performed and rules prescribing the way people should be chosen, trained and promoted for various jobs. Subordinates fight rationalisation in the first area and want it in the second, and supervisory personnel do just the reverse' (p. 161, fn 33).

Crozier therefore notes two types of pressure from workers. There is a constant attempt to evade and manipulate managerial controls as a means to increasing their own autonomy and power (see Terry's 'dynamic of informality', 1977.) However, at the same time, employees attempt to establish rules to regulate and control managerial behaviour towards them. Linking the distinction drawn in the quote above to the division in Weber's bureaucratic characteristics made by Littler (see p. 38), we can say that, in general, employers press for the bureaucratisation of controls over task performance, while employees are more interested in bureaucratic personnel policies. Employers seek specific written rules to govern the division of labour and work performance but like to be free to recruit and reward as they wish. Employees prefer autonomy in work methods but seek the clear, rational–legal regulation of recruitment, discipline, pay and promotion prospects.

Crozier did not imply that employee negotiation shaped personnel policies; indeed, he argued that in his very highly bureaucratised tobacco monopoly, bargaining and the exercise of power had been replaced by bureaucratic regulation. However, when he spoke of bargaining he was apparently referring to small group, individual and shopfloor bargaining. Some of the rules and regulations that enmeshed his plants *were* negotiated, but they had been negotiated between higher levels of the management and union hierarchies and, therefore, at plant level could be seen simply as bureaucratic rules. For example pay, hours and also the rigorously enforced rules on seniority (which restricted management's freedom in the deployment of labour) had been established by centralised collective bargaining. Crozier's analysis suggests that non-institutionalised negotiations may be eliminated as organisations become rigidly structured and highly bureaucratised. However, bureaucracy does not exclude institutionalised negotiations; indeed, bureaucratic structures and rules are often the outcome of institutionalised negotiation. As Lockwood (1958) noted in the context of growing white-collar trade unionism, unionisation and bureaucratisation can be reinforcing and mutually cumulative processes, while Hyman (1979), commenting on the increasingly bureaucratic structures of shop steward organisation and negotiation in Britain in the 1970s, argued that centralised, formalised systems of control have benefits for employees if they give access to otherwise inaccessible decisions.

To what extent are modern organisations shaped by the negotiating power of employees? Only a small proportion of organisational arrangements are under negotiation at any one time: for example, a case study of a GKN forging works found only 4 per cent of all the interactions involving the twenty-eight top managers could be classed as bargaining. (Harper and Argent, 1975). Nevertheless significant bargains from the past leave their mark on organisational arrangements. As we noted in Chapter 3 employers may adopt different bureaucratic strategies in response to differences in employee power. Friedman suggests that bureaucratic personnel policies of 'responsible autonomy' are adopted by large, oligopolistic modern firms in response to employee pressure, while Littler analyses the development of work organisations in Britain, Japan and the USA in terms of the interaction between employer strategy and employee resistance in the period when modern organisations were evolving (pp. 45–9). In Britain, employees have pressed for standardised rules on pay rates and hours, using arguments based on precedent and comparability. However British trade unions have been less bureaucratic in their orientations than those of West Germany, the USA or Japan where bureaucratic personnel policies and internal labour markets have become more firmly established within large corporations. Littler (1983) suggests that because British unions were themselves structured to relate to the British labour markets of the late nineteenth and early twentieth centuries, when British capital was still highly competitve and dependent on market skills, they have seen less advantage in the organisation-related policies of unions formed under monopoly capitalism, with their greater concern for seniority and organisational careers.

WHAT OF THE FUTURE?

Employment relations are increasingly set in the context of large-scale organisation. Business concentration and trade union mergers are likely to continue. There is no sign, for example that the growth of multinational corporations, spreading vertically and horizontally to extend their control over markets for products and supplies, will slacken, though economic or nationalist pressures may modify their form. Given the organisational requirements that accompany this concentration we can safely endorse Weber's prediction that bureaucracy will dominate organisational life.

Bureaucracy will survive, but whether institutional negotiations for employees will continue to be segregated through collective bargaining or will become integrated within organisational structures is difficult to predict for the UK. The trends will be heavily influenced by government policy. If governments adopt corporatist policies at national level, then they are likely to encourage industrial democracy and the integration of employee representatives onto company committees and boards.

Governments cannot avoid playing a major role in economic affairs. The management of the public sector, together with economic policy, whether of a Keynesian or of a monetarist kind, have a direct impact on economic activity and on employment relationships within the private sector. However, although state activity is inevitable in governing a twentieth-century economy, current policy proposals still range from the Thatcher government's monetarism backed by more active restriction of trade union powers to the many variants of corporatism advocated by the present opposition parties. Government policy towards industrial relations is, as we have seen, subject to see-sawing reversals and the eventual outcome is impossible to foresee.

Those who predict a trend towards more corporatist government policies cite in evidence the need for a post-liberal form of interest intermediation because of reduced market competition (Schmitter, 1974, 1977), the pressures for harmonisation within the EEC, or the need to incorporate trade unions into government to contain their disruptive potential (von Beyme, 1980). How stable would corporatist policies be? Schmitter argues that they are already established in Sweden, Switzerland, the Netherlands, Norway and Denmark, that they are emerging in France, Britain, West Germany and the USA, and are no less stable than liberal-collectivist democratic policies. Panitch (1980, 1982) disagrees, arguing that corporatist policies cannot create the degree of consensus necessary for their survival and that fundamental class conflicts will inevitably break them apart. He cites the experience of British incomes policy and notes that divisions between union leaders and their rank and file have emerged as the major source of weakness in the past attempts to harness workers into corporatist structures of centralised control.

Pressures towards corporatism meet many obstacles in the UK. The power of unions and employers is decentralised, a decentralisation which has a long history and deep roots in the industrial infrastructure. The decentralisation and the strength of liberal values both fuel resistance to more centralised controls. Booth (1982) notes that corporatist policies have been adopted on three occasions in Britain in the twentieth century, in each case as a response to national economic crises and with the primary purpose of reducing wages relative to Britain's competitors. However each occasion was followed by periods (1919–22, 1930–3, 1976–81) when corporatist policies were apparently rejected by the electorate in favour of 'sound money' policies. Booth argues that liberal, anti-corporatist values dominate society and, are heavily supported by powerful financial interests, and that while this is sufficient to undermine the credibility of corporatism in the UK it is not accepted as a viable alternative to liberal policies. M. Smith (1982) suggests further reasons why liberal rather than corporatist policies might succeed. Corporatist policies politicise employment relations and so provide a focus for organised resistance, whereas monetarist policies with their associated high levels of unemployment effectively reduce or stifle opposition. Unemployed workers are beyond the scope of the union organisation they need to express resistance or protest, while unemployment reduces the employed workers' resistance to government policies, no matter what their effects.

Whether or not governments adopt corporatist or liberal policies, their approach towards employees can be more or less coercive (see Crouch, 1977). There are many proposals current in the UK for anti-union legislation which would reduce employee bargaining power and limit the ability of workgroups to oppose their leaders. These proposals are backed by the argument that employee bargaining power must be curbed to make Britain more competitive in international markets, and they are gaining wider support. How strenuously or aggressively governments pursue policies to weaken employee control in the employment relationship will no doubt be affected by the depth and length of Britain's economic recession. If the UK fails to adjust to the loss of traditional heavy and manufacturing industries and to invest in microelectronic technology, or if Kondratieff's prediction that the recession starting in the 1970s would last for fifty years (Mandel 1972) then we might expect increased social tensions to lead to more coercive government controls.

The patterns of negotiation and control developed in the UK will depend in part on international levels of bargaining or administration. The growth of multinational enterprises with internationally centralised personnel policies threatens the regulatory hold of national collective bargaining (see p. 172). Multinational companies have so far resisted union attempts to establish multinational collective bargaining, but the exchange of information between national unions has increased and unions have sought to act at the political level demanding international codes and regulations for multinational activity (Weinberg, 1978; Levinson, 1972; Windmuller, 1980). Again, the outcome of these pressures is likely to depend on government policy and the support unions receive from national governments for international, political forms of negotiation and control.

The processes of control over employment relationships have been the subject of intense political controversy within Britain for nearly two decades. With no new consensus emerging, British industrial relations will remain a socially important and intellectually stimulating field.

Bibliography

Abell, P. (ed) (1975, 1978), *Organisations as Bargaining and Influence Systems*, vols I and II (London: Heinemann).

ACAS (1980), *Industial Relations Handbook* (London: HMSO).

Anderson, P. (1967), 'The limits and possibilities of trade union action' in Blackburn and Cockburn (eds) (1967).

Anthony, P. (1977a), *The Ideology of Work* (London: Tavistock).

Anthony, P. (1977b), *The Conduct of Industrial Relations* (London: IPM).

Armstrong, P. J., Goodman, J. F. B. and Hyman, J. D. (1981), *Ideology and Shop-Floor Industrial Relations* (London: Croom Helm).

Bachrach, P. and Baratz, M. (1962), 'The two faces of power', *American Political Science Review*, no. 56.

Bachrach, P. and Baratz, M. (1970), *Power and Poverty, Theory and Practice* (New York: OUP).

Bain, G. S. (1970), *The Growth of White Collar Trade Unionism* (Oxford: Clarendon).

Bain, G., Coates, D. and Ellis, V. (1973) *Social Stratification and Trade Unionism* (London: Heinemann).

Bain, G. S. and Price, R. (1972), 'Union growth and employment trends in the UK, 1964–1970', *British Journal of Industrial Relations,* vol. X, no. 3.

Bain, G. S. and Price, R. (1980), *Profiles of Union Growth* (Oxford: Blackwell).

Bain, G. S. and Woolven, B. (1978), *A Bibliography of British Industrial Relations* (Cambridge: CUP).

Bain, G. and Elsheik, F. (1976), *Union Growth and the Business Cycle*, (Oxford: Blackwell).

Bain, G. and Elsheik, F. (1979), 'An interindustry analysis of unionisation in Britain'; *British Journal of Industrial Relations*, vol XVII, no. 2.

Baldamus, W. (1961), *Efficiency and Effort: An Analysis of Industrial Administration* (London: Tavistock).

Barrett, B., Rhodes, E. and Beishon, J. (1975), *Industrial Relations and the Wider Society: Aspects of Interaction* (West Drayton: Collier-Macmillan).

Batstone, E. (1979), 'Systems of domination, accommodation and industrial democracy', in Burns, T. *et al.* (1979).

Batstone, E., Boraston, I. and Frenkel, S. (1977), *Shop Stewards in Action* (Oxford: Blackwell).

Batstone, E., Boraston, I. and Frenkel, S. (1978), *The Social Organisation of Strikes* (Oxford: Blackwell).

Bendix, R. (1974) (ed.), *Work and Authority in Industry*, (Berkeley Calif.: University of California Press).

Berle, A. and Means, C. (1932), *The Modern Corporation and Private Property* (New York: Macmillan).

von Beyme, K. (1980), *Challenge to Power: Trade Unions and Industrial Relations in Capitalist Countries* (London: Sage).

Beynon, H. (1973), *Working for Ford* (Harmondsworth: Penguin).

Beynon, H. and Blackburn, R. M. (1972), *Perceptions of Work, Variations Within a Factory* (Cambridge: CUP).

Blackaby, F. (ed.) (1980), *The Future of Pay Bargaining* (London: Heinemann).

Blackburn, R. M. and Cockburn, A. (eds) (1967), *The Incompatibles*, (Harmondsworth: Penguin).

Blackburn, R. M. and Mann, M. (1979), *The Working Class in the Labour Market* (London: Macmillan).

Blank, S. (1973), *Industry and Government in Britain: The Federation of British Industry in Politics, 1945–65* (Farnborough: Saxon House).

Booth, A. (1982), 'Corporatism, capitalism and depression in twentieth century Britain', *British Journal of Sociology*, vol. xxxiii, no. 2.

Brannen, P., Batstone, E., Fatchett, D. and White, P. (1976), *The Worker Directors* (London: Hutchinson).

Braverman, H. (1974), *Labor and Monopoly Capital* (New York: Monthly Review Press).

Brewster, C. and Connock, S. (1980), *Industrial Relations Training for Managers* (London: Kogan Page).

Brookes, C. (1979), *Boards of Directors in British Industry*, Research Paper no 7 (London: Department of Employment).

Brown, W. (1972), 'A consideration of "Custom and Practice"', *British Journal of Industrial Relations*, vol X, no. 1.

Brown, W. (1973), *Piecework Bargaining* (London: Heinemann).

Brown, W. (ed.) (1981), *The Changing Contours of British Industrial Relations* (Oxford: Blackwell).

Brown, W. and Sisson, K. (1975), 'The Use of Comparisons in Workplace Wage Determination', *British Journal of Industrial Relations*, xiii.

Brown, W. and Terry, M. (1978), 'The nature of national wage agreements', *Scottish Journal of Political Economy*, vol. xxv, no. 2.

Bullock Report (1977), *Report of the Committee of Inquiry on Industrial Democracy*, Cmnd 6706 (London: HMSO).

Burgess, K. (1975), *The Origins of British Industrial Relations* (London: Croom Helm).

Burkett, B. and Bowers, D. (1979), *Trade Unions and the Economy* (London: Macmillan).

Burns, T., Karlsson, L. and Rus, V. (1979), *Work and Power*, (London: Sage).

Burns, T. and Stalker, G. (1961), *The Management of Innovation* (London: Tavistock).

Cairncross, F. (ed.) (1981), *Changing Perspective of Economic Policy* (London: Methuen).

Caplow, T. (1954), *The Sociology of Work* (Maidenhead: McGraw-Hill).

Castles, F., Murray, D. and Potter, D. (1971), *Decision, Organisations and Society* (Harmondsworth: Penguin).

Cawson, A. (1982), *Corporatism and Welfare* (London: Heinemann).

Chamberlain, N. and Kuhn, J. (1965), *Collective Bargaining* (New York: McGraw-Hill).

Chandler, A. (1966), *Strategy and Structure: Chapters in the History of the Industrial Enterprise* (New York: Anchor).

Chandler, A. D. (1976), 'The development of modern management structure in the US and UK', in Hannah (ed.) (1976).

Chandler, A. (1977), *The Visible Hand: The Managerial Revolution in American Business* (Chicago, Ill.: Belknap Press).

Chandler, A. and Daems, H. (eds) (1980), *Managerial Hierarchies: Comparative Perspectives on the Rise of Modern Industrial Enterprises* (Cambridge, Mass.: Harvard Univsity Press).

Child, J. (1964), 'Quaker employers and industrial relations', *Sociological Review*, vol 12, no 2. 293–315.

Child, J. (1969a), *British Management Thought* (London: George Allen & Unwin).

Child, J. (1969b), *The Business Enterprise in Modern Society* (London: Macmillan).

Child, J. (ed.) (1973), *Man and Organisation* (London: George Allen & Unwin).

Child, P. (1981), 'A study of industrial relations in the insurance industry', (PhD thesis, City University).

Clark, R. (1979), *The Japanese Company* (New Haven, Conn.: Yale UP).

Clarke, O., Fatchett, D. and Roberts, B. (1972), *Workers' Participation in Management in Britain* (London: Hutchinson).

Clarke, T. and Clements, T. (eds) (1977), *Trade Unions under Capitalism* (London: Fontana).

Clawson, D. (1980), *Bureaucracy and the Labor Process* (New York: Monthly Review Press).

Clegg, H. A. (1972), *The System of Industrial Relations in Great Britain* (Oxford: Blackwell).

Clegg, H. A. (1976), *Trade Unionism Under Collective Bargaining* (Oxford: Blackwell).

Clegg, H. A. (1979), *The Changing System of Industrial Relations in Great Britain* (Oxford: Blackwell).

Cliff, T. (1966), *Productivity Deals and How to Fight Them* (London: Pluto).

Coates, D. (1980) *Labour in Power? A Study of the Labour Government 1974–1979* (New York: Longman).

Coates, D. (1981), 'The limits of the Labour left', *New Left Review*, no. 135.

Coates, K. (1980), *Work-ins, Sit-ins and Industrial Democracy* (Nottingham: Spokesman).

Coates, K. and Topham, T. (1980), *Trade Unions in Britain* (Nottingham: Spokesman).

Cockcroft, L. (1977), 'Democrats at the mill', *New Society*, 14 April 1977.

Coker, E. and Stuttard, G. (ed.) (1976) *Industrial Studies 2: The Bargaining Context* (Arrow-Hutchinsons).

Cole, G. D. H. (1923), *Workshop Organisation* (London: OUP).

Commission on Industrial Relations (CIR) (London: HMSO):
    (1972) Report no. 29, Alcan Smelter Site.
    (1972) Report no. 32, C. A. Parsons & Co. Ltd.
    (1973) Report no. 55, Pan American World Airways Inc..
    (1974) Report no. 66, Airline Engineering Ltd..
    (1972) *Employers' Organisation and Industrial Relations,* Study no. 1.

(1973) *Industrial Relations at Establishment Level, a Statistical Survey* Study no. 2.

Crawcour, S. (1978), 'The Japanese employment system, *Journal of Japanese Studies*, vol. iv, no. 2.

Crouch, C. (1977), *Class Conflict and the Industrial Relations Crisis* (London: Heinemann).

Crouch, C. (1979a), *The Politics of Industrial Relations* (London: Fontana).

Crouch, C. (ed.) (1979b), *State and Economy in Contemporary Capitalism*, London.

Crouch, C. (1982), *Trade Unions: the Logic of Collective Action* (London: Fontana).

Crouch, C. and Pizzorno, A. (1978), *The Resurgence of Class Conflict in Western Europe since 1968* (London: Macmillan).

Crozier, M. (1964), *The Bureaucratic Phenomenon* (Chicago, Ill.: University of Chicago Press).

Crozier, M. (1971), *The World of the Office Worker* (Chicago, Ill.: University of Chicago Press).

Dalton, M. (1959), *Men Who Manage* (New York: Wiley).

Daniels, W. (1973), 'Understanding employee behaviour in its context: illustrations from productivity bargaining', in Child (ed.) (1973).

'Devlin Report' (1972), *Report of the Commission of Inquiry into Industrial and Commercial Representation* (London: ABCC/CBI).

Dickens, L. (1975), 'Staff associations and the Industrial Relations Act: the effect on union growth', *Industrial Relations Journal*, vol. vi, no. 3.

Donnison, J (1973) 'The sex of midwives', *New Society*, 1/11/1973.

'Donovan Report' (1968), *Report of the Royal Commission on Trades Unions and Employers' Associations 1965–8*, Cmnd 3623 (London: HMSO).

Dore, R. P. (1973), *'British Factory – Japanese Factory'* (London: George Allen & Unwin).

Dorfman, A. (1979) *Government versus Trade Unionism in British Politics since 1968* (London: Macmillan).

Dubin, R. (1960), 'A theory of conflict and power in union–management relations', *Industrial and Labor Relations Review*, vol. xxxiii, no. 4.

Dunlop, J. (1958), *Industrial Relations Systems* (Carbondale, Ill.: Southern Illinois University Press).

Dunkerley, D. and Salaman, G. (1980), *International Yearbook of Organisation Studies* (London: Routledge & Kegan Paul).

Dunn, S. (1981), 'The growth of the post-entry closed shop in Britain since the 1960s: some theoretical considerations', *British Journal of Industrial Relations*, vol. xix, no. 3.

Durcan, J. and McCarthy, W. (1974) 'The state subsidy theory of strikes: an examination of statistical data for 1956–1970', *British Journal of Industial Relations*, vol. xii, no. 1.

Durkheim, E. (1933), *The Division of Labour in Society* (London: Macmillan).

Durkheim, E. (1957), *Professional Ethics and Civil Morals* (London: Routledge & Kegan Paul).

Durkheim, E. (1962), *Socialism* (West Drayton: Collier).

Edelstein, J. and Warner, M. (1975), *Comparative Union Democracy* (London: George Allen & Unwin).

Edwards, C. (1978), 'Measuring union power: a comparison of two methods applied to the study of local union power in the coal industry,' *British Journal of Industrial Relations*, vol. xvi, no. 1.

Edwards, C. (1978), 'Bargaining at the management–trade union interface: further developments', in Abell (ed.), (1978).

Edwards, C. and Harper, D. (1975), 'Bargaining at the management–trade union interface', in Abell (ed.), (1975).

Edwards, R. (1979) *Contested Terrain* (London: Heinemann).

Ehrenreich, B. and English, D. (1974) 'Witches, Midwives and Nurses: A History of Women Healers (London: Compendium).

Eldridge, J. E. T. (1968) *Industrial Disputes* (London: Routledge & Kegan Paul).

Eldridge, J. E. T. (1971), *Sociology & Industrial Life* (Sunbury-on-Thames: Nelson).

Elliott, R. F. (1980) 'Are national agreements dead?' Occasional Paper, Aberdeen University Department of Political Economy 80:13.

Elliott, R. F. (1981), 'Some further observations on the importance of national wage agreements', *British Journal of Industrial Relations*, vol. xix, no. 3.

Elliott, R. F. and Steele, R. (1976), 'The importance of national wage agreements', *British Journal of Industrial Relations*, vol. xiv, no. 1.

England, J. and Weekes, B. (1981), 'Trade unions and the state: a review of the crisis', *Industrial Relations Journal*, vol. xxii, no. 1.

Fallick, J. and Elliott, R. (eds) (1981), *Incomes Policies, Inflation and Relative Pay* (London: George Allen & Unwin).

Farnham, D. and Pimlott, F. (1979), *Understanding Industrial Relations* (London: Cassell).

Fatchett, D. and Whittingham, W. (1976), 'Trends and developments in industrial relations theory', *Industrial Relations Journal*, vol. 7, no. 1.

Fatchett, D. and Whittingham, W. (1977), *Industrial Democracy: Prospects after Bullock*, Leeds/Nottingham Occasional Papers in Industrial Relations, no. 2.

Flanders, A. (1964), *The Fawley Productivity Agreements: A Case Study of Management and Collective Bargaining* (London: Faber).

Flanders, A. (1965), *Industrial Relations: What is Wrong With the System?* (London: Faber).

Flanders, A. and Clegg, H. (1954) *The System of Industrial Relations in Great Britain*, Blackwell, Oxford.

Flanders, A and Fox, A. (1969), 'The reform of collective bargaining: from Donovan to Durkheim', *British Journal of Industrial Relations*, vol. vii, no. 2.

Flanders, A., Pomeranz, R., Woodward, J., (1968) *Experiments in Industrial Democracy: A Study of the John Lewis Partnership* (London: Faber).

Flink, J. (1976), *The Car Culture* (Cambridge, Mass: MIT Press).

Fox, A. (1966), *Industrial Sociology and Industrial Relations*, Research Paper no. 3, Royal Commission on Trade Unions and Employers' Associations (London: HMSO).

Fox, A. (1971), *A Sociology of Work in Industry* (West Draytton: Collier-Macmillan).

Fox, A. (1974), *Beyond Contract: Work, Power and Trust Relations* (London: Faber).

Francis, A. (1980), 'Families, firms and finance capital', *Sociology*, vol. 14, no. 1.

Francis, A., Snell, M., Willman, P. and Winch, G. (1982) *Management, Industrial Relations and New Technology for the BL Metro*, (London: Department of Social and Economic Studies, Imperial College).

Friedman, A. (1977), *Industry and Labour* (London: Macmillan).

Friedman, H. and Meredeen, S. (1980), *The Dynamics of Industrial Conflict: Lessons from Fords* (London: Croom Helm).

Furstenberg, D. (1969), 'Worker's participation in management in the Federal Republic of Germany', *International Institute for Labour Studies Bulletin*, 6.

Galenson, W. (1981), *The International Labor Organisation* (University of Wisconsin Press)

Gennard, J. (1976), *Multinationals-Industrial Relations and Trade Union Response*, (Occasional Paper: Universities of Leeds and Nottingham).

Gennard, J. (1977), *Financing Strikers* (London: Macmillan).

Gennard, J. (1981), 'The effects of strike activity on households', *British Journal of Industrial Relations*, vol. xix, no. 3.

Gennard, J. (1982), 'The financial costs and returns of strikes', *British Journal of Industrial Relations*, vol xx, no. 2.

Gennard, J., Dunn, S. and Wright, M., (1980), 'The extent of closed shop arrangements in British industry', *Department of Employment Gazette*, January.

Gennard, J. and Lasko, R. (1975), 'The individual and the strike', *British Journal of Industrial Relations*, vol. xiii, no. 3.

Glasgow University Media Group (1976), *Bad News* (London: Routledge & Kegan Paul).

Glasgow University Media Group (1980), *More Bad News* (London: Routledge & Kegan Paul).

Goldthorpe, J. (1974), 'Industrial relations in Great Britain: a critique of reformism', *Politics and Society*, reprinted in Clarke, T. and Clements, L. (eds) (1977).

Goldthorpe, J., Lockwood, D., Bechhofer, F. and Platt, J. (1968), *The Affluent Workers* (Cambridge: Cambridge University Press).

Goodman, J., Armstrong, E., Davis, J. and Wagner, A. (1977), *Rule-Making and Industrial Peace: Industrial Relations in the Footwear Industry* (London: Croom Helm).

Goodman, J. P. and Sandberg, W. R. (1981), 'A Contingency Approach to Labor Relations Strategies', *Academy of Management Review*, vol. 6, no. 1, pp. 145–154.

Goodman, J. and Whittingham, T. (1969), *Shop Stewards in British Industry* (Maidenhead: McGraw-Hill).

Goodman, J. and Whittingham, T. (1973), *Shop Stewards* (London: Pan).

Goodrich, C. L. (1920, 1975) (ed.), *The Frontier of Control* (London: Pluto).

Gospel, H. (1979), 'Employers' labour policy: a study of the Mond-Turner Talks 1937–33', *Business History*, vol. xxi, no. 2.

Gospel, H. (1983), 'Managerial structures and strategies: an introduction', in Gospel and Littler (eds) 1983.

Gospel, H. and Littler, C. (1983), *Managerial Strategies and Industrial Relations* (London: Heinemann).

Gouldner, A. (1954), *Patterns of Industrial Bureaucracy* (New York: Free Press).

Gouldner, A. (1954), *Wildcat Strike* (Yellow Springs: Antioch College).

Gowan, D. (1976), 'The bargaining System' in Coker and Stuttard (eds).

Gramsci, A. (1971), *Selections from the Prison Notebooks* (London: Lawrence & Wishart).

Grant, W. and Marsh, D. (1977), *The Confederation of British Industry* (London: Hodder & Stoughton).

Gray, J. (ed.) (1976), *The Glacier Project: Concepts and Critiques*, Heinemann.

Gunter, H. (1972), *Transnational Industrial Relations* (London: Macmillan).

Hanami, T. (1980), *Labor Relations in Japan Today* (London: John Martin).

Hannah, L. (ed.) (1976), *Management Strategy and Business Development: An Historical and Comparative Study* (London: Macmillan).

Hannah, L. and Kay, J. (1977) *Concentration in modern industry: theory measurement and the U.K. experience* (London: Macmillan).

Hanson, C., Jackson, S. and Miller, D. (1982), *The Closed Shop: A Comparative Study of Public Policy and Trade Union Security in Britain, the U.S.A. and West Germany* (Aldershot: Gower).

Harper, D. and Argent, E. (1975), 'An empirical study of power and bargaining relationships in an industrial organisation', in Abell (ed.) (1975).

Harris, N. (1972), *Competition and the Corporate Society: British Conservatives, the State and Industry, 1945–64* (London: Methuen).

Hartman, P. (1976), 'Industrial relations in the news media', *Industrial Relations Journal*, vol. vi, no. 4.

Hemingway, J. (1978), *Conflict and Democracy: Studies in Trade Union Government* (Oxford: Oxford University Press).

Herding, R. (1974), *Job Control and Union Structure* (University of Rotterdam Press).

Herman, E. S. (1981), *Corporate Control, Corporate Power* (Cambridge: Cambridge University Press).

Hickson, D. and Mallory, G. (1981), 'Scope for choice in strategic decision making and the trade union role', in Thompson and Warner (eds) (1981).

Hill, S. (1974), 'Norms, groups and power: the sociology of industrial relations', *British Journal of Industrial Relations*, vol. xxii, no. 2.

Hill, S. (1981), *Competition and Control at Work* (London: Heinemann).

Hinton, J. (1973), *The First Shop Stewards Movement* (London: George Allen & Unwin.

Hobsbawm, E. (1979), 'Inside every worker there is a syndicalist trying to get out', *New Society*, 5.4.79.

Hyman, R. (1972), *Strikes* (London: Fontana).

Hyman, R. (1975), *Industrial Relations: A Marxist Introduction* (London: Macmillan).

Hyman, R. (1978), 'Pluralism, procedural consensus and collective bargaining', *British Journal of Industrial Relations*, vol. xvi, no. 1.

Hyman, R. (1979), 'The politics of workplace trade unionism: recent tendencies and some problems for theory', *Capital and Class*, no. 8.

Hyman, R. and Brough, I. (1975), *Social Values & Industrial Relations* (Oxford: Blackwell).

Ingham, G. (1974), *Strikes and Industrial Conflict: Britain and Scandinavia* (London: Macmillan).

Jackson, D., Turner, H. and Wilkinson, F. (1972), *Do Trade Unions Cause Inflation?* (Cambridge: Cambridge University Press).

Jackson, M. (1977), *Industrial Relations* (London: Croom Helm).

Jackson, J. (ed.) (1970), *Professions and Professionalisation* (Cambridge: Cambridge University Press).

Jackson, P. and Sisson, K. (1975), 'Management and collective bargaining. A framework for international comparison of employers organisations,' working paper, SSRC Industrial Relations Research Unit, Warwick.

Jackson, P. and Sisson, K. (1976), 'Employers' confederations in Sweden and the UK and the significance of industrial infrastructure', *British Journal of Industrial Relations*, vol. xiv, no. 3.

Jefferys, J. B. (1945), *The Story of the Engineers, 1800-1945* (London: Lawrence & Wishart).

Johnson, T. (1972), Professions and Power (London: Macmillan).

Jones, M. (1977), 'Y chwarelwyr: the slate quarrymen of North Wales', in Samuel (1977).

Kahn-Freund, O. (1954) 'Legal framework', in Flanders and Clegg (1954).

Kahn-Freund, O. (1969), 'Industrial relations and the law, retrospect and prospect', *British Journal of Industrial Relations*, vol. viii, no. 3.

Kornhauser, A., Dubin, R. and Ross, A. (eds) (1954), *Industrial Conflict* (New York: McGraw-Hill).

Kumar, K. (1978), *Prophecy and Progress: The Sociology of Industrial and Post-Industrial Society* (Harmondsworth: Penguin).

Kynaston-Reeves, T. and Woodward, J. (1970), 'The study of managerial control', in Woodward (1970).

Lane, T. and Roberts, K. (1971), *Strike at Pilkington* (London: Fontana).

Lazonick, W. H. (1983) 'Technological change and the control of work: the development of capital–Labour relations in US mass production industries', in Gospel & Littler (eds) 1983.

Levinson, C. (1972), *International Trade Unionism* (London: George Allen & Unwin).

Lewis, R. (1976), 'The historical development of labour law', *British Journal of Industrial Relations*, vol. xiv, no. 1.

Lewis, R. (1979) 'Kahn-Freund and labour law: an outline critique', *Industrial Law Journal*, vol. 8, no. 4.

Lewis, R. and Simpson, B. (1981), *Striking a Balance?, Employment Law After the 1980 Act*, (Oxford: Martin Robertson).

Littler, C. R. (1978), 'Understanding Taylorism', *British Journal of Sociology*, vol. xxix, no. 2, pp. 185–202.

Littler, C. R. (1980), 'Internal contract and the transition to modern work systems: Britain and Japan', in Dunkerley and Salaman (1980).

Littler, C. R. (1981), 'Power and ideology in work organisations: Britain and Japan', Open University Course D207, Block 3, Study Section 22.

Littler, C. R. (1982a), 'Deskilling and changing structures of control', in Wood (1982).

Littler, C. R. (1982b), *The Development of the Labour Process in Capitalist Societies. A Comparative Study of the Transformation of Work Organisation in Britain, Japan and the USA* (London: Heinemann).

Littler, C. R. (1983), 'A comparative analysis of managerial structures and strategies', in Gospel and Littler (1983).

Littler, C. R. and Salaman, G. (1982), 'Bravermania and beyond: recent theories of the labour process', *Sociology*, vol. 16, no. 2.

Lockwood, D. (1958), *The Blackcoated Worker* (London: George Allen & Unwin.

Loveridge, R. (1983) 'Corporate strategy and industrial relations strategy' in Thurley and Wood (eds) 1983.

Lukes, S. (1974), *Power: A Radical View* (London: Macmillan).

Lumley, R. (1973), *White Collar Unionism in Britain* (London: Methuen).

Lupton, T. (1963), *On the Shop Floor* (Oxford: Pergamon).

Mandell, E. (1972), *Late Capitalism* (London: New Left Books).

Marsden, D. (1978), *Industrial Democracy and Industrial Control in West Germany, France and Great Britain*, Research Paper no. 4 (London: Department of Employment).

Marsh A. (1979a), *Trade Union Handbook* (Aldershot: Gower).

Marsh, A. (1979b), *Concise Encyclopaedia of Industrial Relations* (Aldershot: Gower).

Marsh, A. (1982), *Employee Relations Policy and Decision Making* (Aldershot: Gower).

Marsh, A., Hackman, M. and Miller, D. (1981), *Workplace Relations in the Engineering Industry in the UK and the Federal Republic of Germany* (David Green).

Martin, R. (1968), 'Union democracy, an exploratory framework', *Sociology*, vol. ii, no. 2.

Martin, R. (1980), *TUC: The Growth of a Pressure Group 1868–1976*, (Oxford: Clarendon Press).

Martin, R. (1981), *New Technology and Industrial Relations in Fleet Street* (Oxford: Clarendon).

Marx, K. (1976) (ed.), *Capital: A Critique of Political Economy*, vol. 1 (Harmondsworth: Penguin).

McQuail, D. (1977) *Analysis of Newspaper Content*, Royal Commission on the Press, Research Series 4, Cmnd 6810–4 (London: HMSO).

McCarthy, W. and Ellis, N. (1973), *Management by Agreement* (London: Hutchinson).

Michels, R. (1915), *Political Parties* (New York: Dover).

Miliband, R. (1969), *The State in Capitalist Society* (London: Weidenfeld and Nicolson).

Miliband, R. (1973). 'Poulantzas and the capitalist state', *New Left Review*, no. 82.

Millerson, G. (1964), *The Qualifying Associations* (London: Routledge & Kegan Paul).

Mills, C. Wright (1959), *The Power Elite* (New York: Oxford University Press).

Milne-Bailey, W. (1934), *Trade Unions and the State* (London: George Allen & Unwin).

Moran, M. (1977), *The Politics of Industrial Relations. The Origins, Life and Death of the 1971 Industrial Relations Act* (London: Macmillan).

NEDO (1970), *The Report of the Working Party on Large Industrial Construction Sites*, the National Economic Development Office (London: HMSO).

Nichols, T. (1969), *Ownership, Control & Ideology* (London: George Allen & Unwin).

Nichols, T. and Armstrong, P. (1976), *Workers Divided* (London: Fontana).

Nichols, T. and Beynon, H. (1977), *Living With Capitalism* (London: Routledge & Kegan Paul).

Oakeshott, R. (1978), *The Case for Worker Co-ops* (London: Routledge & Kegan Paul).

O'Higgins, P. (1976), *Workers' Rights* (London: Arrow).

Ouchi, W. (1981), *Theory Z, How American Business Can Meet the Japanese Challenge* (Reading, Mass: Addison-Wesley).

Palmer, G. (1974), 'Uncertain councils', *New Society*, 31.10.1974.

Palmer, G. (1978), 'Industrial relations in the news', *British Journal of Industrial Relations*, vol. xvi, no. 7, pp. 119–23.

Palmer, G. and Littler, C. R. (1977), 'The invisible heroes', *New Society*, 24.11.1977.

Panitch, L. (1976), *Social Democracy and Industrial Militancy*, (Cambridge: Cambridge University Press).

Panitch, L. (1977), 'The development of corporatism in liberal democracies', *Comparative Political Studies*, vol. x, no. 1.

Panitch, L. (1980), 'Recent theorisations on corporatism: reflections of a growth industry', *British Journal of Sociology*, vol. xxxi, no. 2.

Panitch, L. (1981), 'Trade unions and the capitalist state', *New Left Review*, no. 125.

Parkin, F. (1972), *Class, Inequality and Political Order* (London: Paladin).

Parkin, F. (1979), *Marxism and Class Theory: a Bourgeois Critique* (London: Tavistock).

Paynter, W. (1970), *British Trade Unions* (London: George Allen & Unwin).

Paynter, W. (1972) *My Generation* (London: George Allen & Unwin).

Pelling, H. (1963), *A History of British Trade Unionism* (London: Penguin).

Perlman, S. (1928), *A Theory of the Labor Movement* (London: Macmillan).

Perrow, C. (1972), *Complex Organisations: A Critical Essay* (Glenview, Ill.: Scott Foresman).

Phelps-Brown, E. H., (1959) *The Growth of British Industrial Relations* (London: Macmillan).

Phelps-Brown, E. (1981), 'Labour market policy', in Cairncross, F. (ed.) (1981).

Pike, F. and Strich, T. (1974) *The New Corporatism* (Indiana: University of Notre Dame Press).

Piore, M. J. (1972), *Notes for a Theory of Labor Market Stratification*, Working Paper no. 95, Department of Economics, MIT.

Pondy, L. (1967), 'Organisational conflict: concepts and models', *Administrative Science Quarterly*, vol. xii, no. 2.

Poole, M. (1980a), 'Managerial strategies and industrial relations', in Poole and Mansfield (eds) (1980).

Poole, M. (1980b), *Theories of Trade Unionism: A Sociology of Industrial Relations* (London: Routledge & Kegan Paul).

Poole, M. and Mansfield, R. (eds) (1980), *Managerial Roles in Industrial Relations* (Aldershot: Gower).

Poulantzas, N. (1973), *Political Power and Social Classes* (London: New Left Books).

Poulantzas, N. (1975), 'Classes in contemporary capitalism', (London: New Left Books).

Poulantzas, N. (1976), 'The capitalist state: a reply to Miliband and Laclan', *New Left Review*, no. 95.

Prais, S. J. (1981a) *The Evolution of Giant Firms in Britain* (Cambridge: Cambridge University Press).

Prais, S. J. (1981b) *Productivity and Industrial Structure* (Cambridge: Cambridge University Press).

Price, R. and Bain, G. (1976), 'Union growth revisited', *British Journal of Industrial Relations*, vol. xiv, no. 3.

Purcell, J. (1981), *Good Industrial Relations: Theory and Practice* (London: Macmillan).

Purcell, J. and Smith, R. (eds) (1979), *The Control of Work* (London: Macmillan).

Richter, I. (1973), *Political Purpose in Trade Unionism* (London: George Allen & Unwin).

Roberts, B. C. (ed.) (1979), *Towards Industrial Democracy: Europe, Japan and the U.S.* (London: Croom Helm).

Roberts, B. C., Loveridge, R. and Gennard, J. (1972), *The Reluctant Militants* (London: Heinemann).

Rogaly, J. (1977), *Grunwick* (Harmondsworth: Penguin).

Roy, D. (1952), 'Quota restriction and goldbricking in a machine shop', *American Journal of Sociology*, vol. 57, no. 5.

Roy, D. (1954), 'Efficiency and the 'fix': informal intergroup relations in piecework machine shops', *American Journal of Sociology*, vol. 60, no. 3.

Samuel, R. (1977), *Miners, Quarrymen and Saltworkers* (London: Routledge & Kegan Paul).

Sapsford, D. (1981), *Labour Market Economics* (London: George Allen & Unwin).

Saville, J. (ed.) (1954) *Democracy and the Labour Movement* (London: Lawrence and Wishart).

Sayles, L. (1958), *Behaviour of Industrial Work Groups* (New York: Wiley).

Schmitter, P. C. (1974), 'Still the century of corporatism?', *Review of Politics*, also in Pike and Strich (eds) (1974).

Schmitter, P. C. (1977), 'Modes of interest intermediation and models of social change in Western Europe', *Comparative Political Studies*, vol. x, no. 1.

Schmitter, P. and Lehmbruch, G. (eds) (1979) *Trends towards Corporatist Intermediation* (London: Sage).

Schneider, E. (1971 edn), *Industrial Sociology* (New York: McGraw-Hill).

Shalev, M. (1980), 'Industrial relations theory and the comparative study of industrial relations and industrial conflict, *British Journal of Industrial Relations*, vol. xviii, no. 1.

Simon, D. (1954), 'Master and servant' in Saville (ed.) 1954.

Smith, A. (1970), *The Wealth of Nations* (refs to 1970 edn–Harmondsworth: Penguin).

Smith, M. (1982), 'Accounting for inflation', *British Journal of Sociology*, vol. xxxiii, no. 3.

Stinchcombe, A. (1959), 'Bureaucratic and craft administration of production', *Administrative Science Quarterly*, vol. 4, pp. 168–87.

Stinchcombe, A. L. (1974), *Creating Efficient Industrial Administrations* (New York: Academic Press).

Strauss, A. *et al.* (1971), 'The Hospital and its negotiated order', in Castles *et al.* (1971).

Strinati, D. (1979), 'Capitalism, the state and industrial relations', in Crouch (ed.) (1979a).

Sykes, A. (1969a), 'Navvies: their work and attitudes', *Sociology*, vol. iii, no. 1.

Sykes, A. (1969b), 'Navvies: their social relations', *Sociology*, vol. iii, no. 2.

Taylor, F. W. (1964), *Scientific Management* (New York: Harper & Row).

Terry, M. (1977), 'The inevitable growth of informality', *British Journal of Industrial Relations*, vol. xv, no. 1.

Thompson, A. W. J. and Engleman, S., (1975), *The Industrial Relations Act: A review and Analysis* (Oxford: Martin Robertson).

Thompson, A. W. J. and Hunter, L. C. (1975), 'The level of bargaining in a multi-plant company', *Industrial Relations Journal*, vol. 6, no. 2.

Thompson, A. W. J. and Warner, M. (eds) (1981), *The Behavioural Sciences and Industrial Relations* (Aldershot: Gower).

Thurley, K. and Wood, S. (eds) (1983), *Managerial Strategy and Industrial Relations* (Cambridge: Cambridge University Press).

Tugendhat, C. (1973), *The Multinationals* (Harmondsworth: Penguin).

Turner, H. A. (1962), *Trade Union Growth, Structure and Policy: A Comparative Study of the Cotton Unions* (London: George Allen & Unwin).

Turner, H., Roberts, G. and Roberts, D. (1977), *Management Characteristics and Labour Conflict* (Cambridge: Cambridge University Press).

Turner, C. and Hodge, M. (1970) 'Occupations and professions' in Jackson, J. (ed.) (1970).

Undy, R., Ellis, V., McCarthy, W. and Halmos, A. (1981), *Change in Trade Unions: The Development of UK Unions Since 1960* (London: Hutchinson).

Vanek, J. (ed.) (1975), *Self Management* (Harmondsworth: Penguin).

Walton, R. and McKersie, R. (1965), *A Behavioural Theory of Labor Negotiations: An Analysis of a Social Interaction System* (New York: McGraw-Hill).

Webb, S. and Webb, B. (1898), *Industrial Democracy*, published by the authors.

Weber, M. (1947), *The Theory of Social and Economic Organisation* (refs to 1964 edn–New York: Free Press).

Weber, M. (1930), *The Protestant Ethic and the Spirit of Capitalism* (London: George Allen & Unwin).

Wedderburn, D. and Crompton, R. (1973), *Workers' Attitudes to Technology* (Cambridge: Cambridge University Press).

Wedderburn, K. (1980), 'Industrial relations and the courts', *Industrial Law Journal*, vol. ix, no. 2.

Wedderburn, K. (1982) 'Tebbit's proposals', *New Socialist*, no. 5, May/June.

Weekes, B., Mellish, M., Dickens, L. and Lloyd, J. (1975), *Industrial Relations and the Limits of Law: The Industrial Relations Effects of the Industrial Relations Act 1971* (Oxford: Blackwell).

Weinberg, P. (1978), *European Labor and Multinationals* (New York: Praeger).

White Papers (London: HMSO):
(1948) *Personal Incomes, Costs and Prices* (Cmnd 7321).
(1962) *Incomes Policy, the Next Step* (Cmnd 1626).
(1965) *Prices and Incomes Policy* (Cmnd 2639).
(1965) *Prices and Incomes Policy: an 'Early Warning' System* (Cmnd 2808).
(1966) *Prices and Incomes, Standstill: Period of Severe Restraint* (Cmnd 3150).
(1967) *Prices and Incomes Policy after 30 June 1967* (Cmnd 3235).
(1968) *Productivity, Prices and Incomes Policy in 1968, 1969* (Cmnd 3590).
(1969) *In Place of Strife* (Cmnd 3888).
(1969) *Productivity, Prices and Incomes Policy after 1969* (Cmnd 4237).
(1975) *The Attack on Inflation* (Cmnd 6151).
(1977) *The Attack on Inflation after 31 July 1977* (Cmnd 6882).
(1978) *Industrial Democracy* (Cmnd 7231).
(1981) *Trade Union Immunities* (Cmnd 8128).

Whitley Committee Reports (London: HMSO):
(1917) *Interim Report on Joint Standing Industrial Councils* (Cmnd 8606).
(1918) *Supplementary Report on Works Committees* (Cmnd 9001).

Willman, P. (1980), 'Leadership and trade union principles: some problems of management sponsorship and independence', *Industrial Relations Journal*, vol. 11, no. 4.

Windmuller, J. (1980), *The International Trade Union Movement* (Dordrecht: Kluwer).

Windmuller, J. and Gladstone, A. (forthcoming), *Employers' Associations in Industrial Relations: A Comparative International Study*.

Winchester, D. (forthcoming), 'Industrial relations research in Britain', *British Journal of Industrial Relations*.

Winkler, J. T. (1974), 'The ghost at the bargaining table: directors and industrial relations', *British Journal of Industrial Relations*, vol. xii, no. 2.

Wood, S. (ed.) (1982), *The Degradation of Work* (London: Hutchinson).

Woodward, J. (ed.) (1970), *Industrial Organisation: Behaviour and Control* (London: Oxford University Press).

Wootton, B. (1955), *The Social Foundations of Wage Policy* (London: George Allen & Unwin).

Zander, M. (1968) *Lawyers and the Public Interest* (London: Weidenfeld and Nicolson).

Index

References in *bold* characters denote chapters that are wholly concerned with the subjects to which they refer.